Qu

Global Stage

Gender, Contests,
and Power

Beauty Queens on the Global Stage

Gender, Contests, and Power

Edited by
Colleen Ballerino Cohen,
Richard Wilk, and
Beverly Stoeltje

Routledge / New York and London

Published in 1996 by

Routledge
29 West 35th Street
New York, NY 10001

Published in Great Britain in 1996 by

Routledge
11 New Fetter Lane
London EC4P 4EE

Library of Congress Cataloging-in-Publication Data

Beauty queens on the global stage: gender, contests, and power/
    edited by Colleen Ballerino Cohen, Richard Wilk, and Beverly Stoeltje.
        p. cm.
    Includes bibliographical references and index.
    ISBN 0-415-91152-4 (hardback). —ISBN 0-415-91153-2 (pbk.)
    1. Beauty contests—Cross-cultural studies. I. Cohen, Colleen Ballerino. II. Wilk,
Richard. III. Stoeltje, Beverly.
HQ1219.B35 1995
305.42'079—dc20

Contents

Acknowledgments

All the contributors to this book began their work on contests and pageants in isolation from each other. The process through which we found others who shared our interests was indirect and unsystematic, depending on personal networks and accidental connections. We do, however, want to thank Michael Herzfeld, who first realized that his friends Colleen Ballerino Cohen, Richard Wilk, and Beverly Stoeltje shared a common interest, and encouraged us to get in touch with each other. Penny Van Esterik was also an early and enthusiastic supporter of this project and worked with us to organize the session at the 1993 American Anthropological Association meetings where versions of many of the papers in this volume were first presented. Marlie Wasserman, our editor at Routledge, has been encouraging and helpful from the very start, especially with editorial suggestions and in keeping us on track and on schedule (or at least close to it). She helped us think through the project and reach consensus, and she arranged the anonymous peer reviews that were so useful in identifying the important themes in the many papers. We are also indebted to Beth Edwards, Cohen's research assistant at Vassar, whose diligent labors and attention to detail made collaboration between the authors and editors a pleasure, despite the short deadlines and a rapid production pace. Thanks as well to Ara Wilson for her inspiring press clippings, to Kendra Wilhelm for background research, to Catherine Sebastian for her great eye and wonderful cover photograph, to Gretchen Stoeltje for her video materials, and to the many students who so enthusiastically offered their knowledge of beauty contests in their own communities and countries. All three editors want to thank their families for their forbearance and encouragement, and, finally, we thank all contributors for being such good colleagues, committed scholars, and exciting people to work with.

Introduction

Beauty Queens on the Global Stage

Colleen Ballerino Cohen and Richard Wilk, with Beverly Stoeltje

While we were in the final stages of editing this book, we received a packet of newspaper clippings on beauty contests from one of our students doing ethnographic fieldwork in Thailand. The clippings were taken from international newspapers during a five-week period early in the summer of 1994, and their topics ranged from the involvement of the 1993 Miss World second runner-up in fixing the results of the Manila Film Festival to the run-away marketing success in the Philippines of photos of Miss Belgium's entry in the 1994 Miss Universe pageant and to the first Croatian men's beauty contest held, according to a photo caption, "while nearby Serb artillery shelled the Dubrovnik region." The *New York Times* articles on beauty contests and pageants[1] over the last twenty years show similar intriguing juxtapositions: The 1975 protests of the Miss Universe contest in El Salvador that were among "the most serious of the events that...sharpened discontent with the Government of Col. Arturo Armando Monina among students, peasants, workers, landowners, the clergy and even the armed forces" (*New York Times* 1975); the 1984 re-voking of Vanessa Williams' Miss America title, and the controversy sparked when one of her songs was played during the 1993 Miss America evening gown competition (*New York Times* 1993); the near-scuttling of the 1976 Miss World contest by contestants protesting South Africa's apartheid policies (*New York Times* 1976); and the 1993 announcement by the African National Conference of "intensive negotiations" with the sponsors of the Miss South Africa contest resulting in "promises of a 'training fund' to groom future nonwhite beauty contest contestants" (Keller 1993).

These press items highlight two striking and related facts about the topic of this book. First, beauty contests are everywhere: they take place around the world; draw local and international audiences; span every conceivable group, interest, and topic; and involve competitors ranging in age

1

from infants to centenarians. Second, as universal and diverse as beauty contests are and as varied as their cultural and historical contexts tend to be, what they *do* is remarkably similar. Whether the competition is for the title of Miss Universe or the Crooked Tree Cashew Queen, these contests showcase values, concepts, and behavior that exist at the center of a group's sense of itself and exhibit values of morality, gender, and place. We live in a world where everyone seems to be watching satellite television and drinking Coke; it is also a world where making, claiming, and maintaining local identity and culture is increasingly important. The beauty contest stage is where these identities and cultures can be—and frequently are—made public and visible.

This book reflects both the diversity and universality of beauty contests by bringing together thirteen studies from different cultural contexts. Their topics range from community queen contests in Guatemala, Nicaragua, Andalusia, Texas, and rural Minnesota to national pageants held in Thailand, Belize, Tonga, and Tibet that select representatives for international competition. They include a study of a queen "rally" in Liberia, a queen and king "show" in the British Virgin Islands, a Moslem Philippine transsexual beauty queen contest, and an ethnographic account by a contestant in a Moscow beauty contest. Understanding how these contests work requires a look "behind the scenes," at both preparations that take place backstage and the local knowledge needed to understand the meaning and symbolism of the staged performances. All the contributors to this collection acquired extensive ethnographic experience in the settings where they worked. In many cases they also spent time with pageant contestants, sponsors, and judges. They read deeply into the history of the contests they describe and explain how each has acquired special meanings and local flavor.

Beauty contests put gender norms—conventionally, idealized versions of femininity—on stage in a competition awarding the winner a "royal" title and crown. Yet beauty contests are not just about femininity, or beauty, or even competition. They evoke passionate interest and engagement with political issues central to the lives of beauty contestants, sponsors, organizers, and audiences—issues that frequently have nothing obvious to do with the competition itself. By choosing an individual whose deportment, appearance, and style embodies the values and goals of a nation, locality, or group, beauty contests expose these same values and goals to interpretation and challenge. This sort of opening or rupture happens when a local aesthetic encounters a foreign model of beauty, when local opinions diverge over who should win and why, and when audience and judges disagree. Beauty contests evoke controversy over qualities that should count in a competition, how women should act, and what the outcome means. Because the form of the beauty contest can be easily replicated and combined with other events, because beauty contests provide opportunities for public expression and negotiation of standards and values, they have proliferated and grown hugely popular. This also makes them rich sites for ethnographic study, for going to the heart of matters often hidden or simply taken for granted.

A Historical Overview

The idealized femininity put on stage in beauty contests is often closely associated with broader concepts such as morality, or with larger social entities such as the "nation." In undertaking studies of beauty contests, the contributors to this book draw on work on feminine allegory and symbolism (Cowie 1990; Driver 1988; Fox 1985; Gutwirth 1992; Warner 1985), on pageantry, performance, and semiotics (Babcock 1978; Bakhtin 1981; Baudrillard 1983; Bauman and Briggs 1990; Certeau 1984; Eco 1976; Moore and Myerhoff 1977), on nationalism and sexuality (Curthoys 1993; Hall 1993; Jayawardena 1986; McClintock 1993; Parker et al. 1992; Yuval-Davis and Anthias 1989), and on the body as a site for naturalizing cultural precepts and enacting power (Bordo 1993; Butler 1991, 1990; Feher 1989; Foucault 1990; Lacquer 1990; Martin 1987; Mascia-Lees and Sharpe 1992; Ortner 1990). Most of us also sought some historical context for our studies of beauty contests, only to find that a comprehensive history of beauty contests remains to be written. The basic outlines of the modern form of beauty contests are, however, fairly clear.

Historically, beauty contests have deep roots extending back into Greek mythology when Eris began the Trojan war with a prize "For the Fairest" (Pomeroy 1975). In medieval Europe "Queens of the May" and other festivities chose men and women to represent royalty, bringing together elements of both high and low culture (Segalen and Chamarat 1983; Banner 1983, 249). In the United States, beauty was recruited in the service of nation-building. When an elder Lafayette returned triumphantly to the United States in 1826, each state chose young women to appear at welcoming celebrations, and they were known for the rest of their lives as "Lafayette Girls" (Banner 1983, 250). Young women were also recruited for tournaments, centennials, fairs, and other public celebrations, but their appearance rather than their selection was the focus of attention. Rivalries between cities were common, but beauty was rarely the issue. The use of women in these ways mirrored practices in post-revolution France, where female figures were used in art, cartoons, and literature to stand allegorically for the egalitarian principles of the new republic (Gutwirth 1992; Warner 1985).

It was showman P.T. Barnum who recognized the popular potential of beauty as spectacle. As an extension of his side show of curiosities, Barnum promoted contests for dogs, birds, flowers, and babies, with prizes for the winners. In 1854 he tried to stage a contest where women would be paraded in front of judges, but he could not get "respectable" women to take part. So he substituted daguerreotypes for the women, and thereby invented an enduring and popular event, which became the mainstay of popular exhibitions and "dime museums." Newspapers later adopted Barnum's idea, and by the end of the century, almost every newspaper held photographic beauty contests, sometimes with more than ten thousand entries (Banner 1983, 255–61). In 1905 the St. Louis exposition led to the first national contest where several newspapers cooperated. The *Chicago Tribune* challenged other cities to match the beauty of its winner, and had a secretary to the dean of the Chicago Divinity School serve as judge, to lend respectability to the event. The contest pulled 40,000 entries from a dozen cities, and the winner's image was used in advertising.

Only when female public bathing became acceptable did beauty contests emerge from the newspaper onto the public stage. Public bathing evolved from the spas of the elite, and was linked, like so many American fashions, with health. Miss United States, held in Rehoboth Beach, Delaware, in 1880 was the first beauty contest of record. The explicit goal of this contest was to attract publicity and tourism to the resort, but it was nonetheless couched in respectability, as evidenced in the first prize of a bridal trousseau (Deford 1971, 108). Subsequent to this event, queen contests became a regular feature of summer at beach resorts on the East coast, and laid the groundwork for building regional hierarchies of events leading to state championships.

Miss America emerged in 1920 in Atlantic City as part of that city's "Fall Frolic," with contestants from both states and major cities. While early contests had much the same form as today's events, they had little of their cultural trappings. For the first twenty years of their development, American beauty contests took place at carnivals and raucous beach resorts, and their contestants aspired toward Hollywood rather than professional careers and college educations. Scandal surrounded these contests almost every year during this period, and newspapers were full of allegations of bribery and corporate influence, of professional models as "ringers," and reports of thugs with guns trying to intimidate judges (Deford 1971).

Little change appears to have taken place in the status or presentation style of American beauty contests until World War II, when they became patriotic and respectable. Throughout the war, Miss America sold more war bonds than any other public figure; the 1945 Miss America, Bess Myerson, symbolized a shift in contests away from their side-show roots and toward professionalism, careers, scholarships, and a definition of beauty that included deportment and citizenship (Dworkin 1987). With this shift, beauty pageantry became part of the culture of middle class civic boosterism. For the past forty years, the Jaycees, Elks, Rotary, and other clubs and community associations have been the main sponsors of America's beauty contests (Deford 1971; Bivans 1991).

The international spread of pageantry has remained undocumented by historians. Anecdotal evidence suggests that Hollywood films and newsreels helped spread the idea of beauty contests to different countries during the 1920s and 1930s. Offshore enclaves that fed the American taste for the exotic—Hawaii and Cuba, for example—may have been the first foreign sites, but the form was also quickly adopted in Europe, especially England, where earlier traditions of festival Queens had never disappeared (Synnott 1989).

The many beauty pageants and contests that proliferated during the 1930s and 1940s as part of decolonization and nationalism in the Third World gradually coalesced into regional contests during the years following World War II. South America, Southeast Asia, and the Caribbean were leading areas. The separate national contests were not unified under a single umbrella until 1951, when the Miss America corporation (a non-profit foundation) invented the Miss World pageant (Synnott 1989, 609). The following year Miss Universe was created by a swimwear company because of a dispute over photographic rights (Kindel 1984, 138). Today the dual structure of world pageants is dominated by major corporate sponsorship arrangements with close ties to media empires. The Miss Universe pageant presently attracts contestants from seventy eight nations, and its festivities are televised live via satellite to countries with an estimated audience of 800 million to one billion people (Miss Universe Press Kit 1991).

Taking Beauty Contests Seriously

Many of us began our work sharply critical of beauty contests, thinking of them as part of commoditization, power, and control—as simply reinforcing narrow cultural expectations and understandings of women, gender, and sexuality. While the popular press and vast segments of the public take beauty contests very seriously, scholars generally do not. Our colleagues often see beauty contests as somehow trivial, frivolous, or vulgar. Many of us attended our first beauty contest while away from home, seeking respite from the rigors of "real" fieldwork. Even when we thought that beauty contests were much deeper, more complex, and more important than we ever expected, we studied them with some trepidation.

Our own contradictory responses to beauty contests are mirrored in the world of beauty contests themselves, where anti-pageants and counterpageants explicitly challenge the dominant standards by promoting different ones (Faludi 1988; Jewell 1993). The same contradictions emerge among feminist critics like Susan Brownmiller, who states that beauty contests are "denigrating...they create unfair standards for women," that they hold "a morbid fascination...I watch them all" (quoted in Kindel, 1984, 138). These same sorts of contradictions emerge in even the smoothest and most carefully staged beauty contests. While pageants are often presented as events of skill and talent, both audience and participants know that money and physical appearance are crucial. Participants do use beauty contests to enhance their communication and presentation skills and to get college scholarships, and viewers around the world applauded the personal triumph of a Miss America over her impaired hearing. Yet many suggest that an increasing number of competitors are undergoing cosmetic surgery (*Bloomington Herald Times* 1994). These contradictions and ambivalences are themselves deserving of analysis and underscore the importance of beauty contests as sites for ethnographic study.

While many scholars fail to take the business of beauty pageants and contests seriously, there is good evidence that assessments of physical beauty play a basic role in the everyday life of most societies. Repeated studies find, for example, that American men and women who approximate the Western cultural ideal earn significantly higher wages than those who do not (Averett and Korneman 1994; Hamermesh and Biddle 1994). The failure to grant beauty pageants serious attention may reflect a reluctance to deal with beauty itself as a serious matter. Yet recent scientific propositions that knowing what is beautiful is the result of hard-wired pathways in the visual cortex mirror in some disturbing ways both similar propositions about intelligence and personality, and mid-twentieth century efforts to develop a physical science capable of defining the perfect human body (Cash and Pruzinsky 1990; Sheldon et al. 1949). Cross-cultural studies reveal wide variability in peoples' assessments of what constitutes a beautiful face and body (Cassidy 1991). Combined with historical research documenting radical shifts over time in beauty ideals (Maschio 1989; Banner 1983), these cross-cultural studies suggest that beauty has everything to do with culture and power (Lakoff and Scherr 1984), and very little to do with a physically objective, or genetically prescribed basis for human notions of beauty (Nichter and Nichter 1991).

The limited scholarly work on beauty contests may also reflect the association of beauty contests with entertainment and popular culture. Yet resistance to beauty pageants and contests is a long-standing practice in the United States, and has been a principle means of articulating and grounding many American feminist principles and movements (Corrigan 1992). Barnum's first pageant was canceled due to popular protest on the grounds of indecency, and established American church groups attacked the Miss America pageant annually for many years, because they thought it vulgar, indecent, and degrading. In 1922, a woman's league attacked the

Miss America pageant as "insulting to womanhood"; modesty, one of the greatest safeguards of the "Morals of Nation," was being endangered. In 1927, the federation of women's clubs asked that beauty pageants be abandoned because they were degrading to "American girlhood" (Deford 1971, 245-47). North American feminists took up many of the same critiques during the 1960's and 1970's, likening a beauty queen to "a prize cow, a slave, or a coveted piece of candy" (Riverol 1992, 1). The famous 1968 protest against Miss America was an important event bringing feminism into popular consciousness (Douglas 1994). Subsequent protests of the exclusion of women of color from the Miss America contest, and of the complicity of beauty contests in imposing dangerous body images on women and promoting self-hatred, articulated key political positions for American feminists.

Cultural critics argue that in treating popular culture as trivial, we risk obscuring the operation of structures of power that are masked by the seemingly frivolous nature of events and images (Mukerji and Schudson 1991). A central issue raised for both contestants and observers of beauty contests is the degree to which they impose control, mapping power onto the bodies of their participants by forcing beauty into a narrow and arbitrary mold. One of the ways they do this is by promoting the illusion that there is, in fact, a beauty standard, that beauty can be measured objectively, and that beauty has a concrete existence apart from the individual. If beauty cannot be reduced to an objective formula or a genetic prescription, it can nonetheless be "naturalized." By promoting a sense of consensus about beauty, beauty contests narrow notions of diversity, reduce the range of possibilities for individual expression, and allow special interests and small constituencies to speak for the majority. Meanwhile, decisions rendered in beauty contests—which by most accounts are seldom objective and replicable (Deford 1971, 41)—make the social, contextual, and subjective appear biological, universal, and absolute.

But culture and power are hardly ever uniformly experienced or seamlessly meshed. Rarely do they conspire effectively to force a single image on consumers or audiences of popular culture (Fiske 1989). Consumers of culture have demonstrated amazingly creative and resistive responses to powerful cultural images and icons (Ang 1985; Mankekar 1993; Radway 1984). Similarly, the work that beauty contests do to suppress culture within nature is never complete. This is why beauty contests are almost always—as the opening newspaper accounts indicate—riven by scandal, discord, and dispute. There is always a division between frontstage and backstage, a rupture between the objective selection of a winner in the main event, and all the other interests that both contestants and viewers know are influencing the outcome: the commercial, the class-based, the personal, the political. It is the "something more" going on in beauty contests that is at the root of their enduring attraction both for their audiences and their ethnographers.

Gender, Contests, and Power

Misreadings, missed cues, and passionate audience responses are as much a part of beauty contests as the standard elements of contestant introductions, fashion competitions, and "royal" promenades. Beauty contests are places where cultural meanings are produced, consumed, *and* rejected, where local and global, ethnic and national, national and international cultures and structures of power are engaged in their most trivial but vital aspects. Each description of a beauty contest included in this book records an encounter between different systems of knowledge and structures of power as they are played out in a public competitive event. Each also demonstrates the complex ways that beauty contests connect to issues and struggles going on in arenas outside of the immediate purview of the contest.

In some instances, the issue at hand and the object of struggle is the beauty contest itself. Mary Moran's study of Liberian queen rallies, Katherine Borland's study of a Nicaraguan India Bonita ("Pretty Indian") contest, and Carole McGranahan's discussion of a Chinese-government sponsored Miss Tibet contest make clear that these struggles are hardly trivial. Often what's at stake are the very terms and values to be used in consolidating a people as a nation and determining the trajectory of the development of a nation-state. In Moran's analysis of changes in a Liberian queen rally over a single year, in Richard Sanders and Sarah Pink's description of public disputes over an Andalusian cultural queen pageant, and in Richard Wilk's overview of the history of Belize's national beauty pageant, beauty contests emerge as tools for articulating different political positions in rapidly changing social and political climates. Many of the studies also find a strong connection between beauty contests and notions of social progress; as Borland puts it in her study of a Nicaraguan contest, "For new nations of the southern hemisphere...organizing a beauty contest now often functions as a badge of civilized, modern status."

That an event bringing women, beauty, and competition together as an important site to represent the nation and its status is itself significant. These studies of beauty contests underscore their role in nationalist projects by asking the question, as Moran does in her analysis of the Liberian queen rallys, "What is it about the privileging of a particular kind of female physical appearance that serves as such a highly charged point of articulation between local and national discourses?" Carlota McAllister notes in her study of a Maya Queen contest that, as events where women are publicly judged, beauty contests project "an idealized national femininity." Beverly Stoeltje's analysis of gender signification in a community festival in Texas demonstrates how idealized femininity is linked to capitalism's social relations of production and how, by standing for some larger entity or ideal, beauty contestants are schooled to their particular social and economic roles. Lena Moskalenko's insider account of a Miss Moscow contest, and Penny Van Esterik's overview of Thailand's involvement in the Miss Universe pageant demonstrate a similar link between women's productive and reproductive roles in society and official notions of beauty and femininity paraded in state-supported beauty contests. Nevertheless, as Stoeltje points out, contestants—and especially beauty queens— are granted a voice to speak publicly, and "the queen's voice may minimize the link to its sponsors and thus to the social obligation to speak for the point of view of those sponsors."

Struggles over beauty contests are also struggles over the power to control and contain the meanings mapped on the bodies of competitors. Mark Johnson's study of transvestite beauty pageants in the southern Philippines and Colleen Ballerino Cohen's study of a male and female contest in the British Virgin Islands point to the important link between precepts of gender difference, and power and privilege. They show how contestants' performances of gender imbue "naturalness" into political constructs like "nation" and "citizen." They also reiterate a point made in several of these papers. That is, as Wilk puts it in his discussion of two Belizean contests, while pageants "can serve the state's goals of 'domesticating difference,' of channeling potentially dangerous social divisions into the realm of aesthetics and taste...they can also fail in getting this message across, and can end up emphasizing and exacerbating the very divisions they are meant to minimize or control."

The problem of sending a coherent message is embedded in the structure of the beauty contest itself. The meaning of representations put on stage are always being negotiated and contextualized in interactions between contestants and audience, and beauty contestants can never fully achieve the idealized role they are performing. The Minnesota contestants described by Robert Lavenda, for example, "sometimes reject the overt messages [of the pageant], sometimes choose to participate for a range of idiosyncratic reasons, and sometimes get a different message from their participation than was intended." Similarly, if the pageant described by McAllister is to accomplish its goal of representing an "authentic" Guatemalan indigenous past, "it must animate the form of the Maya Queen without fleshing her out."

Sometimes slips between what contestants think is required of them and what they actually do, expose the multiple cultural systems and structures of power in which contestants and audiences are enmeshed in their daily lives. The contestants in the rural Minnesota community queen pageants described by Lavenda in this volume are hesitant to reveal an overt interest in winning. Following a principle codified in the globally televised Miss America, Miss Universe, and Miss World pageants, these contestants demonstrate their good character and their willingness to stand for the community at-large by making a show of their support of sister-contestants. One of the contestants in a British Virgin Islands contest observed recently by Cohen appeared to be following the same principle when she responded to an interview question asking who she thought should win, by pointing to a rival contestant. The beauty contest audience registered its immediate disapproval of this move, revealing not just that self-effacement doesn't play well in the British Virgin Islands, but that the contexts within which audience and contestants negotiate meaning are themselves in constant movement.

Western models of femininity, beauty, and civility can and do inform the beauty contests described in this collection. While illuminating hegemonic principles at work in beauty pageants, the studies in this book also pay attention to how local knowledge and practices intersect with and diverge from Western ones, and to what effect. Jehanne Teilhet-Fisk's study of a Tongan beauty contest and Van Esterik's study of a Miss Universe contest in Thailand confirm that the structure of international beauty competitions is a conduit for proliferating western styles, values, and expectations. But they also highlight contrasts among local and globalized notions of beauty and identify the local conditions which enable global styles to be resisted. In Van Esterik's paper, and in Johnson's work on gay beauty contests in the Philippines, we also see how "the appropriation of a desirable yet potentially threatening global cultural other" (Johnson) is used in the on-going contest and debate over *local* identities. These themes of identity, citizenship, and affiliation surface in the contests described by Wilk in Belize, by Cohen in the British Virgin Islands, and by McGranahan in Tibet, where histories marked by colonial expansion, transnational migration and shifting political borders destabilize a homogeneous and bounded image of the nation. Wilk and McGranahan also relate the pageants to the "global reach" of multinational commodities, marketing, and corporate capital.

Conclusion

In looking at beauty pageants, we track the transmutations of a single form as it links localities in new sorts of networks and relationships. Far from being trivial or frivolous, beauty pageants are *typical*, as elements of mass consumer culture, of a kind of entertainment that subtly influences the ways we see ourselves and our communities. On a global scale, pageants and contests are representative of a kind of television-mediated linkage that ties larger and larger segments of the world population to-gether into a single audience; they are part of a global "civic" culture of sports, world music, and entertainment (Hannerz 1989, 1987; Feld 1988; Foster 1991). They make us all part of something larger, at the same time that they assure us of our own distinctiveness. While beauty pageants pro-vide crucial insights into what happens at the intersection of local, na-tional, and global culture, they also remain highly problematic sites. For everything they reveal about the contingency of power and about spaces where power is resisted, they also underscore the persistence of deeply op-pressive and limiting structures and practices—structures and practices rooted in the ideas about gender difference and sexuality paraded on the beauty contest stage.

The papers in this book all deal with beauty pageants on different lev-els. Like the pageants they study, the papers do many things simultaneous-ly and defy systematic categorization. We have put the papers in an order that reflects one of the main axes of variation in beauty pageants, the line that connects every single local event to the highest level of international competition. Beginning with Stoeltje's article on a local Texas rattlesnake festival, we move through papers focused on the way that beauty contests figure in struggles over ethnic and national identities, to those that connect local, national, and international events. Stoeltje's paper also establishes a model for analyzing beauty contests as a forum for negotiating contempo-rary cultural issues. The papers in this book reflect our enthusiasm for what beauty pageants can reveal about the entanglement of gender, con-tests, and power, and the intersecting systems and structures within which most people in the world today are enmeshed. These papers also reflect the excitement that comes from finding people with a shared enthusiasm, and from finding in each other's work new directions for our own.

Notes

Colleen Ballerino Cohen and Richard Wilk wrote this introduction together, and Beverly Stoeltje contributed through the many discussions surrounding the process.

1. The terms pageant and contest are used interchangeably in the literature, and there is no conventional distinction made between the two. In our descriptions, we use pageant to denote the elaborate form of a beauty contest, an event that combines a beauty contest with other entertainments, and "contest" to refer either to the compet-itive component of a pageant or to a competitive event whose singular focus and only "entertainment" is the contest itself.

1

The Snake Charmer Queen
Ritual, Competition, and Signification in American Festival

Beverly Stoeltje

A popular and ubiquitous class of ritual events in which women compete for a fictive royal title, princess or queen, beauty pageants occur on an annual basis in small villages and large cities around the globe. From the Snake Charmer Queen beauty contest, held at the Rattlesnake Round-Up in Sweetwater, Texas, to the Miss Ghana competition, a national event described by one critic as exhibiting "earmarks of Euro-cultural chauvinism," these events attract wide and passionate participation wherever they occur.[1] The Indy "500" automobile race of Indianapolis, Indiana, is graced with a queen, four members of her court and thirty-three princesses, while just fifty miles away in the university town of Bloomington, the Slum Goddess Pageant provides the stage for drag queens to compete in a contest suffused with "dramatic irony," exemplified by the name of the 1994 winner, *Feramona*.[2]

The International Directory of Pageants claims data on over 3000 beauty pageants worldwide. An index of its popularity, these numbers also point to the ease with which the beauty contest can be replicated. A defining feature of popular culture, replication depends on two essential features: a form (1) that can be easily reproduced and recognized and (2) that is easily adapted to local meanings and familiar symbols, values, and aesthetics—those relevant to the producers, performers, and consumers of the contest. Communities, industries, ethnic groups, cities, states, and nations find such a form attractive because it not only involves the local population, but it creates links to other communities and to hierarchies of such events in larger venues (Stoeltje and Bauman 1989).

Ease of replication and the capacity for adaptation make possible a public site in which contemporary issues can be symbolically enacted. Such sites are necessary, for, although modern societies are flooded with communication and abundant opportunities exist for addressing political issues, significant social changes must necessarily be acted out in ritual

13

performance just as they are in premodern societies. Social change requires adjustment, and, more importantly, negotiation. According to Terence Turner, transition, ambiguity, conflict, or uncontrollable elements may threaten a given structure of relations, explicitly or implicitly. Ritual behavior develops in response to such uncertainties and challenges. Through ritual, a specific definition of social relationships and social roles is demonstrated (Turner 1977). Sally Falk Moore and Barbara Myerhoff drew attention to secular rituals and argued that they "show" by acting in terms of social relationships or through the expression of ideas and values that are inherently invisible most of the time. Secular rituals display symbols of social relationships and implicitly enact their "reality"(1977, 14). Moreover, ritual often serves a conservative purpose, enacting and reinforcing social relations closer to the status quo than to the socially innovative, although it should be emphasized that a social group that represents a challenge to the status quo will also utilize ritual in support of its vision. The purpose that ritual serves, however, will be to legitimate the dominant social relations within the group that enacts it. Consequently, scholars most often characterize ritual as legitimating the sociopolitical order of a particular group, whether that group constitutes a hegemonic force or a challenge to the status quo.

In contemporary social life changes in gender roles and identity have certainly challenged the patriarchal structure of gender relations. Consistent with Terence Turner's theory of ritual as a response to a challenge to the status quo, I argue that the beauty contest is a ritual response to changing gender relations. Regarding rituals concerning sexuality, Jean S. La Fontaine pointed out that the distinction between adult and child, and the one between female and male, are fundamental to the organization of any society; they are both socially constructed concepts established through initiation rites. She argues that the core concern of rituals marking adult status is clearly adult sexuality; such rites express ideas concerning reproduction consistent with the values of those who produce them. Importantly, she states that the sexual symbolism of initiation rites is not so much about sexuality per se, but is "an attempt to harness immaterial powers to social purposes," a task accomplished by individuals with specialized knowledge who can mobilize power in ritual action (La Fontaine 1985, 114-16). La Fontaine's analysis provides a useful perspective for the consideration of beauty pageants, specifically, that the beauty pageant functions as a modern secular ritual event concerned with harnessing the powers of young women in modern society. Beauty pageants serve to legitimize the perspective of the status quo with regard to the immaterial powers of young females, publicly identifying them as signs of social and civic institutions, including the family and the business, the community and the nation. The ritual contest in which young women compete against each other for the title of queen serves to link the individual contestants to the sponsoring institution as a representative of it, creating both an ideal standard by which to judge women and defining women's role as a sign of an institution to which she is responsible.

Beauty Pageant as Symbolic Inversion

Democratization and modernization have developed together, supported by an ideology of egalitarianism and the economic philosophy of capitalism. Such an environment might seem to some an unlikely location for rituals that would harness the powers of adult sexuality; nevertheless, young, nubile, unmarried women are the subjects/objects of beauty pageants, events that place them in a public contest characterized by a specific ritual form that introduces them formally to their communities as candidates for womanhood and as competitors for the status of ideal female, the young adult woman who will represent the social or civic community, state, industry, or nation. As we consider the context of beauty contests, let me note again the role of ritual as a response to a challenge that would change existing power relations. As scholars from Emile Durkheim to David Kertzer have observed, ritual legitimates the power relations of the status quo because it unites a particular image of the universe with a strong emotional attachment to that image (Kertzer 1988, 40). The means by which ritual accomplishes that purpose were closely examined by Victor Turner whose many volumes on the subject identified the process by which ritual imbues norms and values with emotions and aesthetics. In his words, in ritual "the irksomeness of moral constraint is transformed into the 'love of virtue'" (Turner 1967, 30).

Pageants that feature a contest of beauty utilize the image of queen, a role that might appear quite inconsistent with egalitarian societies. Queens, like kings, are associated with monarchies, the opposite of democracies, so their appearance in modern societies constitutes a form of symbolic inversion. For the most part, this special kind of ritual has been observed in hierarchical societies where these inversions or reversals elevate the low to the high and vice versa. They license taboo behavior and the expression of the unthinkable during a short period of liminal time. When the ritual/festival/carnival comes to an end, the hierarchical structures or the "normative" standards are restored as the guidelines and standards for social behavior.[3] Modern societies based upon egalitarian or democratic ideologies engage in rituals of inversion or reversals as well. The fictive queen produced by the ritual beauty pageant represents just such an inversion in a democratic society. As in other forms of inversion, the beauty pageant creates a role that has no political power, no earning power (though, of course, many contests have financial awards and lead to future earnings), and no authority to exercise over other people. While some contests add scholarship money and other remunerations associated with everyday life, the significant reward in the majority of queen contests is the status she acquires and its "symbolic capital."[4] Scholarly work in recent years has recognized that the ritual behavior of symbolic inversions can exert an important influence on the norms of everyday life, as participants will carry their experience and their status with them back into the quotidian domains of social life. Indeed, participants in beauty contests are motivated to participate not only by the prospect of winning, but by the glamor of the experience and the status associated with the event, whether or not one is a "winner." If we accept that the beauty pageant qualifies as a ritual that creates a liminal space in which symbolic inversion can be employed to create the fictive role of queen and to harness the social powers of young women, we nevertheless want to know what messages the ritual communicates regarding adult womanhood and what knowledge the contestants have acquired, as well as the skills and roles they have learned as a consequence of their experience. We also want to know how the event relates to the social context constituted by the society and/or nation in which it is performed, that is, to the social relations of power that produced the event. Finally, we want to know what motivates young women around the world to engage in a contest that often "terrifies" them at the same time that it attracts them to its stage. The answers to these questions lead us to consider the principles of enactment utilized by the beauty pageant, or what actually takes place that defines this experience.

Although it derives its form from the reservoir of the ritual genres, a large body of public and private events that follow a specific form and result in a transformation (social, sacred, political, or fictive), the beauty pageant achieves its purpose by mobilizing the mechanisms of signification and competition. Linked together in a unique combination, these processes define the ritual contest of the beauty queen, creating a form that embodies the message and communicating it to both participants and audience. These two mechanisms have been combined in the beauty contest in order to provide the dynamic and the motivation that links together the individual female, specific units of the community, and the community as a whole.

Signification

In the majority of beauty pageants the contestants must be sponsored by some business or social group or political unit. Contests are often arranged in a hierarchy. In a local contest each contestant must be sponsored by an organization or group within the community, and when the queen is selected, she may next be sponsored by the general community or local unit;

At the next level of the contest hierarchy, the winner may be sponsored by the state, and after that by the nation or national entity. In this process a contestant always represents her sponsoring unit, and is linked to it by a relationship of representation. In so doing she performs as a sign.

C.S. Peirce defined a sign as follows:

> A sign, or *representamen*, is something which stands to somebody for something in some respect or capacity....The sign stands for something, its object. It stands for that object, not in all respects, but in reference to a sort of idea. (Peirce in Nöth 1990, 42)

Umberto Eco's comments on women as sign are especially useful in this context. Building on Levi-Strauss's much criticized theory on the exchange of women, he explains (from the male perspective) how women act as signs:

> Because it is only a woman's symbolic value which puts her *in opposition*, within the system, to other women. The woman, the moment she becomes "wife." is no longer merely a physical body: she is a *sign* which connotes a system of social obligations. (Eco 1976, 26)

Elizabeth Cowie argues that although Levi-Strauss linked together his theories of women as the term of exchange in kinship systems and his theory of communication, she believes it possible

> to disengage them in order to open up questions about women's subordinate position on the one hand and the representation of women in signifiying systems on the other. (1990, 51)

Cowie goes on to say that exchange is not itself constitutive of the subordination of women, but subordination occurs because of the modes of exchange instituted. She points out that the terms or items of exchange must already be constituted in a hierarchy of value in order to be available for exchange. Once they are constituted as terms of exchange, they are defined by the mode of the structure of exchange. The woman as sign reiterates the semiotic fundamental, that signs are only meaningful within the system of signification in which they are produced, not as discrete units.

Through the dynamics of sponsorship and representation the beauty contest produces a system of signification. From the actual process of entering the contest, through the preparation for the performance and the contest itself, women are transformed from girls to women and produced as signs.

Competition

Competition, the second principle, functions to create the winner of the beauty contest. As the hallowed force of capitalism and the principle of most public ritual in modern society (sport and politics), competition organizes individuals into rule-governed action that sets individuals against each other until a winner is created. Competition is ideally suited to balance the forces of democracy and aristocracy, of egalitarianism and elitism, for through competition some individuals can be determined to be superior to others. Any form that utilizes the principle of competition sets up its rules and utilizes a form for the process of selecting the contestants and the winners as well. There are those, of course, who argue that competition simply operates "objectively" to select "the best" out of any category, but every competitive activity functions as a system of signification, endowing its constituent elements with certain meanings and values. Analyzing the system in regard to its values, particularly if it draws upon an existing sex/gender system, allows us to analyze the ideological base upon which it rests and to identify the goals achieved by the competition.

Formal competitive events afford a framework that people believe to be rational and operational, which can then be utilized for sorting individuals into hierarchies. Focusing on women's appearance and placing women in a competitive display event that licenses the public gaze on them, beauty contests utilize the principle of competition to determine the "best," the woman who comes closest to the ideal image of a woman in a given context. In that the contestants are measured against an ideal, they also come to represent that image, thereby functioning in a second kind of signification, the representation of the ideal woman.

Up to this point I have characterized beauty contests as a public event that draws from the rich reservoir of the ritual genres for its operating principles, its social functions, and its familiar form. Resting safely behind the performance of all such events, however, is power. We must, then, turn to a consideration of power to address the question of agency that serves as the guiding force in the production of the beauty pageant and the question of signification, what it is that women are representing in the beauty contest and preparing for in adult womanhood.

Michel Foucault argues that analyses of power should not be concerned with the obvious and the official, but with

> power at its extremities, in its ultimate destinations, with those points where it becomes capillary, that is, in its more regional and local forms and institutions...where it is in direct and immediate relationship with that which we can provisionally call its object, its target, its field of application, there—that is to say—where it installs itself and produces its real effects. (1986, 232-44)

Beauty contests qualify unambiguously as local forms that also exist in a hierarchy linking the local to the global. A popular institution where power installs itself and produces real effects, the beauty contest is, however, embedded in a discourse that declares it frivolous or "simply" entertainment, thereby masking the relations of power. Foucault emphasizes the role of discourse in the exercise of power.

> In any society, there are manifold relations of power which permeate, characterize and constitute the social body, and these relations of power cannot themselves be established, consolidated nor implemented without the production, accumulation, circulation and functioning of a discourse. (1986, 227)

Although discourse is constitutive of social life and expresses the relations of power as it is used, its very familiarity may disguise its message bearing capability. As Richard Fardon states, power is derivative of metaphors whose primary senses lie elsewhere and

> is never directly visible, it has to be read off. But its visibility may be promoted through objectifications of power which dramatise its thing-like nature and the concomitant possibilities of localisation and possession. (1985, 7-8)

Elsewhere I have proposed a model for analyzing the flow of power in the ritual genres that attempts to recognize both the creativity of power and the inequality of social relations so often revealed in these events (Stoeltje 1993). The model identifies three sources that frame the performance of a ritual event and which must be taken into account in order to identify the location of power:

1. the evolution of the form
2. the discourse in which it is embedded
3. the organization of production.

The evolution of the "form" runs through time, incorporating influences of specific sociopolitical contexts; the "discourse" includes the language of the performance itself, but also that of any texts concerning it, including those used by the media, and especially the oral traditions which circulate informally; the "organization of production" refers to the organization of forces and energies necessary to materially produce the event, including the decisions concerning the rules, the form, access to the performance and the selection process for determining the outcome. All of these sources function together in any single event to produce the actual performance, and all of these involve choices and decisions that are made by specific individuals at some level during the organization of the event.

Although power operates through these sources, the actual performance event deflects attention away from them, focusing on the action of the subject. In the case of beauty contests, young women are placed on display and evaluated in relation to standards of beauty and behavior;

women and beauty are the subject or target of power that is not visible. It must be "read off."

At this point I would like to turn our gaze on beauty to the Miss Snake Charmer Queen contest in Sweetwater, Texas, and attempt to read off power as it circulates in this particular event and encounters its target, women, directly in the contest.

Miss Snake Charmer Queen/The Rattlesnake Round-Up

From the beginning we should be aware that this event is embedded in the Rattlesnake Round-Up, a local community festival occurring annually in February. Every annual celebration has a stated purpose and a specific symbol (Stoeltje 1992). The rattlesnake serves that function in Sweetwater, a small town located in northwest Texas where the residents are engaged in agriculture and small business. The Round-Up is organized by the Jaycees of Sweetwater, the local chapter of the nation-wide organization of young businessmen. Many of the Jaycees grow beards or mustaches for the Round-Up and wear cowboy hats, jeans, boots, and red vests decorated with a rattlesnake image during the event. One of their activities is guiding out-of-town visitors, some of whom are wealthy tourists, on rattlesnake hunts. At some point prior to the Round-Up all of the contestants in the beauty pageant are taken out on a hunt together.

The Round-Up gathers thousands of snakes together in the City Auditorium for viewing, milking, butchering, and eating. When the Round-Up begins, the snakes are brought to the City Auditorium and placed in "pits," circular bins constructed with waist-high solid fences that permit easy viewing. The live snakes maintain a constant, low-level buzz with their rattles and a stench that no amount of "air freshener" can affect. Throughout the day the Jaycees organize demonstrations in which the venom is "milked" from snakes, snakes are "handled," and snakes are skinned, butchered, cooked, and eaten. Snake products for sale include belts, hat bands, wallets, belt buckles, paper weights and translucent toilet seats with fangs inside them.

Whether one associates snakes with the serpent of the Garden of Eden, bearing knowledge and connoting evil, or with the phallic symbolism so pervasive in popular culture, or with the murky unconscious, snakes reverberate with symbolic messages suggesting the power and danger of sexuality. The concentration of so many rattlesnakes inside a single building and the "handling" and "milking" demonstrations, in which a man holds a snake between his legs and squeezes venom out of the snake's mouth with his hands, create an atmosphere saturated with sexual potency and subtle messages of danger represented by the rattlesnake's venom.

Male and female symbolism come together when the winner of the Miss Snake Charmer contest enters the pit to "handle" a rattlesnake. The rules of the Miss Snake Charmer pageant require that the Queen must go to the Round-Up where the rattlesnakes are gathered together, enter "the pit" with the rattlesnakes and demonstrate for the crowd that she can handle a rattlesnake. A dramatic contrast to the queen on the pageant stage, the queen in the rattlesnake pit must confront the challenge of the snake in her hand.

Miss Snake Charmer Pageant

Held in the evening at the High School Auditorium the Miss Snake Charmer Pageant attracts a huge crowd of family and friends of the contestants. The Round-Up itself can be understood as a community festival. As such it belongs to the classification of the ritual genres, specifically to the celebrations that occur annually, that are designed for the participation of the general population and are built around a familiar local symbol. Festivals characteristically offer a range of events including food, drink, music, dance, and a specific event recognizable as a ritual drama or contest in which some transformation takes place.

The beauty contest that is replicated in so many communities around the world, adapted to the specific places with local symbols and definitions of gender, is the ritual drama of the festival. Set apart in its own location where it can be formally enacted, the pageant presents the young women of the town to the public for evaluation and judges them according to an "ideal" standard, ultimately determining that one of them deserves the title of *Queen*. Replication of this event is made possible because of its form. Like other rituals, the beauty pageant defines space specifically for the purpose of its action, setting up the performers and the audience in a specific relationship; it follows rules that order the action into a sequence creating, in this case, a contest and ultimately a winner. It has defined roles (the announcer, the judges, the contestants, the organizers), and a specific performance in which the contestants must wear apparel designed to attract attention to their bodies. Finally, of course, the action produces a transformation: one of the contestants becomes the queen. These features of formality, of transformation, of performance, are all derived from the elements that constitute the ritual genres, a category of formal enactments encompassing the many variations of ritual behavior—festivals, pageants, drama, rites of passage, celebrations.[5]

Set on the stage of the city auditorium, the Snake Charmer Beauty Pageant opened its program in 1990 with a choreographed musical performance by the contestants, twenty-three high school girls dressed in short skirts and sweaters, and several young male dancers.[6] Like all of the other Round-Up events, the "organization of the production" of the beauty pageant rests in the hands of the Jaycees, but a group of women train and prepare the contestants and choreograph the entertainment. Together they constitute the traditional authorities in the local setting who determine the rules for participation and organize the actual performance/contest. These authorities select the judges who will decide who are the finalists, and ultimately, who is the winner. Power is for the most part invisible for it rests in the hands of individuals who do not appear or appear only briefly at the pageant.

Another kind of authority, however, occupies a position of visible power in the performance in that it provides the discourse for the event, presenting the contestants to the audience and explaining the particulars of each contestant. This position is known as the master of ceremonies.

The beauty contest discourse begins and the form is brought to life when the crowd is welcomed and made to feel a part of the event by the president of the Sweetwater Jaycees. Speaking as a representative of the sponsoring organization that controls the production of the overall event, he introduces the master of ceremonies for the evening, who becomes the Voice of the event, mediating between the contestants and the audience, providing the discourse of the event.

In 1990 the master of ceremonies began with an introduction of the judges for the pageant, all of whom were from neighboring towns, and some of whom were previous residents. They included: (1) a public affairs consultant for a very large manufacturer in a neighboring city; (2) a former contestant who moved to a neighboring city to teach exercise classes and design clothes (3) the president of the statewide Jaycee organization; and (4) the executive vice president of the nationwide Jaycee organization, a native of the town who became a model. Local ties are important in the identities of the judges, but of equal importance is the fact that they are all residents of some other city at the time of the pageant. They exercise a great deal of power as they select the winner of this competition; consequently, while their identity is no secret and, in fact, is publicly announced, they are never introduced to the audience. They are told by the organizers to consider the poise of each contestant in their decision making.

In our effort to read off power in the event, it is significant to emphasize that the judges, who are endowed with the power to select the winner, are selected by the organizers of the event and remain invisible, separated from the audience by a layer of mystification. Yet, they have strong local ties, legitimating them as members of the society; they are not foreigners.

The Snake Charmer Queen Pageant

The Pageant competition is divided into two parts, the "Casual Competition" and the "Formal Competition." The terms *casual* and *formal* refer to dress style. In the Casual Competition the contestants walk on stage and move around like models in a fashion show, wearing dresses that would be classified as "dressy" in a department store. In the Formal Competition the contestants again walk on stage one at a time and move around as if in a fashion show, wearing long formal dresses ("ball gowns" or "evening gowns") made of taffeta, net, or satin, and often strapless or draped off one shoulder. Each of these competitions requires only that the girls walk around the stage, stop, and turn and look over their shoulder at the audience.

Focusing the competition on the contestant's dress and appearance as she walks about the stage not only draws attention to the female body, but appearance and dress specifically serve to define gender. M. Gottdiener states that, "Dress is one way that gender status differences are signified and enforced," and that the act of wearing women's clothing validates the female's subordinate role (1995, 10). Dress functions to communicate about gender and in itself constitutes "a system of sign vehicles that help to regulate the important social division of gender relations" (1995, 10). Certainly the more formal a dress is, the more it distinguishes the female from the male, calling attention to the subordination of women, especially in the formal gown which limits movement. Moreover, the formal gown disengages the wearer from her quotidian context and establishes her as an object of display, to be gazed upon by the audience.

In both competitions the master of ceremonies provides us with the knowledge of who the woman's parents are and who her sponsor is. In the Casual Competition, following this information, he tells the audience the contestant's age, classification in high school, her achievements, her honors, and her affiliations, such as the church she attends. Then he lists the foods she likes to eat in some detail.

Contestants are generally fifteen, sixteen, or seventeen years of age. As mentioned above, one of the requirements for each contestant is that she find a sponsor for herself. One contestant explained to me that girls just simply go to businesses and ask them to sponsor them. She was sponsored by the employees of the business where her father worked. The sponsor then pays the entry fee that ranges between $50.00 and $100.00. Examples of sponsors include the Hair Design, the Rolling Plains Campground, Dairyland, local Coca-Cola employees, a funeral home, a bank, an IGA (grocery store), or a flower shop. In this act of obtaining a sponsor, a young woman experiences a lesson in becoming a sign. She learns that in order to enter this contest she must represent someone other than herself. This involves persuading a company or group that she (or her parents) are worth the entry fee and that it wants to see her riding in the parade wearing the name of its business and representing it, standing for it, in the beauty contest itself.

With the listing of the contestants' achievements and afffiliations, attention is focused on the individual rather than her family or sponsor, but in this category she is evaluated in regard to an ideal standard for women that requires them to be an active participant in their community, a "credit" to their family. Activities in which they participate include: the Christian Athletes, the Honor Society, the Student Council, volleyball, one-act plays, the Mexican-American Club, the church, barrel racing in rodeo, tennis, the West Texas Teen-Ager Pageant, and so on. The contestants' taste in food differs little from that of the larger population: pizza, hamburgers, meat loaf, cheesecake. Yet the inclusion of food preferences into this list acknowledges food as a semiotic system, a variable in the inventory of identity features that describes yet another of the contestants' personal preferences for the public.

In the Formal Competition the master of ceremonies announces to the audience the contestant's hair and eye color and her height. Then, as she walks about on stage for the audience to gaze upon her, the master of ceremonies speaks for her and tells the audience what she likes to do—her hobbies, sports, and extracurricular activities. He also provides a list of the musicians the individual likes, just as he listed the taste in food in the casual competition, and, finally, he provides the information about her plans for attending college. Some plan to attend major state universities, and others expect to attend smaller schools closer to home. A few of the contestants state what subjects they wish to study at the university. In the listing of identity features, drawing on the contestant's physical characteristics, her activities of choice, religion, and educational goals, the audience is offered yet more detailed information about the young woman who is on display. Reminiscent of an auction block in which livestock or antiques or farm equipment are placed on display, described and auctioned off to the highest bidder, the young women are presented to the public, stripped of their privacy; knowledge of them is offered to the audience for their consumption. As the contestants are judged on their poise and beauty on stage, it is not possible to know just how significant any of this information is to the judges.

After each contestant is presented to the audience by the master of ceremonies, the audience is entertained with more musical performance while the judges make their decision, and then the contestants return, and the finalists are announced. Each finalist must then select a question to answer. These concern current political and social issues such as "Do you think it is fair to take money from a rich school district and give it to a poor one?" "What can we do to curtail youth gang wars?" "Should a coach have a right to voice an opinion about decisions of a referee?" "Will more prisons help to solve the crime problem?" "What do you think could be a possible solution to the homeless problem?"

The pageant discourse takes a significant turn as the contestants speak for themselves, and, moreover, speak on subjects concerning the welfare of society as a whole. The message communicated by this segment of the ritual in which the young women are asked to display their knowledge is that the ideal woman who will represent the community should have some knowledge of social issues. In providing a podium for the contestants' voice, the pageant displays some recognition that women are voting, speaking members of society. However, the fact that only the finalists are expected to speak suggests a distinction between a class of women whose opinions are worth hearing and another class whose voice we do not want to hear. As with all symbolic forms, the voice has power, and, therefore, the speaker can use the opportunity to speak independently, to be heard as an individual. On the contrary, the speaker, who represents her family and a business or institution, may feel compelled to represent the views of her sponsor when she speaks, for she will be evaluated by the community on the basis of what she says whether or not the judges consider her words seriously. In either case, public speaking represents one of the skills that women learn in beauty pageants, whether they learn to speak the words their sponsors want to hear or words they feel that they chose independently of a link to particular individuals. In any case, they learn that they will be judged on the basis of their verbal performance by the community/audience.

Having answered their questions, for the most part with minimal information, the contestants leave the stage, the curtain comes down, and the judges deliberate. Meanwhile, the Jaycees' Beard Contest occupies the audience. For this event, the contestants stand on the stage while judges measure, joke with the audience, and eventually determine winners according to three criteria: the longest, the ugliest, and the best looking beards. Although the beard contest occupies a short period of time, it nevertheless offers a contrast to the pageant: the ugly with the beautiful and the male with the female. The message communicated is one that places an emphasis on gender differences, specifically ones that are exaggerated during this ritual inversion.

Having completed this display of masculinity, the beards return the stage to the beauty contest. The curtain rises and the contestants are all present on the stage together, along with the Miss Snake Charmer Queen from the previous year who will crown the new queen. She is introduced and states something to the effect that she "wouldn't trade this year for anything." The woman who directs and organizes the contest appears on stage and expresses her appreciation to her assistants and then presents the Miss Congeniality award to the contestant who was voted the most pleasant to be around by the other girls. Characteristic of many American festivals, this award permits recognition of the relationship among women, stressing the importance of qualities that encourage consideration and politeness among women, which is the opposite of competition, the feature that defines the queen contest itself. This award does not figure in the judging for the queen as it is determined by the contestants.

A second award is announced to the winner of the essay part of the contest. The 1990 essay topic addressed the question, "Which freedom do you treasure the most and why?" Functioning independently of the queen contest, the essay contest again provides an opportunity for women to speak through writing. As a part of this overall event, produced by the Jaycees, it also provides an opportunity for educating the women into a particular understanding of citizenship, once again creating an awareness of the power of public opinion to judge one's words.

At last the winner of the beauty contest is announced, and in 1990 she was the contestant who was runner-up in the previous year's contest. It is a common ocurrence that a runner-up is selected as the winner in the following year, and some believe this continuity has become a traditional practice. The former queen crowns the new queen, and her father comes on stage to give her a kiss. She is congratulated by big crowds of friends, bringing to an end the annual competition for the title of Miss Snake Charmer Queen.

The Ritual of Representation

The beauty pageant replicates a ritual form that creates the context for the formal introduction of young women to their community, state, or nation. In so doing the women are transformed into a special class through the principle of competition. In this class of "contestants," however, each individual must be sponsored by a community unit, creating her as a sign of that unit.

The United States has defined itself as a democracy from its beginning, but foundational to its capitalist ideology is the principle of competition, a mechanism for creating distinctions between winners and losers, elites and commoners. This principle is employed in the beauty contest, a form of ritual inversion in modern societies that teaches women to compete. However, in the contest they must represent a community interest or the community, state, or nation itself. In this link, the social and civic units harness the power of young women, socializing them to their community, state and nation. The selection process for Queen teaches the young women that they are responsible to their community and that they will be judged by their community. First they must obtain a sponsor in order to enter, creating the first link to their community; then they must appear on stage and be described by a male authority to the public; then a few of them will be permitted to speak; and, finally, they will be judged on these qualities. In all of this the goal is the opportunity to become the sign of the community or the nation, to represent the larger body and simultaneously to stand for the ideal woman.

As Turner points out, ritual succeeds by connecting the emotional to the obligatory, by transforming moral constraint into the love of virtue. The beauty contest stimulates intense emotions for the young women who are competing. As each individual appears on the stage, presenting herself and her body for judgment, both by the judges and informally by the audience who clap enthusiastically or modestly for each contestant, she experiences fright, anxiety, and excitement in her moment in the spotlight when the attention of the judges and her community is totally focused on her—her physical dimensions, her eating habits, her dress, her sponsor. One contestant explained that she likes being the center of attention and riding in the parade. But she also found it scary, and it made her (and other contestants too) very nervous. She described her feelings as an adrenaline rush. Now that she has gone to college and no longer competes in queen contests she misses the competition, which she described as "working for something." The enthusiasm, fright, and anxiety experienced by contestants are those emotions that are linked to the norms and values of a community in ritual, the competitive performance event of the beauty contest. It creates the desire in the contestants to compete for the goal and thereby ensures the participation of a significant number of the young women of the community in the ritual event that defines the role of women as a sign of civic and political units and communicates to all that a woman's performance in everday life is on display for judgment by the community.

Power can be read off here in two directions. The first is the means by which power flows through the organizers of the production of the event to produce a ritual performance. The second is the expression of the power of young women who are approaching adulthood and the potential for assuming mature female roles in society. Through the selection process and the performance itself the ritual event establishes that community authority (usually dominated by males, and females who are willing to conform to male standards) will harness the immaterial powers of young women as they approach adulthood, directing those powers and energies toward the community norm. That norm defines woman as a sign of a larger unit and judges her according to her public performance as a sign. In this process the power of norms and values flows through community authority to harness the power of the target, the young women who are the subject of the event.

Two categories of signification are operating as the channel through which power circulates with the purpose of defining gender roles for adult women. One links the individual contestant to her sponsor. In this she represents and acts as a sign of her sponsor. She functions as an index of that sponsor, and she is evaluated as an indexical sign of it as well as of herself.

In the second she is attempting to conform to the image of the ideal woman as imagined by the producers, acting as leaders of the community (or nation), and the close scrutiny of her body, her habits, and her tastes are judged in relaton to this ideal. Each contestant is willing to be scrutinized in order to compete for the goal, not only in the degree to which her body conforms to expectations, but in regard to her behavior and position in the community as well. The Queen, who is the winner of the competition, will not only signify the ideal woman in appearance, but the behavioral traits as well, central to which is the ability to compete against other women and to function successfully as a sign of a social or political entity.

While power in the form of gender subordination of the female finds its target in the contest of beauty, it nevertheless rewards the contestants in the competition with a small measure of power of their own. Limited to the constraints of the sign system that outlines the role of women in modern society, the contestants, and especially the Queen, are rewarded with public recognition. The Queen is granted a voice to speak publicly, although she always speaks as a sign of the unit she represents. Given that hegemonies rarely exert total saturation and that rituals cannot resist the influences of contemporary social issues and still remain attractive, we must note that the beauty contest, too, exhibits indications of change.

Consequently, both queens and their sponsors adapt in selected places and times to the changing norms and values of society, and some queens utilize the power of their position to speak independently, minimizing the link to sponsors and to social norms that would perpetuate the status quo. The new Miss USA, Miss Texas Chelsi Smith, like some other winners in recent years, represents a departure from the status quo and a voice that recognizes social problems. In her first public statement she stated that she plans to draw on her biracial background to teach children about the harms of racism and the importance of self-esteem.

In conclusion, then, we can observe that the beauty contest is a ritual event replicated in communities, states, and nations around the globe, and consequently, that it reflects the social norms and values of those communities through the signification system it produces. As a ritual that targets young women and attempts to harness their powers to social purposes, the beauty contest reflects the uncertainty, change, and contradictions inherent in contemporary systems of gender signification. It identifies both the fundamental principles by which modern society sustains a system in which women are subordinated, and points toward the channels of power potentially available to women for the transformation of systems of gender signification into those which liberate rather than subordinate.

Notes

For a video treatment of the Snake Charmer Queen Pageant, see "Venom in a Jar, A Kiss from the Queen," by Gretchen Stoeltje. I want to express my appreciation to her and to Linka Kinsey Adams for use of materials from their documentary project on the Rattlesnake Round-Up. Also, I want to express my appreciation to Leigh Hoskins, a contestant, for sharing her ideas with me.

1. See the critical article on Ghanaian beauty contests by Lazarus Dempsey Maayang in the special issue of UHURU magazine devoted to consideration of the concept of black beauty.

2. Special thanks are due Jerry McIlvain for introducing and inviting me to the Slum Goddess Pageant during the year of his reign as the Slum Goddess. My thanks also to Joni Matthews, a member of the court, for information on the Indy "500." The term "dramatic irony" was introduced by James Fernandez who uses *irony* to mean something that is asserted but means just the opposite, and "dramatic irony" to mean an incongruity between what is asserted in discourse and the actual state of affairs (1986).

3. See Barbara Babcock, *The Reversible World* for discussion and studies of this phenomenon cross-culturally, and, more recently, Peter Stallybrass and Allon White, *The Politics and Poetics of Transgression*.

4. See Pierre Bourdieu (1977) for a discussion of symbolic capital.

5. See Richard Bauman, *Folklore, Cultural Performances and Popular Entertainments* (1992) for articles on the ritual genres.

6. Since 1990 a talent component has been added to the contest, challenging the contestants to invest more time and preparation in the event.

2

"It's Not a Beauty Pageant!"
Hybrid Ideology in Minnesota Community Queen Pageants

Robert H. Lavenda

My first response to the title of this volume was the automatic response that the people involved with small town pageants always give: "It's not a beauty pageant!" They are quite insistent that the term "beauty pageant" is inappropriately applied to the event that chooses a community queen. To them, to talk of "beauty" is to emphasize physical features when pageants are supposed to find a representative for the community who embodies what local people believe to be the best of themselves: talent, friendliness, commitment to the community and its values, upward mobility. On the other hand, the winners—indeed, nearly all of the candidates—often look so much like the photographs in fashion magazines as to lead outsiders to question participants' claims.

My goals in this paper are to examine the dimensions of these terms for the people I know in Minnesota.[1] I contend that organizers' and participants' insistence on differentiating their event from a beauty pageant is based on their awareness that outsiders may not recognize the difference. They are, in fact, making a traditional anthropological rhetorical move— things that look the same may not have the same meaning, and it is the observer's job to discover the meanings involved. But there is an ambiguity in queen pageants that we will explore here. Why, after all, might outsiders "confuse" the queen pageant with a beauty pageant? I will argue that organizers are trying to reconcile two different and perhaps contradictory prototypes of their event: the debutante presentation and the beauty pageant. The consequence is an event that is ideologically hybrid rather than totalizing and unified, susceptible of several different possible interpretations for outsiders, for organizers, and especially for participants.

This essay is inspired by Bakhtin's discussion of intentional semantic hybrids and historical organic hybrids in language and sociolinguistic world views (Bakhtin 1981, 358-62). His text appears to oppose conscious dialogic engagement of intentional semantic hybrids (as in novelistic

31

prose) to the presumed lack of conscious dialogic engagement in the production of historical organic hybrid world views. But as Emily Schultz points out, "if intentional semantic hybrids are inevitably internally dialogic (as distinct from organic hybrids), this can be interpreted as meaning that organic hybrids are *not internally* dialogic. But it can also be interpreted as meaning that organic hybrids are *not inevitably* dialogic, although they *may* be" (Schultz 1990, 168). In the present case, I wish to argue that queen pageants are dialogic hybrids; that rather than being mired in a kind of false consciousness, organizers have taken elements of beauty pageants and debutante presentations and have, within a frame that is explicitly a play frame, created an event that is a site in which various interpretations flourish and in which a range of socially or personally significant outcomes *may* occur.

The Minnesota Community Queen Pageant as Form and Process

I think it would be well to establish clearly what queen pageants are all about in small towns in Minnesota: how they are organized and carried out, who participates, and so on.[2] Most queen pageants in Minnesota are now part of communities' summer festivals. This placement is relevant to understanding the pageant for two major reasons: first, it frames the pageant as play; second, it connects the pageant with the overarching symbolism of the festival as representing the community to itself and to a wider world. The pageant, which is very much a local event (with one important exception, discussed below) is thus connected with the official ideology of community identification.

Queen pageants begin long before the first candidate sets foot on stage to be introduced. During the winter, the organizers of the pageant begin to plan the pageant. Usually but not always, the organizers are women connected with the business or professional communities as members or as wives of members. Their plans are based on the previous year's pageant; on pageants they have seen when they have accompanied their town's queen and princesses to other towns; and on their own ideas about the pageant, derived both from their creativity and from their familiarity with pageants of other kinds, including such televised national and international spectaculars as the Miss America or Miss Universe pageants. The women involved need to plan for the structure and performance of the event, to approach businesses that have sponsored candidates in the past to solicit their continuing participation, to involve themselves in the selection of the candidates through visits to the high school and publicity articles in the newspaper, and to organize the travels of the new royalty after they have been crowned.

Candidates are selected in one of three ways. First, and most commonly, they are asked by pageant sponsors to compete. A sponsor may ask a daughter, niece, or other relative to run, may ask an employee to run, may ask his or her children for suggestions, may get a copy of the high school yearbook to find possible candidates, or may ask the organizers for help. In other towns, young women who wish to compete must find their own sponsors. The third alternative is for the organizers to find the candidates and match them with sponsors. This is most commonly done by visiting the high school and announcing the pageant, or by soliciting recommendations from teachers, school officials, or members of the business community.

The result of the selection process is first of all, that young women who appeal to members of the small business community become candidates. In order to participate in virtually all Minnesota community queen pageants, young women must be going on to some form of post-secondary education; after all, the prizes are scholarships. Usually, the institutions they have chosen are four-year colleges, although at least one or two candidates in most pageants plans to enroll at a community college, a technical college (Minnesota's name for what is elsewhere a vocation-technical school), or a business college. It is relevant to note that of the some 300 candidates I have seen in the pageants I have attended, almost all of the candidates planning to go to four-year colleges or universities are planning to attend one of the Minnesota or North Dakota state universities. A few plan to attend the leading Catholic women's liberal arts college in Minnesota, even fewer plan to attend the University of Minnesota main campus in Minneapolis, and none has ever been planning to attend a major liberal arts college (on the order of Macalester or Carleton, or one of the elite eastern women's colleges known as the Seven Sisters) or a land-grant university outside Minnesota. Membership in the community's middle class, or upward-mobility into that class, but no higher, are crucial elements in the selection of queen pageant candidates.

One of the fundamental criteria for participation in the queen pageant is a high profile in high school via active participation in many activities: sports, cheerleading, school clubs and publications, youth groups, and so on. This implies, certainly in the minds of the people with whom I have spoken, an outgoing, gregarious personality, as well as a commitment to the school and to the values for which it stands. Thus, candidates expect that all of the candidates—even if they do not know all of them very well—will fit this model. Note that in the context of a small Minnesota town, the pattern of activity is also a marker of social position and upward mobility. That is, it is the number, variety, and nature of the activities with which each candidate involved herself that serve to mark her as a likely candidate for the queen pageant and that serve as a sign of her position in town. Women involved are active in cheerleading *and* sports *and* yearbook *and* band *and* National Honor Society *and* a church youth group. These are achievements that are relevant to the local definition of status. The loner does not usually end up in the queen pageant, no matter how brilliant in her studies or her art she may be. Indeed, the brilliant do not generally compete; as a student once remarked, the best pianist in her school refused to participate in the queen pageant on the grounds that it would cheapen her accomplishments. It is well-roundedness and appropriate achievement that are sought in the candidates.[3]

Once the candidates are selected, a training process begins. There are, to be sure, differences among various towns, but a common pattern is for the candidates to spend several weeks together, sometimes over a month, preparing for the pageant. This involves rehearsals for an introductory song and dance presentation, as well as the pageant itself, parties for the candidates at the homes of organizers or prominent community members, beauty and makeup tips from local women (beauty salon operators or Mary Kay cosmetics representatives), sometimes a trip to a cosmetology or modeling school in Minneapolis or St. Paul for tips on walking on stage, cosmetics, hair, etc. The candidates universally cite this pre-pageant time as the high point of the activity, because it was fun, but also because they got to know the other candidates very well. All indicate that they did not, in fact, know all the other candidates especially well before getting involved with the pageant. This is a significant element in the class and gender-role reproduction aspects of queen pageants, as the majority of the college-bound young women of the town come together for, as it were, the final lessons in social life that their town can give them—instructions on poise, on self-presentation and good grooming, on good manners, on getting along with other members of a small town middle class.

The result of this selection and training process is the annual formation of an elite cadre within the set of young women in the community, an elite that is offered the opportunity to enter the middle-class and upper middle-class elite of the community. I have written elsewhere (see especially Lavenda 1988 and 1992) about class in Minnesota small towns, but will note here that although social class is attenuated in small Minnesota towns, it is not absent. Professionals (including bankers, physicians, lawyers, and dentists), as well as wealthy business people (grocery store owners, pharmacists, hardware store owners, and farm implement and automobile dealers), and other wealthy professional and commercial people may be considered to be part of the community's elite. Their homes are large and decorated in a style distinct from that of others in the community, they are college or professional school graduates, and their travel, vacation, and entertainment choices also set them apart. The set of markers of broad participation in school and church activities, musical accomplishment, suitable clothing, and especially, plans for post-secondary education, highlights the class position that queen pageant candidates have achieved or to which they are striving. The activities surrounding the queen pageant provide them with an early entrance into this world that they are contemplating joining.

As the festival that surrounds the queen pageant begins, the pace quickens for the candidates: there are additional rehearsals, some of which may last four or five hours; there are interviews on the local radio station, visits to nursing homes and senior centers, parties, dinners, or receptions that include their parents. Here there is important variation among communities regarding the placement of the pageant in the festival. A queen pageant at the beginning of a festival has different results than one that ends a festival. In the former case, the emphasis turns early to the winners, and there is very little for the other candidates to do after the coronation, although they always ride in the parade. In the latter case, the emphasis is on the candidates, as they ride in the parade, make appearances at various festival events, and continue to do things together until the very end.

Pageants themselves have a fairly standard format: there is frequently an opening production number, with the candidates singing and dancing; introductions of the candidates; introduction of reigning royalty; talent competition; introduction of judges and visiting royalty; evening gown competition; reigning royalty farewell; coronation of new royalty. Sometimes there are other features: an onstage question for each candidate, chosen from a bowl of questions written by the organizers; a skit by outgoing royalty; a swimsuit competition of some sort, either the Miss America or Miss USA style in which each candidate parades by herself on the stage in a swimsuit and high heels, or a group swimsuit tableau in which all the candidates are together on stage in a beach scene with towels, beach chairs, and so on.

At the pageant, as each young woman is introduced, a universal formula is followed: her name is announced, followed by the name of her parents. Candidates in community queen pageants are grounded in their communities, located precisely in the town's social world. Although this is irrelevant to the actual selection process, since the judges are almost never from the community, it is one of the most important parts of the pageant as a community event. Other aspects of the pageant, most clearly shown in the talent competition and the evening gown competition, also highlight its community dimension. In the talent competition, candidates demonstrate their achievements in singing, dance, musical performance, recitation, or drama, reminding the audience that the town is a place where, as Garrison Keilor puts it, all the children are above average. In the evening gown competition, each candidate walks out onto the stage, turns, walks, and turns again. As she does this, the master of ceremonies reads out her accomplishments:

Mickey is the daughter of Donnie and Jean Lahr. Her school activities included serving on the student council and prom committee, and she was president of the band council her junior and senior years. Mickey was a percussionist in band for seven years, and became active in various ensembles. She was also active in choir where she participated in Triple Trio and Change of Pace. Mickey participated in gymnastics and basketball and ended up her senior year as a tri-captain in tennis, a cheerleader for girls' basketball and a three-time letterer in softball. She was also featured in "Who's Who Among American High School Students" for two years. Also, for the past two years, she has been a Eucharistic Minister at St. Paul's Parish. Mickey plans to attend Concordia College in Moorhead in the field of Psychology.

Throughout this part of the pageant, the audience is invited to recognize the achievements of these young women, whom they know in context, but who are now ready to leave the community. The audience is also invited to make the leap of taking these young women to stand for all young people in the community, a much trickier but important transformation, given what the pageant is about. After all, by extension, the achievements of the candidates are the achievements of the community itself, for it is the community that has formed them and has given them the opportunities to excel.

After the last of the candidates' appearances, usually the evening gown competition, the judges get up and leave in order to begin their deliberations. At this point, the queen pageant changes in character. It has been a celebration, a festival, of the community's young women, a presentation of the latest crop of outstanding young people. Now, the contest takes over, and there is a sensible rise in the level of tension in the candidates and the audience. One of the candidates will become the queen, and two will become princesses. A differentiation will occur; three will be set apart. The debutante presentation part of the pageant is over and the "beauty contest" part takes place.

The time of the judges' absence is usually filled by the introduction of "visiting royalty," the princesses and queen from other communities who have come to town to ride in the parade and attend the coronation. There appear to be nearly endless lines of young women in long gowns who are announced, walk onto the stage, wave, and walk off. To the young people in the audience, however, the introduction of visiting royalty provides a moment for private judging—young women check out the dresses and hair styles, young men look for reasons to visit other towns in search of possible dates. The number of communities represented by visiting royalty can be taken by the host community as a marker of the importance of its festival, and of their town itself: the more royalty introduced, the more important their town. The visiting royalty also provide the entire audience with a way of comparing the representatives of other communities with their own.

Following the presentation of the visiting royalty, the town's outgoing royalty say goodbye to the community, as represented by the audience. By the time the tearful farewells are over, the judges have usually returned, and hand the envelopes containing the winners' names to the master of ceremonies. The candidates return to the stage, standing in a semi-circle and holding hands. The master of ceremonies calls over in turn each outgoing princess and the queen, shows her the name in the envelope, and each young woman then takes a tiara and crowns her successor, frequently after an excruciatingly long and tantalizing performance, particularly by the outgoing queen. She walks up and down the line of candidates, now in front, now in back, holding the crown above each head, sometimes nearly placing it down on a head, only to snatch it away at the last second. Finally, the winner is identified as the outgoing queen suddenly places the crown on the lucky head. There is applause and sometimes cheering from the audience, there are embraces by the new queen and the other candidates, and there are tears from the winner. The new queen, in tiara and sometimes in royal cape, carrying a bouquet of roses, tears in her eyes, walks across the stage and out onto the runway, waving to the crowd. Her reign begins, and she will spend many of the next fifty two weekends, especially in the summer, traveling to other festivals to attend other queen pageants, representing her community in these events.

In the course of my field experience, many times the winner has not been the popular choice. The judges at queen pageants are virtually never from the town hosting the pageant. As a result, they are only able to judge the candidates on what they see and hear: the interview, the talent competition, the evening gown competition, the answers to the questions on the stage, the poise, and the desire to be queen. The factors of interest to the community—achievement, family, personality, commitment, and so on—are either difficult to judge over a weekend or are irrelevant to the job of the judges as they understand it. They are, as best I can tell, usually operating under the beauty pageant prototype. Sometimes, when the judges come from the larger statewide competitions—Miss Minnesota USA or the Minneapolis Aquatennial—they are looking for candidates for their own competitions and so apply the standards of the more conventional beauty pageant. The community, on the other hand, is reading the candidates in a different way, based on their assessment of who these young women are as rounded persons, anchored in the social structure of the community, enhanced by their own achievements. It is important to note that very few of the community queen pageants that I am discussing connect with statewide or national competitions. One or two pageants send candidates to the Minneapolis Aquatennial Queen of the Lakes competition, and only one pageant I have studied is connected to the Miss Minnesota USA program.

Let me turn to two cases in which the conventional patterns were broken, once to the pleasure of the community and once not. Montgomery, Minnesota, is a town of some 2,400 people, many of whom strongly identify with the Czech heritage of many of their forebears. The queen pageant is part of the community's festival, Kolacky Days (named after the Bohemian fruit-filled bun), and is open to young women who have just completed their junior year of high school (this itself is quite unusual). There are sometimes as many as twenty candidates, out of a total eleventh grade population of up to 70 young women. The competition involves individual private interviews with the judges, answering on-stage questions written by the organizers, a talent presentation, and the evening gown event.

Perhaps because the candidates are younger than those at most competitions, but also because of the ethnic fronting that the festival and the queen pageant both represent, the winners do not wear the conventional "royal attire" of evening gown, tiara, and sash. Rather they wear what they refer to as the "Bun Suit," a Czech (or rather Bohemian) style outfit of white embroidered blouse, black vest, and mid-calf length embroidered red skirt. The tiara and sash are supplemental to, and overwhelmed by, the ethnic costume. Here, the iconography is clear: membership in the community takes precedence over the individual (although, it should be noted, at any event at which large numbers of royalty are gathered, the Montgomery queen is always the individual in a crowd of identically evening-gowned young women).

In 1983, there were thirteen candidates. The most popular candidate seemed to be a heavy-set, blonde, young woman, of direct Czech ancestry on both sides of the family. She was, most of the other candidates told us before the pageant, the most likely to win, because she was so outgoing, had a good talent presentation, and was 100 percent Czech. In fact, she sang well, answered the on-stage question articulately, and did win, to much applause and the apparent pleasure of the crowd. In this case, the debutante prototype had greater weight than the beauty pageant prototype, and as far as most people in the community were concerned, that was as it should be. In a crowd of slender candidates, her physical appearance was never mentioned, not even after the pageant, when one of my students talked with a rather disappointed losing candidate. (It is relevant to note that this latter young woman, whose father was an auto mechanic, claimed that, "It's okay that she won but I don't like her attitude. It's always the business people in town, the name families, that win. People like us don't have a chance.") The losing candidate's comment is apposite here: her objection is to the salience of social class and family—in her opinion, the reward should be granted on the basis of individual achievement (although many would have argued that the new queen had, in fact, won precisely on that basis.)

The second case is from Litchfield, Minnesota, a county seat of 6,000 people. Like most queen pageants, the Miss Litchfield pageant is part of the town's community festival, Watercade, and involves young women who have just graduated from high school. In the mid-1980s, the organizers of the queen pageant were anxious to have one of their queens do well in the Minneapolis Aquatennial Queen of the Lakes competition, which conforms more nearly to a classic beauty pageant model, since it lacks a talent competition. Organizers tried a number of strategies to increase their chances. They helped the candidates with their stage presentation, developed a clothing budget for the winner, transformed the swimsuit competition, and brought in Aquatennial officials to judge the pageant. In 1985, the results were nearly disastrous, when the winner was the diffident and shy daughter of one of the brothers who owned the largest business in town, a construction company known throughout that part of the state. She was attractive, slim, and short, had done a good interview with the judges, and had a very beautiful dress that she wore well, but had done poorly in the talent presentation, singing almost inaudibly and barely in tune. Unaware that the talent presentation was just a time-filler to which the judges assigned no points, the audience was shocked when she won. I am not sure that there was a popular favorite that year, but if there was, the winner was certainly not she. While people were leaving the auditorium, angry comments began: her father had bought the judges off, people speculated, since his daughter could never have won any other way. Pageant organizers rushed to arrange a lengthy interview for the head judge with the local newspaper to clarify that no points had been awarded for the talent presentation and to try to explain why the young woman had been selected. In the judge's opinion, the winner was an attractive candidate who would have a real chance at the Aquatennial, where good taste in gowns, physical attractiveness, and a good interview were important.

In Litchfield, the *beauty* pageant prototype had provided the selection criteria for the judges, but the community did not accept these criteria as legitimate for a *queen* pageant. No one in Litchfield objected to the participation of the eventual winner in the pageant—quite the contrary, she was an ideal candidate to be presented to the community along with all the others. But she was not an appropriate *winner*, since the queen pageant model is based on achievement. Indignant townspeople thought achievement included talent. In this case, it did not, but that did not mean that she had won because of who her father was. She did achieve well, but according to criteria that nobody knew about—the Aquatennial criteria.

Because the audience misunderstood what kind of achievement counted, they concluded that achievement had been ignored, leading to the further conclusion that (illegitimate) ascribed social criteria (the debutante model) had been used. As opposed to the situation in Montgomery, most of the Litchfield community considered that inappropriate, since a proper queen should display legitimate middle-class markers of achievement.

Debutantes and Beauty Queens

So let us return to the question of why organizers and participants reject the term "beauty pageant." Candidates in beauty pageants, in the view of community queen pageant organizers with whom I have spoken, are judged not on who they are and what they have accomplished but on the inborn superficialities of face and figure. As one queen pageant organizer told me in 1981, in response to a question about a swimsuit competition: "We're not running a meat market like Miss America here." An appropriate way to judge candidates is exemplified by the Miss Sauk Centre Pageant, which gives 50 percent of the possible points to "Interview and Mental Alertness," 25 percent to "Poise and Oral Introduction," and 12.5 percent each to "Creative and Performing Arts (Talent)" and "Poise and Appearance (Evening Gown)." To be sure, I have heard a judge in Hinckley, exasperated during deliberations, exclaim to her fellow judges, "Look, you want someone tall and thin who looks good waving from a float." But she was a semi-professional judge from another city, and was opposed by judges who wanted to pay more attention to the criteria set out by the pageant's organizers. As one of the masters of ceremonies at the Eden Valley Valley Daze queen pageant put it, "An event like this is part of Americana. It has occurred over many years. It is not a political statement. It is not a showcase for flaunting attributes or beauty. It is a pageant that gives honor, not to each person, but to each one of us, reflecting the contributions each of us makes to our community." Suppose we take him seriously for a moment.

I would argue that, in fact, the organizers are not necessarily looking for the most physically attractive candidate, according to some idealized standard of beauty. What they are looking for is, I think, two-fold. First, they are looking to recognize and train an elite cadre of young women within the town. Second, they are looking for someone to represent the town at a series of similar events held in other small towns around the region.[4] Given these two goals, what kind of event might meet their needs?

One possible model is clearly a debutante cotillion. As it developed in the United States, this event was a way for members of the wealthiest and most powerful class in any city to present their daughters to "Society," which consisted of the other members of the wealthiest and most powerful class in the city. This presentation officially marked their daughters' coming of age, and therefore, their marriageability. There are two relevant points here. First, the most common form of debutante presentation became (and still is) the cotillion, or formal group debut. A group of young elite women, usually just graduated from high school, are presented to society together at an event designed to raise money, contributed by the debutantes' families, for a local charity. The flow of wealth is from the debutante's family to the community, by way of the charity. In some local traditions, mothers and daughters or parents and daughters form a receiving line for guests. In other cases, the organizers form a receiving line and the debutantes are presented to the organizers by their fathers, or the debutantes are formally escorted in by their fathers, or by both parents. Usually, the debutantes dance the first dance with their fathers. The point here, should it require belaboring, is that the debutante presentation revolves around kinship connections within the elite class that pinpoint the debutante's position in society. Indeed, this is all that matters.

The debutante ball, presentation, or cotillion, has a very strong connection in American popular culture (and in fact) with elitism. Movies, shows, plays, articles in newspapers and popular magazines all emphasize the upper-class nature of the debut. Thus, the debutante presentation, and events that model themselves on it, carry with them an inescapable aura of social class, of elitism, of conspicuous consumption. In communities I have studied, communities with an egalitarian ideology, values of hard work and individual achievement, an attenuated class structure, and few, if any, very wealthy families, a formal debutante presentation is socially and ideologically repugnant.

Debutantes achieve nothing; they participate in the cotillion by virtue of the position of their parents. A debutante's physical, intellectual, emotional, athletic, and spiritual characteristics are irrelevant, but these are the very features of a queen pageant candidate that matter most.

The beauty pageant is also ideologically repugnant, as the organizers cited above indicated. Nevertheless, it solves some of the problems of the debut. For one thing, the beauty pageant is a popular democratic form, at least by contrast with the debut. It purports to make its judgments on ascribed characteristics (in this case, physical attractiveness, as defined by a set of locally and temporally relevant standards). Nevertheless, because these traits are believed to occur randomly with reference to social class, women of any social background may be candidates. As well, beauty pageants have rewards. The beauty pageant is a fundamentally bourgeois play form: the winners get material goods in the form of money, trips, cars, scholarships, clothing, modeling contracts, and so on.

But because the beauty pageant stresses atomistic individuals apparently competing on the basis of randomly ascribed physical features, its pure form is unacceptable in a community where everyone knows every-one else, and where, in the social fraction to which organizers belong, sta-tus is supposed to be based on achievement rather than ascription. The question becomes: Along what dimensions can one measure the achieve-ments of the young women belonging, or aspiring, to the small town mid-dle class? Which criteria, acceptable to the petty bourgeois public that or-ganizes and supports queen pageants, justify rewarding the winners with expensive prizes? Indeed, what kinds of prizes are appropriate? In a small town, the solution is not entirely dissimilar to the solution proposed by the Miss America organizers: a pleasing personality, a certain degree of poise and good grooming, and certain levels of skill as measured in the talent competition and the interview are rewarded with college scholarships.[5]

Family, the key to the debut, is not enough at the queen pageant, but neither is physical attractiveness, the key to the beauty pageant. The queen pageant, in order to be acceptable to the community, must reach a careful balance. It must reward what have become appropriate "democra-tic" achievements as it celebrates upwardly-mobile young women, offer-ing to teach them the things they need to know to participate fully in the life of the class fragment they seek to join. Since the beauty pageant is the "democratic" prototype, enough trappings of such pageants must remain so that the queen pageant is not confused with an "undemocratic" debut. At the same time, the most blatant, "unrespectable" markers of the beau-ty pageant, such as the swimsuit competition, must be downplayed or eliminated, so that the queen pageant is not confused with unwholesome flesh-peddling. Here, elements of the "undemocratic" but highly re-spectable debut, such as links between candidates, their families, and their schools, must be highlighted.

This is why it is important to set up the queen pageant in such a way that the correct young women become candidates. If all the young women of the community participated, some would embarrass themselves, the or-ganizers, and by extension the community because they did not meet the achievement standards of class, the ascription standards of the debut pro-totype, and/or the physical standards of the beauty pageant prototype. There must be some achievement or the debut element of the hybrid col-lapses; there cannot be too much achievement or the ideological under-pinnings of the community are exploded (the event then celebrates uniqueness; for not just any young woman could win); there must be some physical attractiveness (however that is locally defined) or the beauty pageant element collapses. That it is difficult to create and maintain this hybrid is illustrated by the example from Litchfield, and by many more in my experience. That these events are hybrids is indicated in their struc-ture, as noted above. The pageant begins in the presentation of the debut and ends in the competition of the beauty pageant.

Pageants as Play

We should now consider the further association of the queen pageant with the community festival, a well-recognized play form. The trappings of the queen pageant can be seen as a kind of protective coloration that allows the organizers and participants to achieve the many practical goals they state (gaining poise, rewarding achievement with scholarships, etc.) in a way that will not offend local sensibilities, including their own. Because the pageant is defined as a form of play, they are doubly protected, since they can always (correctly) claim, "It's play; it's make-believe." In this case, the play frame makes what goes on within it subjective and negotiable. Sheltered within the play frame, the organizers are free both to try to teach the young women who participate what the organizers think they should know, and to present them to the community. The candidates are free to learn what the organizers want them to learn, but they are not obligated to learn or accept it. They are also free to choose other meanings in the pageant, meanings concerned with friendship, with poise, with the need for a scholarship, and so on. The audience is free to take the pageant as a contest or a cotillion, or for that matter as an initiation rite or a rite of elevation. The queen pageant draws its power as a performance from these family resemblances. It is certainly a serious event—festival organizers are a very earnest group of people—but it is also a subjective event, because it is framed as play, and the results follow from its framing as play.

Here I continue to disagree with those who assert that the queen pageant is a ritual rather than play (see, for example, Stoeltje 1983 and this volume) based on the (mistaken) assumption that play is neither serious nor consequential.[6] There are, indeed, consequences for girls and young women in a community in which a queen pageant is found. Queen pageants certainly affect the shape and nature of gender relations in a community, implying a particular approach to emotions, to good fortune, and to the effects of direct self-presentation, to the self as winner or loser, to the queen as she may be remembered in community history. Queen pageants are one among a multitude of influences on women and men of all ages in communities regarding issues of gender.

But the queen pageant is framed as play, and so the contrast between a ritual like a wedding and a queen pageant is clear. In the wedding ritual, people move from one social position in society—single—to a different position—married—and the transformation has social and emotional consequences in terms of sexual access, childbearing, legitimation of children, creation of in-laws, and formation of a social unit on the one hand, and the attitude of the couple toward each other, toward other people, and the attitude of other people towards the couple on the other. In fact, the transformation that occurs within the ritual frame is irreversible: one can stop being married, but one cannot become never-married again. The ritual frame has structural and systemic consequences that are notably lacking in a small town queen pageant in Minnesota.

Nevertheless, the queen pageant does have consequences. They affect individuals, not social systems, and they are indirect rather than direct. A newly married couple may not take their vows seriously, but society does, as becomes vividly apparent when they find themselves arguing over property or child custody during a divorce. Not so with a queen pageant. It is possible to play at the pageant—it's all make-believe, on one level, after all—and it is easy to avoid the social consequences. And some young women do. Some resign before their term is up, some miss events they are scheduled to attend, and some become radicalized in college and reject the gender standards implied in the queen pageant. Almost none remain in the community that selected them.

While it may be the case that at least in certain very specific and limited contexts with no implications for significant systemic action, the status of the winner is changed (she is, after all, "the Queen" when she is visiting other festivals and involved in her own), there is no necessity for this status to last beyond the year in which she serves, nor even to be of much moment during that year. Even her misbehavior or inappropriate behavior (getting pregnant while queen, for example) is not seen as having *social* consequences, or of really changing anything about the community, not even its reputation.

She is, after all, involved in the festival world, a world recognized by Minnesotans as framed in play. In my experience, most communities do not remember their queens and princesses beyond a year or two. Indeed, in 1984, the Pope County *Tribune* published a list of the whereabouts and occupations of the women who had been queens of the Glenwood Waterama since its inception in 1956, since this was not common knowledge. Apart from the 1982-1984 queens who were still students, only two former queens lived in the immediate vicinity; eight lived out of state, and nine lived in the Minneapolis suburbs. Of the twenty-six women who were not still students, four did not give an occupation. Of the others, four were housewives, one had a beauty shop, five were teachers or worked in public schools, one taught gymnastics, one was in real estate, one worked for Minnesota Job Services, one trained horses in Las Vegas, and eight worked in health care as nurses, a dental hygienist, or were connected in some way with hospitals or clinics.

In essence, the queen is a playful representative of her community. If she wishes to emphasize having been queen, that option is open to her. She may also choose to incorporate her experience as little more than a momentary one, like being president of a sorority in college, or of the Chamber of Commerce later in life. She is equally free to forget, to ignore, or to belittle that position (as are other people). This is a consequence of the play nature of the queen pageant—there is no "must" or "will," there is "might" or "may." This loophole, as it were, separates play from ritual.

There are far more profound influences on gender roles than queen pageants, and there are many towns with no queen pageants in which identical gender roles are reproduced. The queen pageant provides a moment in which gender roles *may* become foregrounded, along with a number of other messages of possible social import. But all of the messages can be discounted, if need be, because they are framed as play. Women who choose to participate—and while there may sometimes be pressure to participate, there is never obligation—sometimes reject the overt messages, sometimes choose to participate for a range of idiosyncratic reasons, and sometimes get a different message from their participation than was intended.

Finally, the implication of this ethnographic exercise is to invite us to question totalizing or reductive explanations of events like queen pageants. Such explanations fail to recognize that people often find loopholes in social practices that allow them to escape or reinterpret the official or academically orthodox interpretations. Gender roles are, after all, overdetermined, and towns with and without queen pageants reproduce the same gender roles. But in a small town with a queen pageant, an ambitious young woman, or one who feels overly shy, or one looking to join the small-town elite, or one who recognizes that the skills taught may be useful to her one day, might well choose to compete, *since there are no other venues in which these ends may be achieved.* To assume that the candidates are victims of false consciousness, or unthinking pawns manipulated by the unceasing forces of patriarchy, robs them of their imaginative agency, replacing it with a monologic paternalism that denies the legitimacy of participants' interpretations, experiences, and life goals.

Notes

1. I have been studying small-town Minnesota queen pageants and the community festivals that surround them since 1981, and have attended some twenty five pageants by this point.

2. Other studies of queen pageants in Minnesota are available in Lavenda 1984, 1988, 1991, 1992a. Beverly Stoeltje's extensive writings on community queens in Texas provide an important look at events that appear very similar, but seem to have some significant differences in terms of organization and consequences. See especially Stoeltje 1983, 1987, 1988, 1993.

3. See, for example, essayist Carol Bly's remarks on the nature of appropriate achievement in Minnesota small towns (Bly 1981, 26-31,37).

4. Stoeltje (1988) discusses a somewhat different set of desired outcomes in west Texas.

5. This, by the way, seems to be exactly the problem faced by the Miss America pageant: the contestants, highly educated and ambitious women, are in the competition for the rewards—thousands of dollars of scholarship money, in particular—that it offers.

What have they done to deserve the prizes? When the rewards were smaller, and the position of women different, beauty alone may have been enough. But it stopped being enough years ago in practice, when the talent competition was added. As recent publicity surrounding the Miss America swimsuit competition has shown, the entire event is facing challenges by outsiders and insiders to cease being a beauty pageant in appearance as well.

6. On the subject of play and ritual, see for example, Handelman 1977, 1990, 1992; Lavenda 1992b, 1993, 1995; Csikszentmihalyi 1981; Drewal 1992; Manning 1983; Turner 1974.

3

Homage to "La Cordobesa"
Local Identity and Pageantry in Andalusia

Richard Sanders and Sarah Pink

Introduction

In May of 1981 a journalist in Cordoba, Andalusia, described the opinions about beauty pageants held by Oro Muñoz Gonzalez, a member of a local feminist organization known as the Women's Assembly. He claimed that "To her, beauty contests seem something absurd, ridiculous and insipid....According to her, the countries of higher culture, for example in Northern Europe, have already eliminated these customs, which are now found only in America."[1] The accuracy of her claim (or his) is not in question here,[2] but it seems appropriate to note that by this one comment she was identified with a pro-European, progressive stance, which in Cordoba continues to be pitted against the reactionary or traditionalist politics of the Francoist right as well as of the Andaluz nationalist parties. At issue here is the rhetoric of political positioning, not the objective world history of beauty pageants. The question of women in Cordoba continues to be politicized in a debate that compares, at varying levels of accuracy, Spain's policies for equality, abortion, and so on, with those of "Northern Europe."

The article was published in the midst of a public debate over whether or not to continue the "Queen of the Patios" competition, a beauty pageant in Cordoba which for some twenty-five years had been held under the organizational and financial auspices of the "Ayuntamiento" (city hall). The year was 1981, less than three years after Spain's first ever general elections had swept Franco's "Movimiento Nacional" out of office and put the UCD (Central Democratic Union) in power nationally and the PSOE (Spanish Socialist Workers' Party) in a position of dominance in Andalusian regional politics. Control of Cordoban city politics was taken up by the PCA (Communist Party of Andalusia), with the support of the PSOE; in opposition were the UCD and the PSA (Andalusian Socialist Party).[3] The beauty pageant had been under threat ever since the democratic transition took place, and the Ayuntamiento's attempts to cancel it this year provoked a public argument in which feminism and tradition were at cross-purposes. The following paper discusses the particular pageant in question, the part it played in the maintenance of a source of local identity ("la cordobesa," the Cordoban woman), and the debate over the cancellation of the pageant.

Theory of Pageants

The discourses surrounding the Queen of the Patios competition specifically deny that it participates in the generalized pyramid-contest type. Few of the political commentators and none of the competitors are willing to accept, at least in print, that a generalized feminist critique of beauty pageants applies in this case; each claims some kind of local importance for the pageant which makes it something other than a standard beauty contest. We are interested in exploring this rhetoric of difference; we wish to discuss the ways in which a local, non-pyramidal beauty pageant is used in the construction of local cultural identity and morality. The question then becomes whether or not this pageant is an example of a type of pageant fundamentally different from the pyramidal type, and if so, in what ways.

At the risk of oversimplification, we propose the following typology. First, we propose to take two types of pageant, the local pageant and the international, as extremes on a continuum. The continuum does not necessarily express the degree of integration into the international pyramids of beauty contests; rather, it expresses the degree of orientation outside the local. One extreme, the international, is a contest that is formally, rhetorically, and pragmatically organized in such a way that the winner will move up the hierarchy and away from the local. In such a case the discussion might centre around the degree of standardization within the organization of the contests at all levels; the orientation of the rhetoric of the contest toward local representations to the outside; the pragmatic benefits accrued by contestants or competition organizers through outward-focused competition (overseas modeling jobs, for example, or cultivation of prestige and contacts within an international career). The other extreme, the local, is a self-contained contest in which there is no orientation whatsoever toward outward representations. Here the discussion might centre around the organization of the competition as part of a local setting; the reproduction of local identities through rhetoric; and the pragmatic benefits accrued by contestants or organizers for participation (local political prestige, for example).

The Queen of the Patios competition is closer to the latter extreme. It is formally organized as part of an annual cycle of festival activities. It is also rhetorically of this type: the competition is defended on the basis of local identity, its supporters attempt to separate it conceptually from other kinds of contests and enclose it in self-definition. However, chances are strong that this competition serves pragmatic ends which are outward-oriented: the Ayuntamiento's attempts to attract tourism, for example, or the contestants' use of the local pageant to draw attention to themselves in other arenas. Indeed, because of the pragmatic possibilities which all beauty contests appear to encourage for the cultivation of political prestige and job opportunities, it is unlikely that any contest fits either of the two extremes. But because of the nature of our documentation on the competition, we have confined our analysis to its formal and rhetorical aspects, although we will speculate about the pragmatic outcomes and the possible reasons why these outcomes are hidden.

The following discussion thus consists of two sets of ethnographic material. The first, based largely on participant observation, consists of a description of Cordoba's festival season and the place of the Queen of the Patios within that season. We provide this description to contextualize the debate that follows, both in terms of local political debate and in terms of a wider Andalusian culture, and to illustrate the kind of local cultural manifestation for which a beauty pageant is not out of place. We also identify certain structural patterns within the organization of the festivities which we feel help to maintain the gender identities under debate in the second set of material.

This second set is based largely on archival materials, partly because the debate over the cancellation of the pageant took place in 1981, and partly because the Queen of the Patios pageant was indeed eventually cancelled. We explore the reiteration of the contest's rhetorical orientation by its supporters in the face of attempts by its opponents to restructure its formal aspects. The Communist-controlled Ayuntamiento tried, in 1980, to abolish the beauty pageant but was forced to abandon the plan in the face of strong opposition from the UCD and the PSA. By 1984 it succeeded, but in the year under study, 1981, the Ayuntamiento was trying instead to remove it from city government control. We use the ensuing debate to discuss the construction and maintenance of a Cordoban feminine identity and the use of that identity as a political tool by the opposition. We will illustrate that the moral role model becomes a political symbol for local cultural permanence.

The Pageant in its Festival Context

May is a month of festivities in Cordoba, with each of the first, second, and fourth weeks dedicated to one particular festival. The first week is the "Festival of the Crosses," a festival celebrated all over Andalusia during which large crosses decorated with flowers are placed in plazas all over the city, and each night sees dancing and drinking around these crosses. The second week is the "Festival of the Cordoban Patios," a festival unique to Cordoba during which traditional courtyard houses decorated with flowers are opened to the public in a display of hospitality. The fourth week is "Feria," a celebration which certainly occurs all across Andalusia, but which to our knowledge occurs at the end of May only in Cordoba.

Feria represents the culmination of festivities, and is actually several different events rolled into one. Traditionally it was a livestock market, though this particular focus has been separated from the urban festivals. This is the normal time for bullfights to be held, and there is a huge street festival besides, with a children's funfair and pavilions for adults. During Feria each of the major companies, religious associations, political parties, cultural circles, and so forth, builds its own pavilion with bars for eating, drinking, and dancing.

Each pavilion has an entrance which normally simulates some sort of traditional facade, and there is a competition, organized by the Ayuntamiento, which gives prizes for the most beautiful pavilion, largely on the basis of these facades. There are competitions for patios and crosses as well, each competition organized by the Ayuntamiento, with jurors recruited from within the Ayuntamiento as well as from relevant associations and organizations (for example, jurors for the patios tend to come from the "Association of Friends of the Cordoban Patios," from the Ministry of Tourism, from companies sponsoring prizes in some way, and from local journalism).

The beauty pageant itself was in some ways simply another competition, though perhaps more formulaic than the others. In each of the other three, the competing "thing of beauty" is enlisted by an organization of some kind which then exercises considerable leeway in deciding how to present their particular cross, patio, or pavilion; the potential beauty queen, however, presented herself of her own accord or in association only with her family. To our knowledge, beauty queens were not sponsored or promoted by particular companies, for example, or religious organizations, though it is certainly possible that this occurred without being disclosed through the sources available to us. Of the other three competitions, that of the patios is closest in this respect to that of the women since most patios (though certainly not all) are presented for competition by residents of the houses—both patio and woman are presented from within household or kin groups, while cross and pavilion are presented by wider groupings. Later we will discuss the moral links that bind these various "things of beauty" and the reason that she is "'Queen of the Patios."

Beyond this, the organization of each competition is conducted from start to finish by the Ayuntamiento, which establishes the criteria for qualification and disqualification, organizes the inscription, selects the win-

Audience shot of the "woman only" bullfight. Photo © Sarah Pink

ners and losers, and awards the prizes. The process is similar in each case: there is a deadline for entering; there is a period of testing, during which a jury of "illustrious people" selected by the Ayuntamiento decides which candidates have been successful; there is a prize-giving session, again organized by the Ayuntamiento, which normally takes place in the Ayuntamiento's own pavilion toward the end of Feria; and there is a short period or moment during which the winner is displayed. In the case of the beauty contest, the queen's moment of display, the "Homage to Cordoban Woman," occurs during a bullfight that is situated in the larger event.[4]

Because the beauty contest was cancelled, the queen no longer presides, but this bullfight continues to play what is considered by many to be an essential part in the May celebrations. It is not a full-fledged bullfight: in name it is a "becerrada," a promotional bullfight held so that young trainee bullfighters can display their skills and gain experience performing in public.[5] This particular case differs from a normal becerrada in that the audience receives more attention than the bullfighter, to such an extent that the event is known simply as "the Cordoban woman." It was begun in 1902 by "Guerrita," a retired Cordoban bullfighter. Nationally famous, he carried the ideal bullfighter's image of an unpretentious but socially skilled and popular character with a liking for beautiful women. With the financial and organizational sponsorship of his bullfighting club he is said to have created this event to provide a festive occasion for the enjoyment of "beautiful Cordoban women." The audience is almost exclusively made up of women, as all men apart from organizers and performers are excluded. In practice, however, a man with strong interest and the appropriate contacts will gain entry by the porters' door and be allowed to stand by the ringside. Historical anecdotes also mention men disguising themselves as women in order to enter.

On the afternoon of the event roads are jammed by horse-drawn carriages bringing "traditionally" dressed women to the becerrada. These women are very much on public display both before their arrival and during the pageantry of their eventual entry to the bullring, when the carriages do a circuit of the ring and photographs are taken both of the carriages and of traditionally dressed women on foot, often with an important male figure. These are duly published in the newspapers the following day. The role of the Patio Queen was similar: she was paraded and photographed in the dress she won, and then with her "attendants" went to sit in the presidents' box with the male official, "el Presidente," who presides over all bullfights. Although these women were sometimes referred to as "Las Presidentas," in fact they did little more than accompany the official. The audience expresses Cordoban feminine identity in a less restrained manner; in direct contrast to the passivity of the paraded women who "adorn the carriages," the audience becomes an unruly mob. Norms of female behavior are transgressed by the throwing of female underwear to the "triumphant" performers. Young boys are the recipients of enormous bras thrown by women whose actions are accompanied by musical renderings of Cordoban female identity, embodied in the song, "Soy Cordobesa": "I am a Cordoban woman from head to toe…." Indeed, it may be argued that the whole event turns the conservative male definition of Cordoban femininity and social order upside down: the dignitaries (Queen of the Patios and her entourage) are women; the performers are children; the audience is female and out of control; the atmosphere is carnivalesque, in contrast to the deadly serious character of a "real" bullfight. Nevertheless, the personification of feminine morality, the Queen of the Patios, is not deposed, and the integrity of "traditional" beauty symbolically reigns.

Quotes from feature articles in the local paper help illustrate why she is the Queen of the Patios, as well as the link between this competition, the becerrada, and the other festivals of Cordoba, "the patios, crosses, and Feria." A description of a winner illustrates the linking of images which lies behind the choice of a young woman to "represent" the patios: "It's her, Ana Gutiérrez—sixteen years old and proud to be Cordoban—the most beautiful of the patios, or rather, their queen, and there she is, with that radiance that shines in her face, as the flowers shine in that patio which won the competition....Two winners: a sweet girl/woman and a beautiful patio. And with them a magnificent poster could be made representing our month of May, because that pair woman/patio is like the symbol of a way of understanding living which here and now is still valid."[6] The girl/woman image, linked metaphorically with patios and with flowers (one queen is described as a "flower in vitality"[7]), is at times explicitly linked with Spring: "In May in Cordoba, it is not only the colouring of its flowers and the radiance of its streets, patios, and plazas. The Cordoban woman also forms a part of that enchantment that God gave us to enhance even further this Springtime of festivals."[8] This set of related images lies at the heart of the Cordoban festivities; it is the support for the entire structure of festival events, and it is here that the perceived difference between the Queen of the Patios pageant and other beauty contests is located.

Political Debate over Cancellation

In 1981 the Ayuntamiento shifted the organizational burden of the Queen of the Patios competition to the "Federation of Cordoban Peñas (clubs)," although it continued to finance the competition. Initially those parties that controlled the Ayuntamiento, the PCA and the PSOE, attempted to suppress the entire competition, but ultimately the Ayuntamiento would provide the necessary finance while declining to organize it itself. Meantime a PSOE councillor attempted to justify his position in the local paper, arguing that declining participation coupled with pressing financial needs in other areas were his only reasons for opposing the pageant: "I am not opposed in any way to any kind of popular festival."[9] Responding, supporters of the contest argued that the decline in participation was itself the fault of the Ayuntamiento: the president of the Ayuntamiento's Festival Commission, himself a member of PSA, claimed that "since the celebration was not approved, the registration for participating in it was never opened;" and besides, according to the 1980 winner, "this year I haven't heard anything [about it] either on the radio or in the newspaper."[10]

So the conflict between political parties within the Ayuntamiento spilled out into the local press, and the supporters of the Queen of the Patios beauty pageant poised themselves for a fight against the feminism presumed to lie behind the move:

> The Ayuntamiento has turned feminist on us....Our municipal representatives from the PCA and the PSOE voted against the proposal [to finance the beauty pageant], because they believe that these kinds of events are degrading for the Cordoban woman. So now they're going to discover the Americas. And it's not that I want to get into dogmatic, doctrinaire or ideological arguments, but there are plenty of pretty girls who want to participate in this traditional competition. And of course, they don't think that these kinds of social displays are degrading for women. Besides, one

thing is clear, that the Cordoban woman is a female without parallel in beauty, and that is one thing which not even our feminist
Ayuntamiento is going to change. And the worst thing is that if
this competition doesn't happen, then neither will there be a
"Festival of Homage for the Cordoban Woman" because it is also
a sexist and "fascist" event....And if we start counting we'll arrive
at the conclusion that bullfights are also atrocities, and so they'll
be abolished....Ultimately, from all this we end up with street
demonstrations and "marimachos" (butch women), which appear
to be the fashion at the moment. All that remains for me to say is
that this brief little article is to inform the councillors for PCA
and PSOE that the majority of Cordobans like bulls, women, and
beauty contests. Do I make myself clear?[11]

In this narrative a number of rhetorical arguments are used to support
the beauty pageant. First, the writer claims that the participants themselves do not feel that the contest humiliates women; a variant of this argument is that the women themselves do not feel humiliated for having
participated. This argument is repeated elsewhere, in the newspaper interviews with the winners, who in the course of the printed portion of the
interview are routinely asked one or two questions designed to reveal that
they are willing and enthusiastic participants. Second, the writer holds
that the Cordoban woman will remain an unparalleled beauty whether or
not the competition takes place. This claim appears to operate here as a
populist argument largely designed to elicit agreement; however, it is also
a typical reference to the stability of Cordoban female beauty, a constant
theme throughout debates over the competition and in journalistic interviews with winners. Third, the writer claims that the abolition of this tradition will lead to other abolitions, right into the heart of traditional
Cordoba, leaving only demonstrations and "masculine" women. The
mention of Guerrita's becerrada is a persistent theme because on another
occasion (1986) the becerrada itself was cancelled, raising similar protests
against feminist politics and the destruction of both tradition and the
uniqueness of Cordoban identity.[12]

Intriguingly, in this case the reduction to the extreme involves not
only the denial of celebration and of tradition, but also the dominance of
oppositional politics in which women take on male gender. For this writer
the world is upside down when women enter politics. The commentary is
clearly designed to appeal to an audience for whom local identity and tradition are more important than "progressive" politics: comments about
"marimachos" and assertions of the Cordoban taste for bulls and women
are not calculated to win over the opponents. Against it is part of a commentary from the following year, a letter to the editor from an opponent

of the pageant, similarly preaching to the converted, this time an audience opposed to traditional gender identities. Both writers blame the Ayuntamiento, but it is worth noting that each declares tacit support for two of the parties by explicitly criticizing the other two.

> I couldn't get over my shock when I read in the newspapers of this capital city that this year we are going to have the "Queen of the Patios," a decision which, it would seem, the councillors of the Ayuntamiento (PSA and UCD) have taken....Gentlemen of the PSA and UCD, is it that the electoral campaign has atrophied your minds? Is it that with this you're going to win more votes from the women? The indignation which seizes me, and which I am certain cannot be solely mine when we are used for that clowning around, the product of twisted and reactionary minds [sic]. Dear Sirs, we women are fed up with being used as erotic instruments, when at the same time we are marginalised in the workplace, being paid lower salaries than those of men....I am certain that the "queen" of the patios will be a beautiful young girl, well dressed—oh, pardon!—undressed would be better so that the gentlemen can appreciate the exuberant beauty, she must be a typical Cordoban girl, with black hair...almond-shaped eyes...pride of our land, who will be shown off like some "bicho raro" [fantastic creature] in other competitions.[13] "With this they will have a clear conscience that they have done something for the women of our land." The gentlemen of the press who last year carried on against the Ayuntamiento for its suppression of the "merriment" will this year be content.[14]

Again, political parties are blamed, this time those parties further to the right. The chief rhetorical strategy employed is to contrast the "erotic" object with the exploited worker/wife: this time the stable Cordoban femininity is nothing but ideology. It is the sarcasm in the exploration of the erotic object which is most effective, the parodying of the views of the supporters. The image of Cordoban beauty is this time said to be an image held by "twisted and reactionary minds." The writer wholly rejects the idea of a distinct local identity.

The whole political problem therefore pivots on this notion of a distinct Cordoban femininity, with all parties required to take a position on the importance of this identity. Those parties that instigated the cancellation of the beauty pageant find themselves accused by their political opponents of applying the views voiced above to an event which, according to the opponents, marks a deeply held local identity; the irony is that the opponents who find themselves combining forces under the banner of a local femininity include the UCD, an umbrella party of national centralism reputed to have absorbed the ranks of Franco's traditionalist politicians, and the PSA, an Andalusian regionalist party campaigning for increased regional autonomy. The PSOE and the PCA back down because they do not wish to be seen publicly denying the reality of a Cordoban femininity; thus the importance of the local gender identity as a political symbol is made clear. Yet its use as political symbol is never articulated by any of the various commentators; instead, they constantly return the focus to the moral qualities supposed to be threatened by the "feminist Ayuntamiento."

A politician from PSA puts it this way: "Really, this is not a beauty contest, in the sense that these girls aren't dressed up in swimsuits or bikinis, to be objects of consideration for juries, nor are there economic interests in showing a woman-object." He argues that "Those of the PSOE and PCA have been thinking that the selection of the Queen of the Patios is a beauty contest. But what has always been done has been more than choosing based on physical qualities, placing these next to moral qualities and looking for a woman to represent the average Cordoban. I think that it is a friendly competition because in it competes a succession of girls with the hope of representing Cordoba and obtaining the gypsy dress."[15] A winner similarly argues that the Queen of the Patios competition is distinct: "It's not a beauty contest, as they say it is, but rather something which is done for representing the Cordoban woman in the festivals of Cordoba. I participated in Miss Andalusia and that is something totally different...." According to Ana Maria, to be elected Queen of the Patios is a joy for any Cordoban woman, "and if a woman feels manipulated it is because she wants to feel that way. If you have any personality at all, nobody manipulates or uses you, that much is obvious."[16] Another winner puts it this way, in response to her interviewer:

> Yes, I know that there was the Queen of the Patios, Miss Contacts, Miss Saint Cyr, but...I've never wanted to compete in discos and all that because it's more...you have to put on a swimsuit, you have to do this, you have to do that....And because it isn't something worthwhile, like the culture or the roots of Cordoba. Representing the patios is something beautiful. [The interviewer says] That's right, and the other competitions are tackier. [She responds:] Could be. It's that here it's not just beauty that counts, but grace....From my point of view, I don't feel used, I feel Andaluz and I look to represent the beauty of Cordoba, at least officially. I'm not antifeminist or anything, just a normal, everyday girl.[17]

Emphasis on the distinctiveness of the Queen of the Patio competition is used in these arguments not only to elevate it above the ordinary beauty contest, but also to argue that feminist criticisms of beauty pageants cannot be applied to it: she's not "antifeminist," but she holds that "representing patios is something beautiful."[18] The Queen of the Patios is a focus for moral values, the winner is selected on the basis of moral qualities and of grace, not just physical requirements, and the winner's role as representative of the city and the patios is a worthy task. For each winner it is representing the local which distinguishes the competition; one of the winners frames this in terms of local values, "grace" and "being Andaluz." In response to her interviewer, another winner goes further, describing it as a local tradition which can be used to promote the city: "Do you think that these kinds of competitions are degrading for the rights of women?" [She responds:] "No way, no way. Its only contribution is to elevate her even more, besides it seems absurd to me that they are trying to suppress this show. This tradition cannot be lost, because it is very beautiful and festivals must be preserved exactly as they are. Besides, I think that with this the city is promoted even more."[19]

The idea that the Queen of the Patios competition elevates rather than degrades women is explored further by an older government worker, who describes what the competition used to be like: "I don't think that the woman was diminished at all. Quite the reverse, because these girls were respected to the extreme. Besides, listen, the jury was composed of illustrious personages....Here no one permitted himself the luxury of playing a joke on them, and besides, the beauty of the Cordoban woman was exalted. It was something of the people, which is to say it wasn't, shall we say, something from high society."[20]

For those who see it as a popular local tradition, the beauty contest must be maintained. As a vehicle for local moral values, it is to be upheld and contrasted with ordinary beauty pageants. And in these capacities it can be used to promote the city, it helps the city present itself to tourists in its best light. In this connection it is useful to mention that one contestant is described as a "living postcard,"[21] while another remarks on the hypocrisy of the Ayuntamiento for using images of women on its promotional posters while simultaneously undermining the beauty pageant.[22] Thus supporters of the pageant speak of the governing parties' "false understanding of feminism," while at the same time asserting that they themselves are normal people who agree with some aspects of feminism, but not at the expense of denying their values and traditions.[23] They endorse a localized structure of morality symbolized and represented by the Queen of the Patios; by supporting the pageant and the gender roles discussed earlier in the description, they associate themselves with the politics of local culture and seek to oppose themselves to the prevailing centralized, socialist politics.

Conclusion

The preceding discussion illustrates how local popular culture is mobilized by certain political parties to challenge the prevailing political order. Those politicians, journalists, and participants who support the beauty pageant call on the unchanging nature of Cordoban femininity in their rhetoric of support, holding that there is no contradiction between the aims of feminism on the one hand and the celebration of local beauty on the other. The concept of beauty is not limited to the physical, but is held to incorporate moral values; Cordoba is represented through the celebration of the morality of its women and girls in a way which is consistent with the Andalusian thought that Julian Pitt-Rivers describes in his 1950s fieldwork: "Moral judgements are expressed in terms of beauty and ugliness, the idiom of the feminine ideal" (Pitt-Rivers 1963, 89).

With reference to the connections drawn earlier between the festivals of the crosses, patios, the beauty pageant, and the Feria, the pageant is closest in this regard to the patios. The contrast between the two sets of competitions is strong. In the competitions for Feria and the crosses, extra-kin associations compete through the construction of distinctive yet appropriate, temporary structures in public places. In the patio competition and the beauty pageant, kin groups compete through the presentation of "things of beauty" which embody permanence as well as temporal growth and change. In the patios there is a great emphasis on the maintenance of flowers on the walls, a task which falls to the older woman in the course of keeping the house. Indeed, the structural parallels might be extended to include a contrast between the young woman celebrated by the pageant and the old woman celebrated by the patio competition. Each year the newspapers focus on a few of the women who keep the houses involved in the competition for that year, describing in tones of respect how they have devoted years to keeping a beautiful patio despite ill health and desertion by the young. These two images, the virginal, flowering youth and the consistent household caretaker, are two ends of one morality; intriguingly, the "toiling" woman between young and old is absent from the equation. The "Homage to the Cordoban Woman" becomes the forum for the unification of these two images, an event of pageantry designed so that Cordoban women will celebrate themselves in terms of images acceptable to Cordoban males, and that the Queen of the Patios, the epitome of the "ideal" woman, will remain on her pedestal reigning over the everyday experience of social reality.

Each of the three events, the beauty contest, the patio festival, and the becerrada, is widely perceived as a "popular" festival. As a moment for the reiteration of local cultural values, each is open to exploitation by politicians and parties eager to be seen to supporting "the people." For this reason the debates revolve around the perceived abandonment of popular culture in favour of progressive, or "false," feminism, and any such abandonment will continue to be tempered by the political rhetoric it generates as various politicians attempt to capitalize on the inherent contradictions. We hold that it is useful to view local politics, at least in Andalusia, as very strongly influenced by a popular culture which is continuously renewed via the political culture itself. The Queen of the Patios competition was a local event through which particular urban politicians and urban women in general derived local prestige; it involved the representation of the morality of the city's women, directed towards others in the city as well as towards the outside. The becerrada symbolically confirmed the prevalence of this ideal womanhood and the subjugation of the expression of an experienced reality of hard toil and little thanks for it. Even the most vehement critics of the beauty pageant pointed more than anything else to the hypocrisy which lies in the discrepancy between the ideal Cordoban woman and the reality of daily life for Cordoban women; this proved a more effective criticism than any abstract discussion of objectification or degradation. An anthropology of beauty pageants must address these local discrepancies first, before general arguments can be made.

Notes

Funded by the Economic and Social Research Council, this essay is based on the field-work of two researchers, whose time in the field amounted to sixteen months and twenty-two months respectively. We wish to thank those colleagues and friends whose comments have proved invaluable in the preparation of this paper.

1. *La Voz de Córdoba*, 19 May 1981, 16. We have done our best to verify that the overall sense of our translations is correct and have at times allowed awkward English to support a closer approximation.

2. Of more interest is the question of whether she in fact made that claim; journalistic distortion of interviews and "facts" will be addressed briefly later in this paper, but in general we take the position that we are not interested in whether or not a reported fact or comment is accurate, rather that it is reported at all, that it is reported instead of other facts or comments, and that it is reported using certain rhetorical devices rather than others.

3. UCD: Unión de Centro Democrático; PSOE: Partido Socialista Obrero Español; PCA: Partido Comunista de Andalucía; PSA: Partido Socialista Andaluz. The UCD as a huge coalition party operating as a "safe" voters' option, rapidly lost face after the transition as it was incapable of projecting a unified vision; the PSOE would take power nationally after the general elections of 1982 (Hooper 1986, 35-46). Cordoba itself was unique as the only city in the nation to elect a Communist majority to its Ayuntamiento.

4. "Homenaje a la Mujer Cordobesa." Three sources have been used for the material on this particular becerrada: oral histories, historical bullfighting literature, and the almost yearly newspaper articles. All sources echo the same account of this history, and no alternative versions are on offer.

5. A becerrada is not regarded by "aficionados" (bullfight enthusiasts) to be a "real" bull-fight. Performers are normally males between ten and sixteen, not fully grown, and the "bulls" are around one year old and may be of either sex; thus the becerrada in-volves neither the skill nor the danger of a "real" bullfight.

6. *Diario Córdoba*, 13 May 1983, 1.

7. *Diario Córdoba*, 23 May 1984, 32.

8. *Diario Córdoba*, 17 May 1992, 12.

9. *La Voz de Córdoba*, 19 May 1981, 16.

10. *La Voz de Córdoba*, 19 May 1981, 16.

11. *Diario Córdoba*, 5 May 1981, 6.

12. Aside from the importance of the Homage to the Cordoban Woman in local culture, it seems likely that Guerrita himself is equally important as a symbol of Cordoban identity. As a highly successful national figure he projected Cordoba onto the national stage.

13. "Bicho raro," literally "rare creature," does not hold the English sense of "rare beau-ty"; rather, it carries the connotation of strangeness, like freaks of nature put on dis-play in a circus.

14. *Diario Córdoba*, Sunday 16 May 1982, 4.

15. *La Voz de Córdoba*, 19 May 1981, 16.

16. *La Voz de Córdoba*, 19 May 1981, 16.

17. *La Voz de Córdoba*, 26 May 1982, 20.

18. This does not mean that the Cordoban morality cannot be played out against and contrasted to the relative lack of it in national pyramidal competitions: When recently Eva María Fernández, "Miss Cordoba," was only awarded second place in "Miss Spain," an investigation was proposed. "Morally Eva has won," argued a commentator, suggesting "irregularity" in official mechanisms. Local Cordoban beauty and morality is again pitted against outside corruption.

19. *Diario Córdoba*, 21 May 1981, 14.

20. *La Voz de Córdoba*, 19 May 1981, 16. Mitchell (1991, 56-67) describes the "Maja" model which emerged in the last century. This refers to the "traditional" young woman, whose style of clothing and morality is constructed as an embodiment of the morality of "the people," which was considered perhaps more reliable than the less local and less watchable "high society."

21. *Diario Córdoba*, 13 May 1983, 1.

22. *La Voz de Córdoba*, 19 May 1981, 16.

23. *La Voz de Córdoba*, 19 May 1981, 16. Also *Diario Córdoba*, 23 May 1984, 32.

4

Beauty, Women, and Competition
"Moscow Beauty 1989"

Lena Moskalenko

Introduction

This essay is intended to give a different perspective on beauty contests from that of the other essays in this volume. I describe some of my experiences in the first modern pageant in Russia, "Moscow Beauty 1988." My goal is to further general discussion of the relationship between gender and national politics. While the second part of this discussion is very subjective, I place my own experience in a broader historical and social framework in the first part of the essay.

First I discuss gender ideologies and ideals of beauty as they have changed since the turn of the century. Next, I briefly discuss political and social changes that occurred after the October revolution of 1917. Finally, I show the gradual transformation of certain values and ideals throughout the Soviet era. In this section I attempt to answer a number of questions:

- Why were there no beauty pageants before Perestroika?
- How was beauty understood in pre- and post-Revolutionary periods?
- What was the relationship between "official" and "real" notions of beauty?
- How was women's work related to beauty?

Before 1917

Tzarist Russia was a vast country with a population over 160 million people, out of which only slightly more than 3 million were urban workers (Rosenberg 1989). The rest were mainly peasants living in villages all over the country. The "overwhelming" minority of the population was constituted by the aristocracy, clergy, intelligentsia, and businessmen. This minority lived for the most part in capital cities such as Moscow, St. Petersburg, and Kiev. Generally, the level of urbanization was not very high, and many small Russian towns resembled large rural settlements with peasants' ideology, ideals, and attitudes in contrast to the large cities with considerably different views and ideals.

My point is that in pre-1917 Russia there were two cultures: the peasants' Russia and the noble, rich, and highly educated Russia. There were accordingly two different ideals of female beauty. The one which dominated rural Russia was not unlike the ideal common in Western Europe before the twentieth century: the maternal role was idealized, and being fat was considered healthy and erotic. "Womanhood was equated with motherhood" (Freedman 1988, 48), thus the ideal female was big and heavy, with a big bottom and a huge bust. More than that, in peasant Russia women with big breasts were also considered more tender and generous than the lean and skinny with flat chests.[1]

In contrast, amongst aristocrats the ideal female was much slimmer and taller, with long, "nervous" fingers, and thin waists. Although these women were also expected to produce children and be subject to their husbands, they had more freedom and more choice. That is not to say that they could do with their lives as they pleased (Amphiteatrov 1905). For centuries the brutal and wild Russian reality could not accept educated and emancipated women; women in some sense, were very much like children who "are to be seen and not heard."

After the October Revolution of 1917

In October of 1917 the Bolshevik party of Russia took power and overthrew the existing provisional government. V. I. Lenin (1870-1924), the leader of the Bolshevik Party, stood at the beginning of the great historical transformation of Russia from capitalist state into a socialist (and later communist) state. To defend the achievements of the Revolution Lenin needed the support of all social groups. He also realized that women constitute nearly half of the Russian population; thus their support was crucial for the success of the Revolution.

> It is impossible to win the masses for politics unless we include women. We must win the millions of working women in the city and village for our cause, for our struggle, and in particular the communist transformation of the society. Without women there can be no true mass movement. (V. I. Lenin 1917, cited in Halle 1933)

His oft-quoted phrase, that every cook should learn to rule the state, may sound paradoxical now but I do believe that it was his intention.

One might argue that in general the so-called "women's question" was solved immediately after the Revolution of 1917 when women obtained equal juridical rights with men:

- equal employment opportunities
- equal pay for the same job (work)
- equal civil rights (to vote, to stand for election)
- the adoption of the law on abortion[2]

A few years after the Revolution Lenin proudly announced that there were no longer any laws in Soviet legislation placing women in a dependent or unequal position with respect to men (Halle 1933).

Thus, the state attempted and largely succeeded in giving Russian women equal legal rights with men, rights for which women in developed capitalist countries had to keep fighting.[3] At least by law women in Russia became economically and socially equal to men. At the same time very little was done in order to make domestic work easier and less time-consuming. Soviet Russia needed not only Party members and industrial workers, but mothers and wives; somebody had to give birth, nurse, shop, and cook.
[4] Inevitably the new legal rights intended to relieve the "situation of double enslavement" of women in Tzarist Russia (Lenin, Collected Works, 39: 194) ended by replicating them in what was commonly called work "on two fronts" or the "double burden."[5] Legally women were given the material and legal power to become equal to men, but were actually expected by everyone, both the state and the common population, to continue to perform the economic roles of pre-Revolutionary times. Thus, metaphorically speaking, the only right taken away from them was the right to be feminine, to have the means and time to look after themselves, and, after all, to be beautiful, "to be women" in a higher sense (Halle 1933, 196).

The Big Confusion

I recognize that this notion of femininity may sound problematic, but sadly this is not the place for philosophy. As I showed earlier, there were two different ideals of female beauty before the Revolution. After the Revolution there was apparently only space for one. But which one?…One of the ultimate goals of post-Revolutionary social and economic change was the creation of a new society where all citizens would be equal, and where there would not be any more exploitation, suppression, poverty, or misery. The old capitalist machine and the elitism which supported it were to be dismantled, and the wealth of the state would for the first time truly be the property of the people. As part of this the state attempted to make its cultural heritage—architecture, art, literature, etc.—freely accessible to all. Ironically, the unintended consequence of this was that as the people became "owners" of this heritage and thus had access to it, they inevitably tried to participate in it, adopting the ideals of their former masters. But what the state needed was not weak and feeble intelligentsia and thin, long-fingered women—the state needed workers. In a sense, then, a reversal came about by which, even as the people began to aspire to the old bourgeois notions of beauty, the state tried hard to maintain the old ideal of a working female, the mother and the wife.

However, the Soviet ideal of womanhood was a working woman, achieving astonishing results; one of the most powerful images was the image of a woman-textile worker breaking records in labour productivity (Rosenberg 1989, 67-70). The most popular female Soviet film stars, Lubov Orlova and Larisa Ladynina, became famous after playing the roles of a textile worker and a collective farmer. It was not the looks of those actresses that brought them fame and popularity but their ideologically correct image, supported by the Party and the state. The beauty of work was the only beauty that mattered. But I should say here that the state could not afford to abandon the other ideal entirely. It now tried to combine both in one. Both Orlova and Ladynina perfectly matched the bourgeois image of beauty, but their physical beauty was now used to support the politically correct idea of beauty.

So because of the strength of the state and its propaganda, combined with the strength of pre-Revolutionary popular tradition, the reversal mentioned earlier was slow to take hold. In the public eye the ideal woman continued to be a hard worker, a faithful wife, and a good mother. There was a definite social assumption that a beautiful woman would inevitably fail as a hard worker and a good wife and mother, as she was "spoilt" by her beauty from the early days. A common Russian saying delivers this message: "Do not be born beautiful, be born happy." Also, beautiful women were breakers rather than makers of households. For instance, it was considered immoral to be unfaithful to one's wife, but men did have mistresses, and it is interesting to note that in plays, films, and books those mistresses were usually portrayed as more attractive and beautiful than the deceived and cheated wives. Nevertheless, public opinion and social propaganda were firm—to be beautiful was very close to being "bad." To this extent Soviet ideology mirrored popular values; the tragedy was that the Party took it to extremes, enforcing this ideal on the society to the point where it became illegal not to work.

On paper, then, Russian women were liberated, emancipated, and freed, but the reality was that over the course of the Soviet period they were firmly enslaved by the "double burden." Ideally, they should have had the right to choose between work in the public sector or at home, but in reality they had no choice. They were trapped both by the new political system and the old system of tradition. Besides this, even as they were increasingly acknowledging the ideals of a romantic and feminine female, they were progressively deprived not only from the ideological but also from the physical means to maintain their natural beauty. On the one hand, exhausting work led to rapid aging. Even in 1988 it could still be said that

> Almost 3.5 million women are working in conditions which do not meet the labour norms and rules, such as in smoky, dusty shops with high noise levels and unfavourable temperature ranges. Country women become prematurely aged through working from dawn till dusk, without days off or holidays. (Pukhova 1988)

On the other hand, there was no means of looking after one's appearance. Compared with that of the developed capitalist countries, the cosmetics industry in the Soviet Union had been allowed to decline. The range of skin care and beauty products was very limited and was only available in urban areas. This meant that the majority of the female population of the former USSR, while they might have chosen to care about their appearance, were not usually able to do so.

What Was Offered by Perestroika?

What Soviet women did not know was how to relax and enjoy themselves both physically and emotionally. Their lives were highly constrained by the penetrating state morality and ideology. There was only one moral code as far as the state was concerned—the Communist moral code, and the state worked very hard to suppress any other types of morality. To make it absolutely clear, there was no state ideology of physical beauty, as the state ideology was not very clear on what a woman should be apart from a good worker and a loyal citizen. Interestingly, even now femininity itself is described in advice books for teenage girls as follows:

- the rich, internal world, the soul of a person, which could be hidden behind a very ordinary appearance;
- one's looks, surely, are the start, followed by...
- good posture;
- a gracious walk;
- the absence of excessive bodily movements and gestures;
- tenderness;
- good manners; and
- quietness (for example, it is wrong to laugh loudly).[6]

On the same page one may read that "a loyal, hard working, kind girl is much more attractive than a cold and selfish beauty queen who looks only after herself." It should by now be clear that the whole idea of a beauty contest was inconsistent with the body of Soviet gender ideology, and as will be shown later, public attitudes were not supportive either.

With Gorbachev's rise to power a new stage in the social and politi-

cal life of the former USSR began. The Iron Curtain was lifted, and glas-
nost (openness) brought to the wider population knowledge about the ac-
tualities of the past and the present of Soviet life, exposing its unrevealed
aspects. With the sudden and unpredicted exposure of the Soviet people
to Western propaganda, consumer goods, and advertising, women came
to recognize all that had been denied them during previous periods of
Soviet life. The new expression, "human factor," was rather unexpectedly
injected into Russian political terminology, and almost out of the blue it
was supposed to dawn on Russian people that we were all human and
therefore all different. Suddenly we were given the freedom to realize that
we have different views, different feelings, different tastes, different emotions; that not everything in life is black and white; that human social life
is multicolored, and there is no place for ready solutions and set decisions;
that the leader might be wrong as well as the majority; and, finally, that to
be oneself and to be honest with oneself matters the most.

The state's attitude to family was being rethought, along with the role
of women in society. In 1987, Communist Party General Secretary
Gorbachev wrote that:

> ...women no longer have enough time to perform their everyday
> duties at home. We have discovered that many of our problems—
> in children's and young people's behaviour, in our morals, culture
> and in production—are partially caused by the weakening of the
> family ties and slack attitudes to family responsibilities. We are
> holding heated debates, in the press, in public organizations, at
> work and at home, to put the question of what we should do to
> make it possible for women to return to their purely womanly
> mission.

It is in the context of a search for a new role for Soviet women that the
first beauty contests took place.

And Now About Beauty Queens

The first Russian beauty contest, "Miss Moscow—88" ("Moscow
Beauty—1988"), came as a flash of lightning. I do not recall it being widely advertised, and I even had an impression that all the preparation for the
final show happened behind doors closed to the general public. I got this
impression as a postgraduate student in sociology; at the time I used to
look through the central press regularly and I did not see any advertising
for the contest. Also, the year after I asked some of the participants of
"Moscow Beauty—1989" if they had taken part in the previous tournament, and the common response was: "I would have done if I had known
about it."[7]

The first beauty contest was sponsored by the up-market German fashion magazine *Burda Moden*, whose owner and editor, Mrs. Burda, was an honorable member of the jury.[8] Attractive Russian girls found immediate admirers among film producers, fashion photographers, foreign investors, fashion designers and so on. For instance, the winner, Masha Kalinina, signed a long contract with *Burda Moden* and later appeared on the pages of that magazine. "Moscow Beauty" was expected to become an annual event where prizes were free travel passes for trips abroad, cash, and luxurious (by Russian standards) gifts. The contestants were now able to take up advertising commitments for foreign firms, which would bring in foreign "hard" currency.[9]

The announcement of the "Moscow Beauty—89" contest appeared on the pages of various newspapers long before the first round. As we found out from the organizers, more than 5,000 girls came to participate, including myself, largely inspired by my sister, who kept saying: "Look at the winner of 1988, Lena, you are more beautiful. Just lose some weight, and you will be the champion." She was ever so confident, but I had many things to consider before committing myself to the tournament.

To participate in a beauty contest at that time to a large extent meant to go against the still-prevailing public opinion that only indecent and disgraceful girls took part; girls who did not mind being seen by millions of TV viewers in swimming costumes marching on the stage; girls whose moral values were well below public standards; girls who were more associated with prostitutes than beauty queens. The public debate on this issue was mainly presented primarily by *Moskovskiy Komsomoletz* (the organ of the Young Communist League of Moscow) along with other papers. Some people thought (including members of my family and some of my acquaintances) that at a time when the state economy was in decline, when millions lived below the poverty line, and when social stability had started to collapse, that all the population should unite in a joint effort to overcome the hardships of everyday life. That is why it was seen to be immoral to throw huge sums of money at something as useless as a beauty contest and also to participate in one.

But at the same time there were others who were saying that yes, our life is miserable and grim, and yes, we must concentrate on our political, economic, and social problems, but that does not mean that there should not be any shine, any sparkle in our lives; so, let us forget about our misery at least for an hour of TV coverage of a beauty contest, let us see at least a few smiling and happy faces amid the total gloom and despair.

I was in my second year of a Ph.D. course writing a thesis on the cooperative system in Russia after the Law on Cooperation, adopted in 1988. My ambition was to get a degree in sociology, and I thought that participation in that contest would take too much of my time. But suddenly I had the idea that on the one hand, the beauty contest is a unique social experience, and on the other, I could be a participating observer and even write about my experience afterward. I was not in the least put off by public opinion, by the possibility of being accused of shamelessness, or of being compared with prostitutes. I did not care what comrade P. or comrade M. thought about me; I was confident in my friends and a few relatives, in their support and approval. It was a challenge, after all, and I have never refused to take one.

So I made the decision and attended the first round at the selection center nearest me. After I passed the first round, like every participant, I would have to sign a contract indicating that I would not accept any offers from any film producer, agency, etc., without the knowledge and consent of the contest organizers, nor would I sell any photographs made in due course of the competition. In this contract there was clear information on how much money in cash prizes each participant would receive for reaching the various levels in the competition. I also had to confirm that all information about me was correct, that I was a true Moscovite, that I was over eighteen, or had I not been, that my parents agreed to my participation. But all of this came later; at the initial stage I only had to turn up and be selected.

The official structure of the competition was as follows: (1) there were three rounds before the grand final, which only six participants would reach; (2) as it was a "Moscow Beauty" contest, only Moscovites of the ages eighteen to twenty-four could take part; (3) in the first round girls were selected by a jury of five or six people. There were several sets of judges working in different parts of Moscow: the jury that selected me consisted of one of the editors of *Moskovskiy Komsomoletz* (a woman), a fashion designer, a photographer, a representative from "Sputnik" (a young international tourist organization), and a choreographer. As I understood it, the same procedure for selection applied in a few other places around Moscow. Those who were selected in the first round were invited to a big meeting where further announcements and instructions were made, and the above-mentioned contracts were signed.

In the second round a rather big show was planned. Each of the contestants had to perform three different elements in front of the group of judges: first, they participated in a fashion show, presenting one of the designer outfits; second, they danced to music in a swimming costume, including some required elements in the dance; third, they made a short advertisement or presentation about some traditional piece of craft work or something that had to do with Russian history. After the show, in which some 130 girls participated, the judges came up with a list of 32 who would go further to the semi-final, in a few months' time and after special training.

This training included a two-week trip to the Crimea for sunning, a photo session, and for learning elements of runway and make-up application, plus intensive physical training and a fitness program. During our trip to the Crimea and most of the time henceforth, girls had bodyguards protecting them against any possible incidents. In the Crimea local people found out that we were the participants of the "Moscow Beauty" contest, and they started treating us with contempt. I heard insulting words and was even called a prostitute on several occasions. But the young men from "Mosgosinkasso" (a security organization similar to Brinks) traveled with us everywhere and created an atmosphere of security.

Preparation continued on the return to Moscow. The semi-final show was to consist of the following parts: (1) a line-up; (2) a fashion show; (3) a presentation as a TV reporter of one of the architectural attractions of Moscow (chosen and filmed beforehand); (4) a dance to music in a swimming costume; and (5) the so-called "Ball of the Queens," where we had to walk along the stage accompanied by a male member of a Moscow ballet-dance troupe as though we were being presented to the court. After every part of the show the jury was supposed to mark the performances of every contestant, and the results were shown on a big screen above the stage. The jury for this round was more or less the same as that of the second round, only bigger with representatives of the sponsoring firms and organizations. Because the actual contest was constantly interrupted by rock and pop singers, dance troupes, circus numbers, and so forth, the group of thirty-two girls was divided so there were two "evening concerts," rather than one contest. After the second evening six girls were chosen to enter the grand final show, where there was no jury and the public was supposed to choose the winner by phoning in.

During the first round I met many different girls with different backgrounds, from different social groups, aging from seventeen to twenty-four. I was on friendly terms with many of them. We often discussed things like: Why did they come to participate? What do they want to achieve? What are their objectives? The answer was already there. For most of them the contest was the only way to bring some changes to their lives, to break away from a routine and mundane existence, to feel important and recognized, to become a Queen, a Princess, to see the world. Some, surely, had different objectives. One girl said that she wanted to prove to her husband that she is beautiful, because he did not respect her femininity and charm; some sought public (mainly male) recognition and admiration. Media coverage and generous prizes were promised, and the whole enterprise looked very attractive.

Although the contest was called "Moscow Beauty" the participants were told that to be just beautiful is not enough. You should be well-spoken, intelligent, graceful, friendly, have a good personality, and also have the characteristics of a true Moscovite. Nobody knew exactly what that meant. I was not sure myself. It was difficult to assess the differences between, say, a "true Moscovite" and "true Kievliynka" (a girl from Kiev). I would imagine, apart from language, the requirements would be the same. But the organizers kept repeating that it was far more important to "be Moscovite" than it was to fit the Western standard measurements: to be taller than 170 cm, to weigh less than 60 kg, and to have measurements close to 90-60-90 cm (bust-waist-hips). The reverse turned out to be true: out of around 5,000 girls about 130 reached the second round, and it did not surprise me that although the overwhelming majority were tall and slim, few were well-spoken, and very few indeed cared about the image of a true Moscovite, not knowing what it was.

However, for me it was becoming more and more obvious that beauty was not the only important factor, as other forces (which had little to do with being a Moscovite) came into play. After the second round thirty-two girls were chosen to continue the competition. At least six of them had previous experience in modeling and runway, which gave them a certain advantage in the semi-final as they knew how to present themselves on the stage and had important skills in runway performances. Their experience was due to the fact that there was already a small fashion industry in Russia. I think that one of the true objectives of the contest was the promotion of Russian beauty abroad, and that this could be one of the reasons why professional models were allowed to participate. It also became clear that a few girls already had friends on the jury before the contest and that a few made friends among the organizers of the show during preparations for the semi-final. I myself was approached by men on the team: one a director of the show, promising to help me get to the final in exchange for the obvious favours. From then on the beauty of the beauty contest disappeared for me.

Knowing who was on the jury, who was the main sponsor of the contest, and which of the girls had powerful people behind them, it was not too hard to predict who would be chosen for the final and, more importantly, that in the final it would not really be up to either the girls or the general public to choose the winner. There must have been some other logic for choosing the winner. I am sure that most of the contestants from the last thirty-two could have won by objective requirements alone. But only six were to reach the final, and only one was to become "Miss Moscow—89."

"Moscow Beauty," after all, was not a parade of intelligence and decency—it was a display of Western-style physical beauty. Not surprisingly, the majority of the jury members were men.[10] Men have different tastes. Some like blondes, some like brunettes. Some like big, chubby women; some like tall and slender women. Some prefer easy or outgoing personalities; others prefer shy and quiet ladies. So, there could not be one set of criteria by which the winner would be chosen. There must have been something other than just the personal preference of the members of the jury. Thinking further, any beauty contest is not just a show, not just a festival of smiles, legs, and dresses, it is business. It is a business where big money is at stake, and there are no coincidences in business. So, I thought, there must be somebody, or some institution, with the most powerful single vote. The days of the Communist Party were numbered, so it must be someone else. Who or what could it be? I decided in favour of the chief sponsor; partly, because it seemed very logical, and partly, because there is a saying in Russia: "Those who pay choose the music."

A West German company, sponsoring the first "Miss Moscow" contest in 1988, had introduced as a first prize a two-year contract for modeling in West Germany. The winner was tall, very slender, and dark and thus had all the qualities of the Western European attractive model. Now in 1989 the main sponsor was the Polish company "Medimpex," and the winner was a blonde with a Polish surname.

However, aside from the likelihood that the entire competition was a set-up, it seems pretty clear that the jury was not as blind to "Western" measurements as it claimed to be. The final thirty-two had their various body parts measured several times over in the preparations for the semi-finals, and free access to gyms and swimming pools were arranged. At the same time, no girl remained in the running whose physique deviated in any significant way from the norms, the importance of which the organizers had so expressly denied in the beginning.

For some girls, and especially for those who believed the organizers' comments in the beginning, the results of the whole competition were very disappointing. They were in tears, and some were hysterical. They thought their lives were finished, their not-yet-begun careers were in ruins; they imagined that nobody would ever take them seriously again. They could not stop thinking that they were ugly, worthless, and fat(!), and all that because of false expectations. After the contest I came to the idea that it would be very useful if organizers were to set up some sort of psychological service for the participants to prevent inevitable stresses, nervous breakdowns, and tears.

Even for the years of 1988 and 1989 those young women were extremely brave. As stated above, public opinion was not very supportive, and the girls taking the risk were to a large extent condemned by at least part of the society. Some of them even kept it a secret from their parents and friends and tried to avoid TV and newspaper reporters. But it was worth taking that risk. The timing was right: Russia was "undoing the curtains" and opening up to the West.[11] The chance to be noticed, to get a modeling job or a part in the film was there. As traditional female wisdom teaches: a woman's face is her fortune, her sex appeal the bait, her body the promised pay-off.[12]

I also kept it a secret, not from my family and friends but from my department of sociology. I was not sure what to expect from fellow academics. As it happened I was partially right to be cautious. After the contest it became known in the university that I had not only participated but had reached the last thirty-two, and many male colleagues were very excited by the news. They were saying: "We knew you were pretty but now you are a queen!" Women were not as friendly; they looked at me suspiciously, and some of them could not help inquiring how I managed to get that far and whether I had been forced to do something I had not wanted to do. I was very open and sincere talking about the contest, and I mentioned my intention to write about it. Both men and women thought it was a good idea.

After 1988 numerous beauty contests began appearing all over the country. Every town, every city, every republic, every region was desperate to have its own beauty queen: "Miss Russia," "Miss Siberia," "Miss Almaty," and so on. People's imagination went further and further: "Miss Charm," "Miss Biggest Smile," "The Student's Star," and even, a couple of years later, "Miss Bust" (broadcast nationally on TV).

To organize a beauty contest became very fashionable, to participate became normal, and to win was prestigious. Born with "Perestroika," new Russian businessmen soon realized that beauty is in demand, that the beauty business is a very profitable business. Every "Miss..." had a team of so-called managers who demanded high commissions in exchange for "organizing the schedule." There were no established modeling agencies in Russia, and the first Russian models were very vulnerable in this respect. I am referring in this instance to the incident with the first "Miss USSR," Yulia Sukhanova, who by her own words was ripped off by her manager, whom she had not even chosen herself.[13] There was nobody to protect the rights of young models, to defend them legally; the whole business of fashion and modeling on any large scale was in its cradle.

First tears, first worries, first failures, and first achievements—everything is in the past now. Public opinion, like a tamed bear, is tired of surprises and is reluctant to react to anything that does not affect everyday life. Beauty contests have become routine. If people do not care who is ruling the country, who is sitting in the Parliament or who runs the City Council, then they certainly cannot care who wins this or that beauty pageant. Only those involved stay interested, and if "Miss Moscow" was once the subject of conversation on every corner, now there are some other more important things to discuss: how to earn money, where to find cheap food, what is going to happen to the country in the future?

Conclusion

Time passed and fashion went with it. The "Miss Moscow" beauty contest, which was supposed to have become traditional, is nearly forgotten. Now and then some other beauty competitions take place; Russian girls are sent to different international beauty contests and from time to time return home with good results. But Russian culture, as it seems to me, did not adopt beauty contests. To the Russian tradition they remained as strange as they were before. Beauty was never contested in Russia. As I understand it, in Russian culture beauty is not something to show, something to offer, something to portray—beauty is something to discover. It requires the effort, the subjective effort of learning and exploring beauty.

Needless to say that in every country, in every tradition there are certain and unique (for that part of the world) standards of beauty. More than that, beauty is not all about one's face or facial features. Anton Chekhov said that in a beautiful person everything must be beautiful—your face, your clothing, your character, and (what is more important) your thoughts. All those elements will be different not only in different countries but in different areas and regions of one country. How can it be, then, that we have "Miss Universe," "Miss World," or "Miss Europe" beauty contests? Do we not all know that different countries have different standards of beauty, and that therefore beauty pageants that attempt to span cultures can only be political farce? For instance, if this year an American girl is the winner, then next year it must be a European, and the year after next, probably, a girl from Asia.

On the other hand it is evident that in the modern world national differences are more and more ignored by "the global culture," which is especially clear in advertising. The standards of physical beauty are becoming standardized throughout the world, on many occasions against the will of the common population. I would argue in favour of preserving those differences. Otherwise, we may as well simply allow a computer to come up with the "universal" face and "universal" measurements of her body, and let the same computer decide which of the contestants is closer to those "universal" standards. At least that would be a "fair" judgement; and before joining the competition each girl would decide for herself whether she would like to be close to the standard or would rather be different.

No, I do not think that a universal physical beauty exists. But maybe we should not take all these competitions, pageants, and contests so seriously. Maybe it is just a little bit of fun and glamour in our life, some entertainment to enjoy, not meant to engage our brains, which can always be engaged in some other challenge. Who knows?

Notes

1. N. Lizko in "Do We Need A Political Party for Women?", *Gazeta Dlya Zhenschin*, 1994, 11-12:5. This remains a common point of view and can be found in countless publications.
2. See Halle 1933 and Rosenberg 1989 for more detail.
3. For more detail, see Barrett 1980; Evans 1982; Pateman 1988; Pinchback 1981 (especially the sections on suffrage movements, and struggle for emancipation); and Thomis 1982.
4. For more detail on the Soviet ideology of gender, see Kharchev 1977; Kharchev 1979; and Mashika 1989.
5. "Double enslavement": one, by the state, the Tzar, the landlord; the other, by Man, Father, Husband. "Two fronts": one, eight hours at work for the state, for the society; another, to fulfill all domestic obligations.
6. L. Pinigina 1994, 126. I have selected this example as a typical expression.
7. I personally participated in "Moscow Beauty—1989."
8. There is no history of beauty contests in the former USSR, as physical beauty was never a subject for competition.
9. See *Pravda*, 26 June 1988.
10. For more on this topic, see Chapkis 1988, 14.
11. Chapkis 1988, 39.
14. Chapkis 1988, 139.
13. See *Sovetskaya Rossia*, 1990.

5

The India Bonita of Monimbó
The Politics of Ethnic Identity in the New Nicaragua

Katherine Borland

In the modern world, beauty pageants constitute potent forms of mass entertainment. National and international contests have multiplied rapidly, and advances in the technology of communication have resulted in their reception and digestion by peoples in remote areas of the world. For new nations of the southern hemisphere, in fact, organizing a beauty pageant now often functions as a badge of civilized, modern status. Small town residents of Nicaragua watch the televised broadcasts of the Miss America Pageant, the Miss World Pageant, and even their own Miss Nicaragua Pageant. In the indigenous neighborhood of Monimbó, Masaya, television viewers know and appreciate the standards applicable to the big pageants and even critique the shows when the tall, blonde, blue-eyed American girl (or her closest stand-in) does not win.

Yet, in local beauty pageants audiences apply a distinctive set of criteria when choosing the winner. As in many towns, these pageants constitute performance forms organized and produced within the context of a festival. Like other festival activities, they provide an arena for voicing underlying conflicts and tensions affecting the community. In such a context, the pageant is best understood as a local adaptation, a refashioning of a dominant cultural form to the particular needs for representation within the community.

The India Bonita contest of Masaya is one of a number of events marking the arrival of the patronal festivals in honor of San Jerónimo. As a celebration of indigenous concepts of beauty, it contrasts with a second Masaya beauty contest that crowns the Festival Queen and her runners-up: Miss Folklore and Miss Congeniality. This second contest includes judged rounds for deportment, talent, a personal statement, and wardrobe changes, and aspires to the modern, transnational model for pageants. The India Bonita contest, on the other hand, attempts to recover and celebrate all that is truly "traditional" in the local environment and is designed primarily to select the best female performer of the local folkdance, the *marimba*.

Monimbó Indians comprise about a quarter of Masaya's total population of 80,000 and are concentrated in one large neighborhood on the south side of town. The presence of this indigenous community has strongly influenced the cultural life of Masaya. In fact, it is the arts and practices of the Monimbó community that have earned Masaya its identity as the "Cradle of Nicaraguan Folklore."[1] Despite their active participation in Nicaraguan political life, Monimboseños continue to view themselves as a separate, marginalized culture group within the nation. Moreover, they consider their festival practices to be a visible and powerful means of asserting a positive and distinctive cultural identity. Over the last thirty to forty years, a Nicaraguan folklore revival has elevated their once maligned, indigenous folkdance to the status of a regional, and later, a national treasure.[2] Yet, as the *marimba* was revalued and popularized among mestizo Nicaraguans, Monimbó performers were correspondingly devalued.[3]

For this reason Monimboseños view the performance of *marimba* by noncommunity members as a form of cultural appropriation similar to previous appropriations of Indian lands and labor by the dominant classes. Recently, they have begun to organize themselves politically around the banner of ethnic identity. Yet, as Susan De Valle suggests, ethnicity "may act as a factor of unity *at one moment* in the political struggle, yet ethnicity cannot be conflated with any particular political ideology" (1986, 67). In 1991, the India Bonita Contest became the focus of a struggle by Monimboseños for the right to reclaim the neighborhood's cultural traditions. All Monimbó cultural activists were united in this struggle. Nevertheless, supporters of the two political parties—the Sandinistas and and the Union of National Opposition—had very different understandings of the tradition, and their strategies for asserting their authority contrasted strongly. By tracing the history and changing structure of the India Bonita Contest, we can examine how this event functions as a forum for discussions of ethnic identity and political power.

The Birth of the India Bonita Contest

Changes in the San Jerónimo Festival Queen contests over time reflect changes in residents' differential participation in Masaya's patronal festival.[4] Prior to the 1960s, a rigid class structure divided high society, working class, and Indian groups in the town. The "criollos," affluent families of Spanish or mixed descent, resided in the town center and distanced themselves from Masaya popular culture. For the San Jerónimo festival, they organized a number of exclusive events, such as costume balls and horse shows. Some patronized street dance and masquerading performances, while others disparaged them as "Indian" customs, but none regarded these displays as part of their own cultural heritage.

Also living in the town center and in neighborhoods spreading to the east and west, working-class mestizo residents participated actively in the patronal festival processions and cultural performances. Yet, while they were often no better off economically than Monimboseños, mestizos considered themselves socially and culturally superior to their Indian neighbors. Monimboseños occupied an area of the city characterized by a rural ambience and a lack of basic infrastructure. While they generally avoided the town center, Monimboseños descended in large numbers to perform the traditional dances and masquerades that had made the San Jerónimo festival famous.

In this period only one festival queen contest, the Darrera de Cintas, was organized at the city level. Felipita Cermeño, Sandinista cultural worker and a descendant of one of Masaya's elite families, describes the event in this way:

> In the festival what was normally done was the election of the Queen, which was accomplished through a ribbon contest. So the candidates arrived there—I was a candidate one year—but we were young people of society, understand? So they invited us to be a candidate in a horse race, a ribbon race, mounted on horses, and the one who had the most ribbons [at the end] was the one elected Queen of the Patronal Festivals. That's how it was done in my epoch....So the Queen, they gave her a party and crowned her with her group of maids, but it was a party that not everyone participated in.

The Carrera de Cintas, then, functioned as a rather exclusive popularity contest, the girl who collected the most ribbons being declared the winner.

By the late 1950s, a new set of circumstances began to affect the way in which indigenous cultural traditions were perceived by the town elites. An international growth in the formation of folkdance troupes led to the development of contests among youth of various countries, sponsored primarily by voluntary organizations and government tourist offices. In 1960, the Nicaraguan Lions Club sponsored the first National India Bonita Contest. This contest was designed to select a representative of Nicaragua's picturesque folkloric traditions and was held in Masaya.

Leopolda Palacios (Pola), a nineteen-year old Monimboseña, was chosen by local Lions Club officials to be the Masaya candidate. Although Doña Pola was a member of a noted family of marimba musicians, she had never performed with a festival dance group. At that time she worked as a domestic for a prominent Lions Club family. This, along with her physical attractiveness and indigenous features, appears to have accounted for her nomination. The Lions Club committee contracted a coach to train her in the dance, and she won the contest.

At its inception, then, the India Bonita Contest represented a cultural form devised by middle- and upper-class folklore enthusiasts, who took responsibility for selecting and training their representative of indigenous culture.[5] The contest was subsequently transmuted from a national to a city-wide affair and was celebrated annually in Masaya.

The Transfer of Festival Practices in Masaya

Simultaneous with the emergence of the India Bonita Contest, members of Masaya's social elite began to participate actively in the San Jerónimo dance performances. They adopted *marimba* dancing as part of their Masayan cultural heritage and gave it new value. As town center residents began to dance, however, they introduced stylistic variations and more elaborate costumes, distinguishing their own performances from those of the Monimboseños, who continued to be socially stigmatized.[6]

A complicating factor in the transfer of dancing practices from Monimbó to town center residents was the rise of fixed, town center "Negras" groups. Historically, the "Negras," all-male dance groups in which half the dancers impersonate women, has been understood to bring the *marimba* to its highest form of perfection. Monimbó mixed-sex "Inditas" and all-male "Negras" groups had traditionally constituted loose associations of dancers, who organized themselves in order to "pay a promise" to San Jerónimo (usually for having cured a sick relative or farm animal). Thus, group membership was fluid, and performances by specific groups were occasional in nature. In contrast, the town center "Negras," were established primarily for cultural reasons. Directors gave their groups names, determined a particular date for their performances in the festival calendar, and performed annually. In this way they established a fixed identity that allowed them to build a performance reputation over time.

As town center "Negras" began to dominate the festival arena, they distinguished the "Negras," which they now claimed as a town center tradition, from the less spectacular "Inditas," which they associated with Monimbó. René Chavarría, a town center "Negras" director, explains:

All the traditions of Masaya city are eminently indigenous, and this culture has come to us through the Indians. And over time, we have given them a certain gayer, more folkloric flavor. What happened is that we've made transformations in the city center; we've given the costumes brilliance; we've modified the dance quite a bit. And today, the "Negras" dance is of the city center.

Young mixed-sex groups that were also forming in the town center adopted the "Negras" costume aesthetic, creating a new form of festival dance group, the "Baile de Fantasía." As these town center groups multiplied, the participation of less affluent Monimbó dance groups, especially the "Inditas," declined.

Among the town center dancers were a number of young teachers who were interested in popularizing the *marimba* by institutionalizing folkdance instruction in the schools. In 1965, they founded the Masaya Folklore School, which offered mandatory, weekly dance classes to all Masaya schoolchildren. Thus, *marimba* dancing became a celebration of Masaya's rather than Monimbó's distinctive cultural heritage. By the 1970s, the Masaya Folkdance School had taken responsibility for organizing the India Bonita Contest, which became a competition among candidates from each Masaya High School. Monimboseñas, if they attended high school, continued to compete. Yet the India Bonita title was no longer the exclusive property of Monimbó.[7]

Constructing a National Culture, 1979-1990

After the revolution the Sandinista government initiated a national folkdance revival of its own. Anxious to celebrate the "people's" culture and to present a strong front in the face of a perceived invasion of foreign, largely North American, cultural forms, the new government set about popularizing folk traditions. Marimba dancing, which had already been "discovered" by the early folklore revivalists, became a major vehicle for representing the new Nicaragua's culture of resistance.[8]

Government assistance to grass-roots, traditional dancers was funneled through local Popular Culture Centers (CPCs) and soon led to the multiplication of festival dance groups in Masaya, especially among less affluent residents. Thus, while the folkdance revival of the 1960s had marked an elitist development, the revival in the 1980s broadened festival participation among all Masaya residents.

At the same time the national government supported the formation of a number of folk ballets, based in the nation's capital.[9] These ballets introduced staged reviews of folkdance traditions from around the country and choreographed pieces, loosely based on folk traditions. Receiving the lion's share of government funding, the folk ballets quickly professionalized. They introduced elements of classical ballet and modern dance into their performances, creating a hybrid form of *marimba* that they then projected, through staged performances and televised broadcasts, to national and international audiences.[10]

Masaya dancers, however, strongly objected to the folk ballets' stylistic innovations. *Marimba* dancing in Masaya was understood to project a serious, stately, graceful image. In contrast, Managua-based dancers had quickened the pace of the dance and performed in a way that Masayans found clownish and undisciplined. Since the Monimbó community continued to view these dances as an expression of its unique cultural style, the folk ballet modifications were downright insulting.

In order to combat the distortions being introduced at the national level and reassert regional control over the aesthetics and practice of the dance, Masaya cultural organizers decided to promote and expand the traditional context for *marimba* dancing, the San Jerónimo Festival. Ernesto Ortega, Mayor of Masaya from 1984 to 1989, placed festival production on a new footing by establishing a Patronal Festivals Committee at City Hall. This committee strengthened existing groups and activities by having them work collectively to raise funds for cultural performances, and it solicited suggestions for new cultural activities to enhance the festival as well.

The Revival of the India Bonita Contest

In 1987, the Patronal Festivals Committee decided to sponsor contests to elect the Festival Queen, her runners-up, and the India Bonita of Masaya. These queen contests revived the older Carrera de Cintas and India Bonita contests but placed them on a new, more popular footing. The contests were open to any young woman who registered at City Hall. A large platform stage was erected in the central park, and the general public was invited to attend free of charge. Held on a separate day after the Festival Queens Contest, the India Bonita Contest became a distinctive event. And it was this second contest that elicited the greatest enthusiasm and participation among Monimboseños.

By the late 1980s, several children's and juvenile groups had come into existence in Monimbó. These groups now imitated the town center dance aesthetic, yet, as recently formed groups with limited financial resources for costumes, they were considered less accomplished than the town center groups. Thus, they faced a problem: how to prove that they too had quality as dancers. The annual India Bonita Contest provided an arena uniquely suited to this need.

The only performance setting in Masaya where dancers are evaluated by a panel of official judges, the India Bonita Contest offered an opportunity to compete that was relatively free of class bias. While three criteria are used to determine the winner—oral expression, physical appearance, and dance skill—the contest was popularly understood to evaluate *marimba* dancing. Thus, the young dancer who won the contest was understood to be the best *marimba* dancer in Masaya.

Former CPC director, Felipita Cermeño, explained that the contest was initially designed as a competition among youth from the city's seven neighborhoods. Nevertheless, Monimbó is the only neighborhood that developed a separate eliminatory contest. A project of the Folklore and Sports Association of Monimbó (one of eleven Sandinista community improvement committees in Monimbó), this contest is supported by donations from better-off residents and out-of-pocket contributions from association members themselves.

Sandinista community activist and dance director Carlos Centeno explains:

> Four years ago, Sergio Luna and I organized this neighborhood contest always trying to maintain the traditions. As a dancer, I was interested in making sure that we had a place [in the city-wide competition]. The Sandinista Defense Committees began to hold elimination contests in other neighborhoods in order to massify folklore, but there was little actual participation....The difference was that the girls who arrived from other neighborhoods to participate [in the city-wide competition] had been chosen, but they didn't have the title of India Bonita of their neighborhood as in Monimbó. After the contest, that was it. Our idea was different. We wanted a permanent representative. And the following year, just as in the city-wide contest, she would appear and give up her crown to the new winner. We called ten, eight, six as a minimum, to come and compete to represent their neighborhood....And so there are actually two "India Bonitas," one of Masaya and one of Monimbó.

The neighborhood-level contest caught the imagination of Monimbó residents partly because the India Bonita herself represents Monimbó traditions and identity. During a period when their claim to a distinctive cultural heritage was being challenged by nationalizers and folkdance enthusiasts, the contest served to reassert Monimboseño's authority in matters of traditional culture.[11]

Indigenous physical features are privileged in the city-wide India Bonita contests, and, while girls with Indian features can be found in all Masaya neighborhoods and among all social classes, this focus certainly gives Monimbó an advantage. In addition to physical traits, the contestants are judged for the traditionality of their costumes. Arguably a late invention, the India Bonita costume was introduced during the period when *marimba* dancing began to be staged as a folkloric display. Yet the colors and style of this dress are constantly being fixed by popular memory. Modern contestants concern themselves even with questions of the appropriate number of rows of rick rack, tucks, and pleats "traditionally" used by the "India."[12]

Moreover, make-up and bottled perfume are discarded for this per-

1990 India Bonita of Monimbó and Masaya, Alba Ligia Sanchez Colomer, pins the ribbon on the 1991 winner of the neighborhood elimination contest, India Bonita Matilde Socorro López Puoy.

The 1991 India Bonita of Monimbó goes in procession to the city-wide contest. Alcalde de Vara, Vincente Jimenez (far left) and neighborhood contest organizer, Carlos Centeno (back right) accompany 1991 and 1990 India Bonitas of Monimbó.

formance, and young contestants search for older women who can still make the mix of herbs for the traditional scent used by Indian women. Hair is arranged in traditional braids, and feet are shod in *caites*, the indigenous sandal. Preparations for the contest, then, provide Monimbó girls a chance to reexplore native notions of beauty as they seek to create an aesthetic largely abandoned in their modern, everyday world. As gift-giving remains an important aspect of social and festival practice in Monimbó, Monimbó contestants select some traditional item—home-made foods or crafts—to carry with them as a gift to the judges.

When the neighborhood India Bonita goes to the city-wide contest, Carlos Centeno explains:

> She goes in procession from here to there, with marimba and firecrackers, with chicheros (a brass band) if we can afford it. The procession is made up of the winner with her crown and ribbon, the Alcalde de Vara (the indigenous mayor of Monimbó, now largely a symbolic figure), and the other companions behind who participated in the [eliminatory] contest.

The eliminatory contest, then, has been elaborated to a much greater degree than parallel activities in other neighborhoods. These elaborations—gift-giving and a procession—represent forms of display that occur in most neighborhood festivals, indicating that the preparation and presentation of the Monimbó candidate has itself been festivalized according to an existing neighborhood model.

Creating a New Marimba Aesthetic

Several months before the September contest, young women in Monimbó begin to rehearse for the upcoming event. They contract a private coach or join a group that Carlos Centeno organizes in order to develop mastery in the dance. While most contestants have already danced in festival groups, they must now concentrate on perfecting the *marimba* as a solo performance. When he coaches young women for the contest, Don Carlos emphasizes staging considerations and displacement as important refinements that the girls must learn. While these aspects of training demonstrate the influence of folk ballets on the evolving dance aesthetic, Don Carlos emphasizes that adaptations to the stage must not interfere with the traditional sequence of steps in a given musical piece.

Comments at these rehearsals reveal, in fact, that the contest functions to enforce distinctions between a developing local dance style for women and the influential "Negras" and folk ballet aesthetics. At one rehearsal, a young coach cautioned the dancer never to cross her arms in front of her as the "Negras" dancers do. At another rehearsal a young woman was criticized for holding her skirt extended with her palm out, "Negras" style, rather than toward her body. Finally, young dancers are constantly cautioned to slow down and reduce the number of turns they make, corrections aimed at ridding the dancers of folk ballet distortions. Thus, the India Bonita Contest has allowed for a positive revaluation of the "Inditas" dance which has been historically devalued due to its association with female as opposed to male performance styles and indigenous as opposed to town center aesthetics.

Political Polarization and Constructions of Tradition

Ideally, contestants arrive at the city-wide India Bonita Contest from seven different city neighborhoods. Monimbó contestants who lose at the neighborhood level are free to and do sometimes register in the city-wide contest. Yet Carlos Centeno, organizer of the Monimbó eliminatory contest asserted, "It has never occurred that those who lost at the neighborhood level won at the city level. In four years, the two who won there [had already] won here." Nevertheless, the two India Bonita contests remain fraught with difficulties. Even though a panel of judges evaluates the dancers, aesthetic criteria are loose enough to allow alternative notions of who really dances best.

In 1991, a new group of Monimbó culture workers operating in the UNO controlled City Hall, were engaged in an attempt to capture the leadership of existing cultural institutions from Sandinista activists. Like other Monimboseños, they decried the distortions of the dance tradition effected by the national folk ballets. Yet, unlike Sandinistas, who identified the *marimba* as an expression of indigenous cultural resistance, these UNO supporters viewed the dance as part of their catholic heritage. They publicly criticized Sandinistas for having separated festival dance performances from their religious core, arguing that Monimboseños had originally danced only to pay a promise to the Saint. In addition, they accused Sandinista artists of having profited financially from the dance, because they had accepted government aid in order to mount their festival performances. Finally, they pledged to restore the India Bonita Contest to a "traditional" model—the 1960 Lions Club event.

Speaking for the City Hall Office of Culture, Monimboseña Anita Vivas López asserted that the India Bonita Crown belonged to Monimbó but that dancing ability ought to be secondary to physical appearance. The winning candidate, she said, should be the girl who best exemplified the physiognomy and characteristics—grace, composure, simplicity—of the race. This racialist argument for Monimbó's ownership of the contest *and* the dance implies that ethnic identity is an inherent trait rather than a matter of performance or practice. Office of Culture workers refused to recognize the legitimacy of the neighborhood eliminatory contest, claiming that it was a Sandinista event. They selected and prepared their own candidate, the daughter of a close friend, who did not participate in the neighborhood contest. Six contestants entered the Monimbó contest, and Matilde Socorro López Putoy (Coco), a dancer in Carlos Centeno's festival dance group, won.

In contrast to the neighborhood contest, which was held at an outdoor dance hall in Monimbó, the city-wide contest was moved indoors to the Masaya Social Club, and a five cordoba admission fee (equivalent to one American dollar) was instituted.[13] There, new criteria for the selection of the Masaya India Bonita were announced to the dismay and confusion of the audience. The MC announced three times that the event was not a dance contest, so contestants would not be eliminated simply for making a mistake in the dance. He carefully explained that the goal was to select the most representative Indian, not the best *marimba* dancer.

When each contestant was announced and her affiliation given, the recently crowned India Bonita of Monimbó was presented simply as a representative of Carlos Centeno's dance group. Don Carlos protested, and the MC later reintroduced Coco as the elected India Bonita of Monimbó. However, he subsequently observed that five of the six contestants were Monimboseñas, and declared that all contestants had an equal chance of winning the city title. Despite the announced changes in contest criteria, contestants proceeded to compete in successive rounds of dancing.

Yet, as candidates were eliminated, the political nature of selection became apparent. In the first round, one non-Monimboseña, and two Monimbó dancers who had entered and lost the neighborhood contest were eliminated. Coco, the India Bonita of Monimbó, was eliminated in the second. The final round became a competition between Carla Díaz and Marta Zúniga Gómez, the City Hall candidate. Both were from Monimbó, yet neither had participated in the neighborhood contest. Ultimately, Marta won the contest.

The general confusion provoked by the announced changes in contest criteria, subsequent criticism of the way in which Office of Culture workers had consulted with the panel of judges during the contest, and a new policy of charging admission all provoked widespread dissatisfaction. Although dance directors were divided as to whether the winning contestant actually danced best, all agreed that the nature of the contest had been subverted by the new policies of City Hall culture workers.

In fact, by 1991, the city-wide contest had become an arena for a struggle among Monimboseños for a distinction that all Monimboseños considered the rightful property of their neighborhood. The question being decided was no longer whether Monimbó candidates danced as well as or better than mestizo candidates from other neighborhoods, but whether the Monimboseños working at the City Hall Office of Culture or those working as Sandinista community organizers had the power to select and control the representative of Masaya's indigenous identity. The judges for this contest were drawn from a pool of Masaya authorities on the dance, yet the majority of candidates arrived at the Masaya Social Club from Monimbó.

UNO Office of Culture workers, however, had won the contest at a price. Even those members of the dance world who demonstrated a preference for UNO politics objected to the nonpopular, undemocratic turn the contest had taken. Don Rigoberto Guzmán, a highly respected town center "Negras" director and a strong UNO supporter, objected to the admission fee, explaining:

> They talked there of giving life to folklore, to fill the youth with enthusiasm, and in these popular presentations, they shouldn't exploit the people in that way. Because I saw many people turn around and leave because they didn't have the money to pay for the ticket....

In Monimbó a rumor arose that someone had been given a complimentary ticket by Office of Culture workers. The single complimentary ticket quickly turned into five and then into the conviction that the Mayor's Office had packed the audience in Marta's favor.

The privileging of physical features over dance skill in the 1991 contest functioned in part to mask the politicization of the selection process. It also seriously undermined the contest's potential to serve as an objective determination of quality in the dance. Moreover, when I asked residents to ignore the question of Marta's dance skill and comment on her qualifications as an indigenous beauty, they concurred in the opinion that she did not qualify. An older Monimboseña sympathetic to the UNO party explained that beauty was more a question of attitude than of actual looks. In the neighborhood, Marta had a reputation for being aloof and not particularly respectful of her elders. Immediately after the contest Alba Ligia Sanchez Colomer, 1990 India Bonita of both Masaya and Monimbó, returned the gifts of five cordobas and a shawl that she had received from the Mayor's Office the year before. Her mother, a UNO supporter and friend of Office of Culture workers, explained that these tokens were returned in order to disassociate the family from any questions of favoritism, elitism, or personal gain surrounding the contest.

One week later the newly elected queens appeared publicly for the first time at a social dance. As the queens proceeded around the arena, almost no one in the audience applauded. When they danced during intermission, a ripple of quiet disapproval spread through the contingent of Monimboseños with whom I was sitting. Whispers of "Don't they dance badly?" and "She doesn't know the piece" were exchanged. More than representing an unbiased opinion of the dancers' skill, these comments reflected the popular conviction that the girls had not received their titles fairly.

Conclusion

The India Bonita Contest of Masaya offers an alternative to dominant models for beauty pageants, where local residents and contest participants can explore indigenous notions of beauty. These notions involve much more than physical features; they include the ability to perform traditional culture, primarily through the dance but also in terms of behaviors that demonstrate membership in the community—gift giving, friendliness, and respect for elders. Yet the contest has become important for Monimboseños not as a protest against hegemonic models for female beauty. Instead, the India Bonita Contest provides a space for contesting the more immediately felt appropriation of Monimbó traditions and identity by mestizo folklore revivalists in Masaya and the nation. By 1991, all neighborhood cultural activists agreed that winning the India Bonita crown for the neighborhood was of utmost importance.

Nevertheless, the community's nascent ethnic political movement was divided by the same political polarization that affected Nicaraguan society as a whole in the 1990s. UNO Office of Culture workers, intent on unseating their Sandinista rivals in the cultural as well as the political realm, refused to acknowledge the evolving nature of the event and attempted to return the contest to an original model in which indigenous blood was privileged over dancing ability in the selection process. They also refused to acknowledge the legitimacy of the neighborhood eliminatory contest as a developing community tradition. And they conferred upon themselves, as organizers of the event and representatives of the community, the right to choose Masaya's India Bonita. Yet the Monimbó community was less than satisfied by the outcome of this literal return to traditional models. UNO and Sandinista supporters alike recognized that indigenous identity is earned not ascribed; it is a matter of social practice and performance rather than of mere biological inheritance.

Notes

1. For a more extensive discussion of Masayan folklore, see Peña Hernández 1968.
2. For more on the the Nicaraguan folklore revival, see my dissertation 1984.
3. See Lombardi-Satriani 1973 for more on the process by which intellectual and political groups appropriate and distort the culture of the subaltern classes.
4. For discussions of differential participation in festivals along social class and ethnic lines, see Turner 1986; Rosensweig 1983; and Vogt 1955.
5. Rigoberta Menchú provides interesting comparative commentary on a similar contest

organized in her native Guatemala. She points out that the girls selected for the contest were hispanicized Indians who worked as servants in the town. As a rural Indian, Menchú finds their claim to represent the indigenous tradition farcical. (Menchú 1984)

6. See Michael Thompson 1979 for a theoretical discussion of how the transfer of cultural items from a lower to a higher social class is effected.

7. For a comparative discussion of Mexico's institutionalization of folkdance, see Nájera-Ramírez 1989.

8. The notion that *marimba* dancing exemplified cultural resistance is based on the idea that the dance originally parodied the dance styles of Spanish residents. Dancers, especially "Negras," continue to employ white-face masks during their performances.

9. See Nájera-Ramírez 1989 for comparative information on the rise of Mexican folk ballets.

10. See Barbara Kirshenblatt-Gimblett 1991 for a discussion of the use of folkdance troupes to present a modernized, homogenized and romanticized version of national culture.

11. See Royce 1982 for a discussion of how cultural distinctiveness is emphasized among marginalized groups as pressures to assimilate to the larger culture increase.

12. The early festival costume worn by "Inditas" festival dancers consisted of a loosely fitting, embroidered silk *huipil* or blouse worn over a length of striped cloth wrapped tightly around the hips. The current India Bonita costume is a matching blouse and long, flowing skirt of light-colored muslin, whose cut is similar to the attire used by early twentieth century Indian servant women.

13. This change in the location of the contest had been initiated the year before by UNO culture workers. However, the practice of charging admission was new in 1991. Prior to 1979, when it was nationalized, the Social Club was an exclusive, private club serving members of Masaya's social elite.

6

Negotiating Style and Mediating Beauty
Transvestite *(Gay/Bantut)* Beauty Contests in the Southern Philippines

Mark Johnson

Introduction: The Local Context of Gay Internationals

Transvestite beauty contests are by all accounts an emergent and growing phenomenon in mainland and insular Southeast Asia and the Pacific (Mageo 1992; Van Esterik this volume), and are ubiquitous throughout most of the Philippines (Cannel 1992; Whitham 1992). In this paper I am concerned with the meaning of the *gay* or *bantut* beauty contests in the context of the Muslim Tausug and Sama communities of Zamboanga City and Jolo in the Southern Philippines. In particular I shall focus on the way in which the *gay/bantut* contestants symbolically mediate for local communities the appropriation of a desirable yet potentially threatening global cultural other, and have become central to the ongoing negotiation and constitution of an inviolable Muslim identity.

I would just make a brief note here about the terms *gay* and *bantut* in local usage. Whereas in Britain or North America the categories of transsexualism, transvestism, and homosexuality are carefully distinguished, in most parts of the Philippines as throughout much of this region, such distinctions are blurred (Hart 1968). Locally, those men who call themselves *gay* almost universally define themselves as "women stuck within men's bodies." On the other hand, the *bantut*, as these men are more widely designated amongst the Muslim Tausug and Sama, are considered both to be impotent men as well as men who act like women. Thus, the *gay/bantut* may, in the first instance, be thought of within the general rubric of transgender or gender defined homosexuality, defined by Murray (1992: xxi–xxii) as a situation when a "sexually receptive partner is expected to enact some aspects of the feminine gender role: to behave and/or sound and/or dress in ways appropriate to women in that society." However, as I suggest below, part of what is at stake in gay beauty contests is precisely the meaning of local *gay* gender and sexuality.

89

There are two classes of *gay* competitions in the Southern Philippines. These are community (*barangay*) level contests, such as the one described below, which are usually held in the open air on any available communal property, and annual city-wide (*municipal*) competitions such as the *Miss Gay International*, Jolo (in Sulu), which are usually held in indoor auditoriums such as the Notre Dame de Jolo gymnasium. The main difference between the competitions is in the composition of the audience, the number and status of financial sponsors, and the number and status of the judges, reflecting overall the greater "prestige" value of the municipal contest. What this does not reflect, however, is a formal system or structure of competitive ranks through which one moves, for instance, from being a local community winner to municipal, regional, national, and thence on to a international arena. Gay beauty contests are thus completely local events in the sense that there are no organizational linkages with larger metropolitan centers either in the Philippines or abroad.

Interestingly, however, while gay beauty contests often coincide with local calendrical celebrations, and while contest titles, such as the *Miss Gay Habena*, will sometimes include the name of the community in its title, most contests are organized around the theme of an international beauty pageant. Competition titles in the town of Jolo over the past few years include *Miss Gay World*, *Miss Gay International* and *Search for Miss Gay World*. Moreover, what links these otherwise formally unrelated gay beauty pageants together is that it is by and large the same set of gays who organize and repeatedly enter and re-enter these "internationals" in what is said to be a gay obsession with "exposing one's beauty."

The structure of the shows articulates with a much longer performative tradition in Sulu where the *bantut*, who were and still are regarded as excellent musicians, singers, and dancers, would in some instances travel together from village to village or even from island to island performing at wedding celebrations (Kiefer 1967; Nimmo 1978). Transvestite men are widely recognized as having played an important role both as ritual specialists and performers throughout this region (Van der Kroef 1954; Peacock 1968; Errington 1989, 124; Murray 1992; and see for instance Nanda 1992 who documents a similar tradition in South Asia). Within the last twenty years, however, transvestite men have emerged in Sulu (as elsewhere in the region), as possessors and purveyors of "beauty" and "style" (*istyle*). Not only have they come to dominate a burgeoning beauty parlour business, but also they are the principle organizers, orchestrators, and choreographers of women's beauty pageants as well as a myriad of other similar events such as school talent shows. Following Peacock (1968), I argue that this is but a contemporary transformation and re-emergence of a ritual transvestite role.

Transvestite beauty contests are, like the *gay/bantut* who themselves represent various subjectivities, undoubtedly multi-layered and polysemic texts. Yet, if *gay* beauty contests are ritual performances, then the overall trend towards including "world," "universe," or "international" in the title is indicative of the central focus of these ritual performances; that is, the encompassment of a potent and significant global otherness (Friedman 1990, 321), which here, as in many other parts of the world, is primarily conceptualized in terms of America.

Miss Gay Super Model (of the World), 1991

I begin with a description taken from field notes of the first among several gay beauty contests which I attended and which I consider to be representative of gay beauty contests in general.

April 17, 1991
Today was the day of the *Super Gay Model of the World*. I have been told about this contest for weeks now, and for most of the gays I know it has overshadowed the Hari Raya festivities marking the end of Ramadan, the Muslim period of fasting and prayers, which concluded just one week ago. The contestants had pre-registered for the contest, filing a 15 pesos registration fee and photograph, and filling out a form that looked something like this:

Miss Gay Super Model
Name: Ms. Regine Valasquez
Country representing: Ms. Czechoslovakia
Age: 18
Height: 5'11"
Vital Statistics: 36-24-36
Sign: Virgo
Ambition: "To be a certified public accountant"
Personal motto: "Simplicity is beauty"
Ideal man: "Tall, handsome, intelligent"

The contestants had also been given a list of the various awards that they would be competing for. In addition to the overall winner and four runners-up, prizes were to be awarded in the following categories: best in national costume; best in evening gown; best in cocktail dress; best in runway; promising new model; darling of the crowd; Miss Photogenic; "Miss Lux," for best in skin complexion (Lux being a brand of soap); and "Miss Rejoice," for hair (Rejoice being a brand of shampoo).

The contest was held in the small, predominately Muslim community of Cawit about 13 kilometres out from Zamboanga City proper. The venue was a small dirt basketball court, which sat opposite the local mosque. A small makeshift wooden stage had been constructed, including a somewhat precarious looking runway, which consisted of odd bits of timber, packing crates as well as wooden Pepsi and Coca-Cola bottle containers. At the back of the stage was a wall over which was draped a cloth and on to which the title, *Gay Super Model 91*, and other decorations had been pinned. On either side of the stage were large speaker boxes from which mostly western pop music was playing. There was one incandescent light mounted on a pole and a small spotlight mounted on a Coca-Cola container at the end of the runway.

Immediately in front of the stage was the table for the board of judges, chaired by the headmistress of the local school. Towards the front and pressing up against the judges were young children and young men, whilst sitting directly in front of the stage to one side were two beautifully turned out gays, who it turned out were the previous year's queen and first runner-up. To one side of the stage was another row of benches and chairs occupied by various sponsors—mainly local village business persons and members of leading families in the community, such as the wife of the *barangay* captain and councillors, and so forth, while toward the periphery were older men and women from the surrounding community, including one man who I was told was the local Imam, although I did not confirm this.

The contest began with each contestant in their "ethnic attire" or "national costume," as it was alternately designated, called out on to the stage and presented as Miss Germany, Miss Canada, and so onto an electric orchestrated theme song. The contestants then walked to the front, the song fading somewhat into the background, and said a few words into the microphone, usually a repeatedly practised English speech, such as Ms. Czechoslovakia's: "Good evening ladies and gentlemen, honored members of the board of judges, my name is Regine Valasquez, and I am representing the beautiful country of Czechoslovakia. May I wish you a pleasant evening, and I hope that you will enjoy my beauty." Then, with an added touch of *gay/bantut* flair, "Thank you and I love you all." Ethnic attire was followed by cocktail dress, summer and sports wear—including high cut or French cut bathing suits and two piece bikinis—and finally the evening gown. The latter was accompanied by soft music, over which each contestant's details ("biodata"), as provided on the registration form, was read.

The emergence of the *gays* brought with it a mixture of cat calls such as "sexy" or "*arte*," genuine appreciation expressed by clapping, and/or comments made to one another about the "talent" of the *gays*, as well as laughter and mimicry of any stutters, stammers, or long pauses in their speech. Whilst the majority of the dresses, like the stage performances, were truly convincing, reflecting the time, money and hard work gays invest in the contests, some of the costumes were not quite all together, and

Candidates for the Miss Gay Super Model (of the world) including Miss India (in the center) pose in their "ethnic attire."

Contestants modeling "cocktail" dresses.

in several cases the dresses were so short that they left either the front or the rear portion of the model's underwear exposed. In another case all the nylon had gathered together at the ankles of the contestant, which brought uproarious laughter from the audience. This same mixture of appreciation and hilarity continued throughout the evening and gave the proceedings a certain satirical feel.

Following the costumes and presentation of the minor awards, the judges choose ten candidates for the *Question and Answer* portion. This was to be the basis from which the five finalist were selected, and they in turn were asked another set of questions. The questions, which were all given in and had to be answered in English, included topics related to politics and the contestant's designated career choice. For example, contestants were asked, "If you were President Cory Aquino, would you let Imelda Marcos return to the country?" "Why do you want to be a nurse?" In addition, however, contestants were asked questions which explicitly played on *gay/bantut* gender and sexuality, such as, "What effect can *gays* have on family planning?" "What would you do if you found out your boyfriend was a *gay* like you?" Although the responses to these latter questions in particular often elicited the most laughter, a well answered and articulated question on any topic was met with as much if not more audience support than a beautiful dress. Moreover, as the primary basis for the assessment of "intelligence," the *Question and Answer* portion accounted for 50 percent or more of the total score awarded by judges.

By the time the five finalists had answered the last set of questions, it was 3 a.m., and the contest had lasted over seven hours. Finally, the runners-up and winners were announced, each preceded by a taped fanfare and drum roll (which had to be rewound prior to each announcement). Miss Philippines was declared *Miss Gay Super Model of the World*, and somewhat anti-climactically for the crowd at least, she was presented with the tiara by the previous year's winners. Hugs and kisses were exchanged all round by the winners and losers, whose postures and tears were reminiscent of those in the Miss America contest.

Beauty and the Legacy of the American Mandate

Rather obviously the forms and idioms of beauty circulated in *gay* beauty contests in the Southern Philippines are informed by a western (predominately American) produced image of glamour and beauty, whether they are the locally televised Miss Universe and Miss America pageants or Hollywood movies and television programs. As such, *gay* beauty contests have a familiar resonance about them, from the music of Andrew Lloyd Weber and Madonna, amongst others, to the "ethnic" costumes that faithfully reproduce familiar stereotypes: island countries equated with flowery skirts, sarongs, and swimsuits and African countries with appropriately "primitive" attire, including charcoal-darkened skin and leopard-spotted tights.

Running parallel to and informing this global cosmopolitanism as much as the American media's version of it, is the Manila based Filipino media's production of superstars (*artista*) such as Janice de Belen, Regine Valasquez, and Sharon Cuneta. It is the names of these stars that are appropriated by *gays* in the beauty contests, and more than Hollywood stars, they are who people watch on television, in the video houses, and in the cinema. As Cannel (1992, 342) notes, all of these Filipino stars represent to a certain extent an already domesticated west, a global cosmopolitanism situated and transformed by local sensibilities. This also highlights the extent to which the particular constitution of the imagined global "other" is informed and structured not just by a diffuse world of goods and information, but by specific political articulations and, in this case, the particular institutions (the media no less than the Philippine state) established during and after the American colonial regime in the early part of this century.

Educational institutions in particular were a key part of the implementation of the so-called *American Mandate*, which, as outlined by then-President McKinnley, had as its stated aim to, "develop, civilize, educate or train the Moros (Muslim Filipinos) in the science of (democratic) self government" (Gowing 1983, 319). Currently they are among the major local sponsors of such events.[1] Not only are schools often the venue for gay beauty contests, but also professional educators frequently appear on the board of judges. Moreover, education itself is one of the primary referents of beauty contests. In this respect, Wilk's (1995 also this volume) recent comparison of sporting competitions and beauty contests and his illustration of the Double-Dutch League Jump Rope Championships with its educative emphasis on discipline, self-development, and "developing self-respect" resonate with the close and ongoing association between education, beauty contests, talent shows, and other performative events within local school curriculums.

Looked at from this perspective beauty contests are filled with instances of stylistic and verbal discourse that are clearly embedded in colonial ministrations. Beauty is about education and the mastery of the English language. Beauty is about good citizenship and professional orientation. Beauty is about sportsmanship with winners democratically decided on the basis of clear criteria.

The point is that the images of beauty purveyed in the beauty contest are rooted in, articulate, and index a particular conceptual order of the world. Moreover, there is no discontinuity between the images of glamour and the images of education. Both are part and parcel of the same conceptual order. Thus, it is neither surprising nor coincidental that "beauty" is articulated by and associated with those very institutions which were seen as necessary for the implementation of the American Mandate or that local persons perceptively see these institutions as the locus of and for the *ilmu' milikan*, that is, the knowledge-power of the American.

In short, beauty is another idiom for and indexical sign of the *ilmu' milikan*, which together (beauty, America, and the *ilmu' milikan*) form the primary idioms within which this global other is conceptualized. But whilst beauty as with the *ilmu' milikan* is something that local persons desire and to some extent aspire to, it also represents, if not an immediate political threat, at the very least an opposing order of relations to the *ilmu' Islam*, that is, the knowledge-power of Islam.

Between Islam and America: The Politics of Local Muslim Identity

When a child is born in Sulu, the placenta, which is considered to be the primary and elder sibling of the infant, is placed in a coconut shell and either buried or hung from a nearby tree. In addition, a piece of paper with a portion of the Koran written in Arabic and a scrap of an English language newspaper will also be included with the placenta. This is done, it is said, so that the child will grow up to possess both the *ilmu' Islam*, the knowledge-power of Islam, and the *ilmu' milikan*, the knowledge-power of the American.

Ilmu', widely appropriated throughout insular Southeast Asia from the Arabic *ilm*, meaning knowledge, has been translated in Southeast Asia to mean magic or esoteric knowledge (Geertz 1960, 88, Keeler 1987, 81). *Ilmu'*, like *mana* in other Pacific cultures, is at once spoken of as "power" inherent in certain words and objects that can be possessed and transferred, and at the same time affixed as *ilmu'an*. It is used as a stative verb—a statement about someone being effectual, successful or realized (Keesing 1984). In short, to be *ilmu'an* is to be filled up with *ilmu'* and to "possess" indexical signs of power such as strength, firmness, invulnerability, or beauty.

However, *ilmu'* signals more than simply the indexical signs of an indeterminate form of power. Rather it is always part of or attached to a larger system of meanings or signification, a conceptual order of the world, such as Islam or America, which amongst other things articulates a particular set of political and ideological relations. It is in this sense that *ilmu'* may be considered a local system of knowledge-power (Endicott 1970; Anderson 1972, 43).

I have elsewhere outlined in some detail what I regard to be the major historical movements and transformations that establish the precedent for, even as they impinge on, the current configuration of knowledge-power (Johnson, n.d.). The point I would make here is that the implementation of the American Mandate at the beginning of the twentieth century is like the appropriation of Islam in the fourteenth and fifteenth centuries, out of which emerged the Sulu Sultanate. It not only signalled a new universe of indexical signs of potency in the form of material objects, language, titles, and so on but also signalled a new system of discriminatory signs or "criteria" that attempted to fix, and through which persons attempted to fix themselves and others in, the relations of signification (Wilk 1995).

This is precisely the place where a fundamental contradiction arose since the *ilmu' milikan* was seen to represent a certain order of relations not just distinct from but antagonistic to an Islamic identity. That is to say, Islam was not simply an ideology that legitimated the traditional Sulu polity. Over the course of several hundred years and largely in contrast and in conflict with the militaristic advances of the Spanish colonial government, it had become the idiom within which persons understood and asserted their significance within the universe. The dissolution of the sultanate, moreover, did not in any way effect a similar diminishment of an Islamic identity. Rather, whereas previously persons were incorporated into Islam largely through their participation in the sultan's *barakat*, later, as the sultanate became ineffectual, persons became individually responsible for the defense of the *dar-ul-Islam* (Majul 1973, 353-56). This shift marked a new and ongoing phase in the crystallization of an individualized Muslim identity within and through which the individual could and did participate directly through martyrdom in the divine order and blessing (Kiefer 1988).

Not surprisingly, the American colonial regime met with some of the fiercest resistance from the Muslim Tausug and Sama (Tan 1977). Among the measures that met with the strongest opposition were the attempted implementation of compulsory education and the cedula, a registration tax that required all adult males between the ages of 18 and 55 to pay one peso per year. The payment of the cedula was seen by many as tantamount to conversion, and Kiefer (1988, 65) reports that as late as the mid-1960s certain older persons refused to walk along roads built through the money raised by such tax for fear of being transformed into a Christian.

Thus, the appropriation of the *ilmu' milikan* was never simply a question of acquiring the vitality, or *mana* of the Americans, but was also a question of identity. Moreover, while the major developments and incidents of the twentieth century have been characterized as being alternately one of collusion or resistance (Tan 1977), this fundamentally glosses over the fact that both are moments in an overall process with which local persons have been occupied over the last century: that is to negotiate the contradictions of an identity defined as much by the active appropriation of otherness as by its at times violent refusal to be overwhelmed by otherness.

That this contradiction exists is seen in the fact that persons have attempted to construct a theoretical framework which allows them to retain their Muslim identity whilst freely participating in the *ilmu' milikan*. Kiefer (1988, 65) describes this framework as follows:

> To the question, "Why does God permit these infidels to conquer us?" the answer they gave was that sometime in the past God gave both the Tausug and the Americans a choice whether they wanted paradise on this earth or paradise in the afterworld. The Americans naturally chose paradise in this world, and the Tausug paradise in the afterworld. This was the basis of a perfect working misunderstanding, although the Filipinos were left in limbo.

In what was clearly an extension of this reasoning, I was told on several occasions that the differences between the Tausug or Muslims and the Americans could be related to differences between the knowledge-power or *ilmu'* of *Nabi Isa* (the Prophet Jesus) and the knowledge-power or *ilmu'* of *Nabi Muhammad* (the Prophet Muhammad). That is, *Nabi Isa* is seen as the *pangikutan* (forerunner of, a kind of ideal type) of the American inasmuch as his power was said to be demonstrated in the world healing the sick and so forth, whilst *Nabi Muhammad* was concerned primarily with the proclamation of and struggle for true religion, and his rewards lie in the afterworld.

This marks an interpretive point of departure, for it is clear that there has been and continues to be an attempt to carve out a theoretical space for the appropriation of the *ilmu' milikan*. However, there are two further points to be made in this respect. On the one hand, it is clear that the *ilmu' milikan* is no longer strictly about America or Americans. Rather, America and the *ilmu' milikan* is the historically salient idiom within which a certain global world order is thought or imagined. On the other hand, since the incorporation of Sulu into the Philippine state, the problem of an ethnic or religious identity has also been increasingly linked to the question of political autonomy. The most recent and forceful expression of this has been the Moro National Liberation Front (MNLF), which was, during the early and mid-1970s, able to transform various ethnic Muslim identities into a fledgling national identity and mobilize, for a period of time, a concerted, armed separatist movement (Noble 1976; George 1980; Che Man 1990). As I suggest below, the valorization of *gay/bantut* engenderment and their emergence as central figures in the mediation of local identity and the appropriation of cultural otherness is crucially tied to these recent historical events.

On Being "Over-exposed": Beauty, Political Violence, and the Transformation of Gender

I suggested in the introduction that *gays* define themselves transgenderally. While this is often related to being the receptor in homosexual relations, being beautiful and creating beauty clearly emerge not only as pivotal to *gay* understandings and expressions of femininity, but also to the wider conceptualizations of the *bantut* as neither real men nor women. This is articulated both within the everyday discourse and practice of the beauty parlours, as well as within the context of beauty contests. It was the latter that was often talked about by *gays* as being their greatest opportunity, as one *gay* put it, to "expose my beauty so that the world will know that I am really a woman."

Clearly this notion of "exposing" one's beauty is central to understanding both the *gays* and *gay* beauty contests, and Cannel (1992, 365), in what could almost be an exact description of the discourse of *gays* in the Southern Philippines, notes:

> The *bakla'* [read *bantut*] in fact often seem to assimilate their identity to a language of visibility and hyper-visibility, referring to themselves as "apper" (an appearance) and talking about their power to seduce as "exposing themselves." A common *bakla* greeting is to say "How is your beauty?" instead of "How are you?" and to substitute in ordinary conversation the phrases "my beauty" for "myself" and "your beauty" for "yourself."

The first point to be made, however, is that while beauty is used by *gays* in self-reference, so too *baran*, which in the first instance denotes the physical body, is more widely used in speaking of one's self, as in the construct *baran ku* or *baran-baran ku*—which is a normal way of saying "me myself." In answer, for instance, to questions such as where do you get your ideas for *istyle* (style), I was frequently told by individuals, *baran-baran ku hadja*—meaning "just myself." The body is important not simply because it is the second term in the construct *ginhawa-baran* (*baran* or body being the locatable container of the immaterial spiritual quality and potency signified by *ginhawa*). Rather, the body is important precisely because this immaterial quality and potency is only apprehended by its effects or presence—that is to say its physical manifestation. Thus, the body is a primary site for the inscription of cultural truths, be it Islam or America, as well as being an important site for self-transformation (see Foucault 1980, 124-25; Errington 1989; and Cohen this volume).

This is clearly seen in the notion of *singud/singuran*, which might be translated, "to imitate/imitation." *Singud* is often, although not exclusively, used in reference to *istyle*, which like "beauty" signals a similar concern with things defined as American. What is intended in *singud* is more than simply imitation, but rather an active process of appropriation. Many persons, in fact, used the English word "capture" interchangeably with it, so that I was often told, by young persons especially, that even while they could not always understand an American movie or television program, they would watch them so as to "capture" or *singuran* the *istyle*—the speech, clothes, mannerisms, and so forth, of the program.

That *singud* implies more than simply imitation is also seen in the transmission and acquisition of the *ilmu' pagkausug*, the knowledge-power that renders one in the state of continuing manhood. This *ilmu'* is part of the religious and ritual instruction that either accompanies or follows the circumcision of young boys called *pagIslam*, to enter into, or become Islam. The *ilmu' pagkausug* is critical in as much as it completes the necessary transformation of boys into men, instilling the virtues and quality of bravery and courage or *isug* (Kiefer 1972, 53), which among other things is indexed in a body's strength, firmness, and sexual potency. The point is that *singuran* is spoken of with reference to *ilmu'* (usually in the form of Arabic words that are uttered, chanted, or spat out) not simply as a process of imitation, but as a process of internalization and as an external process through which one is dressed or clothed in power.

"Exposing" one's beauty in the beauty contest (as with the incessant "checking" of one's beauty and the "making" of beauty that occurs in the beauty parlours) is similarly seen to signal this active process of transformation. Exposing one's beauty is neither an uncovering to reveal something hidden, nor simply a process of covering over to conceal that which must remain hidden, but is rather an active process of objectification, which through the literal application of layers upon layers of signs of beauty enacts an ontological transformation.[2]

This logic links beauty and the project of gender transformation, conveyed in statements made by *gays*, such as "I want to expose my beauty so the world will know that I am a woman." But it also informs the statements, made by other persons, about the *bantut* being, as one man put it, "over-exposed." Indeed, it is here that the historical conjuncture between the valorization of *gay/bantut* gender and sexuality and recent political events becomes apparent (see Johnson, 1995).

Gay beauty contests are a relatively recent phenomenon in Sulu, coinciding with a rise in beauty parlours and a perceived overall increase in the number of *gay/bantut*, so that as more than one person said to me, *simung sung na mas mataud in manga bantut dayn sin manga usug* (soon there will be more *bantut* than men). Significantly this rise in the number of *bantut* is traced back to the mid-1970s, and in particular to the bombardment and burning of the town of Jolo in 1974 by the Philippine navy and the subsequent period of Christian Filipino military governorship which came to be known as the GHQ or General Headquarters.

According to the majority of residents in the town, military abuses were rife and largely went unchecked. Soldiers would patrol the streets looking for a *kursinada*, that is, a Muslim Tausug whom they could "target" or "salvage," a common term used throughout the Philippines to describe the summary execution of individuals. One explanation given by many persons as to the rise in the number of *bantut* was that as a result of such abuses, some men began to lose their *isug* and their normally assertive manner through imitating (*singuran*) the style of and becoming transformed into the flaccid and impotent *bantut*.

On the one hand, having lost their *isug* and by extension the *ilmu' pagkausug*—the knowledge-power of continuing manhood that is identified with as it is defined by the defense of Islam—the *bantut* are defined as unrealized or "not-men." On the other hand, as a result of the ongoing process of appropriative imitation or "exposure," they have been overwhelmed and transformed by a potent otherness, so that the femininity the *bantut* are seen to embody and exemplify is not that of a "real woman."

Here we confront the very equivocal nature and ambiguity with which the *bantut* are locally regarded. The one term that consistently arises more than any other word in relation to the *bantut* and which signals the apparently contradictory sensibilities which define their transgenderal expression is *maarte*. On the one hand *maarte* is precisely about *istyle*, the *usu* or the trendy, beautiful and glamorous. On the other hand, *maarte* crosses over into the affected, pretentious, and vulgar. Moreover, when not directly related to the *bantut*, *maarte* often centred around categories of women, from the *burikat* (women of loose morals who are thought to wear excessive make-up and dress indecently) to the *puta'* or prostitute. These categories of women are frequently cross-referenced both with Tagalog film stars (*artista*) of the *bald* (risque) variety, as well as with foreign women in the *fighting fish* or X-rated video movies, whose *istyle* of sex is something that men on the one hand talk about capturing (*singuran*) but which can only be safely enacted with prostitutes, outside the scope of normal sociality and recognized sexuality.

Significantly, however, while prostitutes are located on the margins of the social geography, the *bantut* are allowed into the central arenas of social life. The point is that having been "over-exposed," the *bantut* represent a negotiable form of otherness in which the threat of contamination is largely contained by their engenderment as unreproductive women and impotent men. The *bantut* thus stand as the symbolic complements to the Muslim warriors in the maintenance and preservation of an impenetrable social identity and the encompassment of a potentially overwhelming force. Indeed, in an ironic twist, it is now the *bantut* who go on "patrul" in the marine barracks just as it is now the *Bisaya'* soldier who is widely seen as being the number one *kursinada* or target of what is commonly said to be the voracious sexual desire of the *bantut*, thus inverting the violent relationship that existed between the Christian military and the Muslim Tausug.

Viewing the Denouement: Gender and Power in the Tragic-Comedy of Gay Beauty Contests

Gay beauty contests are, as I suggested at the outset, multi-layered and polysemic texts, which I can only begin to explicate here. This multi-dimensionality represents various elaborations of lived contradictions, which are posited, as differentially experienced and contested, in the various idioms of the *ilmu' Islam* and the *ilmu' Milikan*, and in which the *gay/bantut* have emerged as central mediating figures.

What *gays*, who regard the contests with utmost seriousness, are contesting (both amongst themselves as well as with the audience) is not only their possession of beauty but also the nature of the transformation that they see themselves enacting through "exposing" their beauty: specifically, their claim to be women. On the one hand, *gays* identify themselves with progressive, educated, independent, glamorous, sophisticated, and cosmopolitan women, as signalled among other things in their "biodata" by the appropriation of superstar's names, educational qualifications, body measurements, as well as in the elaborate stage performances and the wearing of "cocktail" dresses, "evening" gowns, and swimsuits. At the same time, *gays* will often project a shy, quiet, self-effacing image of femininity, defined primarily in terms of motherhood and domesticity. *Gays* may also identify themselves with an image of a "modern woman of traditional virtue" as exemplified for instance by Cory Aquino. This is expressed not only by the frequent reference to familial and civic responsibility as a function of professional employment as teachers, nurses, doctors, and so forth, but is also signalled by the importance given to the displays of national and ethnic costumes in every *gay* contest (see Blanc-Szanton 1990, 379-83).

In aligning themselves with these images of femininity and in juxtaposing the glamorous with the maternal, what *gays* are specifically attempting is to distance themselves from associations with the vulgar, indecent, and the *over-exposed*. Yet it is precisely in this regard that *gay* attempts are thwarted by the audience. The *bantut* are regarded in the first place as impotent men (a point challenged by the *gays*), signalled amongst other things by their bound penis. This is a frequent point of comment, both amongst men and women, who sometimes suggested that the reason it was so easy for the *bantut* to conceal their genitals is because they were so small. On the other hand, the more the *gay* contestants strive to present themselves as respectable, if cosmopolitan women, the more the

M.C., usually a straight man or woman, will seek to draw out their homosexuality, often with barely hidden references to anal intercourse. Such comments, while reinforcing the protocols of engendered sexuality and often under the pretence of supporting the so-called "third-sex," reinforce the image of the *gay/bantut* as inverted and unreproductive men and women.

At the most general level one might see the comic tension surrounding the *bantut* beauty contest and the *bantut* beauty queens as embodying, "the tragic aspect of personal and community life—the frustration of unobtainable aspirations and desires" as I wrote in a preliminary report from the field (see also Cannel 1992). However, this tragic comedy is not primarily about the unobtainability of an idealized "American" dream of glamour, unlimited consumption and democracy. Rather, the *bantut* beauty contests, amongst other things, allows people, if not to directly challenge the specific political and economic conditions under which cultural otherness is confronted, at least to symbolically circumscribe the domain of cultural otherness and thus control the limits of transformative appropriation through its inscription onto the bodies of the *gay/bantut*. That is to say, it is in these beauty contests, that the *bantut* are repeatedly constituted not only as being the repositories of beauty, but also as those who have been *over-exposed* to and overwhelmed by the beauty of otherness: the boundaries of local identity are made explicit and a global otherness made negotiable by its objectification and reconstitution with the *gay/bantut* in the space of liminal sexuality and gender (see Turner 1968; Kapferer 1988).

Notes

This essay is based on Ph.D. research carried out in Zamboanga and Sulu over a period of approximately 18 months from 1991-1992. I should like to thank the National Museum of the Philippines, the Notre Dame de Jolo, and the CISCUL center (Coordinated Investigation of Sulu Culture) for research assistance and affiliation in the field. The research was financially supported by a University of London Research Studentship as well as by an Overseas Research Student Award. This paper has benefited from comments and suggestions made at various post-graduate and departmental seminars in the anthropology department, University College London. In particular I should like to acknowledge Daniel Miller, who has provided guidance and insight throughout my research and writing, as well Fennala Cannel (LSE), whose account of the *bakla'* in Bicol, Luzon, resonates with and has helped shape my own analysis of the *gay/bantut* in the Southern Philippines.

1. One of the earliest recorded "beauty queens" (1920?) was Princess Indataas, whose father (Datu' Tambuyong) had led part of the local resistance against the Americans, but who, herself, was one of the first Muslim schoolteachers (Orosa 1923,107; Gowing 1983, 306).

2. Cannel (1992) argues for a similar process of self-transformation in relation to spirit possession as well as transvestite beauty contests in Bicol. See Miller (1994) for a comparative instance and more general discussion of style and ontological transformation.

7

Authenticity and Guatamala's Maya Queen

Carlota McAllister

Introduction

I first attended the Rabín Ahau in 1988, during the presidency of Vinicio
Cerezo, who was Guatemala's first civilian head of state in fifteen years.
My companions, members of Guatemala's landowning elite, and I arrived
late to a crowded arena with a fashion-show runway in its center.
Indigenous women in ceremonial dress, introduced by the names of the
towns they represented, danced one by one up the runway to the stage
while their incense burners slowly filled the room with heavy smoke.

The proceedings were disrupted when a guacamaya (a large tropical
bird), chained to its perch on the backdrop, fell in the middle of Vinicio's
speech. Stage hands scrambled up the papier-mâché volcanoes of the
scenery to where it hung helplessly, squawking in counterpoint to
Vinicio's thumps on the podium and cries of "Guatemalans! We are a people of two bloods!" The Indian queens' speeches were a sobering contrast
to this nationalist comedy. One after another they shouted that the blood
of the ancient and glorious Maya coursed through their veins and that
they would no longer tolerate oppression by *ladinos*, non-Maya Guatemalans. I had never heard anyone in Guatemala make such a radical statement. Clearly, this event begged anthropological analysis: it offered nation and blood, ritual and power, conflict, and, most seductively, an
opportunity to explore the powerful pleasures Guatemala grants those
who claim her as their own.

The Rabín Ahau, Daughter (or Granddaughter) of the King in
Q'eqchi', is elected annually in a pageant held in Cobán, Alta Verapaz,
Guatemala. To be Rabín Ahau is to be *Reina Indígena Nacional* (National
Indigenous Queen), the representative of the indigenous race before the
nation, and communities from around Guatemala send candidates to
compete. Nineteen ninety-three was the twenty-second year of the
pageant and the silver anniversary of the folkloric festival of which it is the

crowning event. The fifty-four candidates present were judged, according to the program for the event, on the following bases: (1) authenticity of race; (2) authenticity of *traje típico* (typical costume); (3) expression in their own language; (4) expression in Spanish; and (5) authenticity in dancing the *son* (a "traditional" indigenous dance, see Borland this volume). I asked a juror to define "authenticity": how would she know it when she saw it? The authentic, she told me, "represented something *really real* of a people or of a person."

Nationalism is more than dry ideology: it is a "structure of feeling" (R. Williams 1977) which, internalized by the subjects of political entities, fills them with ineffable love. The premises that produce and reproduce the sentiment of nationalism are economies of pleasure (Parker et al. 1992). Pageants, which project an idealized national femininity, directly engage these economies. Yet internal divisions as well as international relations structure the national imagination. The Rabín Ahau is above all queen of her race and consequently her election is not a beauty pageant. Beauty has a quality of universality: the beauty queen makes human femininity flesh. Miss Guatemala, invariably among the whitest of the nation's young women, is Guatemala's version of the feminine (see Hendrickson 1991 for a discussion of this pageant). The Indian Queen's task, however, is not to prove that Guatemala can compete on equal footing with other nations, but to represent what makes Guatemala most distinct: her tradition, her Indian past. Authenticity marks the Maya Queen's particularity as an aesthetic property, subordinate to the truly beautiful.

Nation, Race, and Authenticity

Chatterjee (1986) characterizes postcolonial nationalism as "[a] different discourse, yet one that is dominated by another" (1986, 42). That is, it implicitly opposes colonial domination, framing the opposition by affirming a distinct collective "subjectivity" (1986, 38). However, this difference is conceived in the Enlightenment terms of the autonomous, rational, self-actualizing subject, terms that derive from the colonial heritage postcolonial nationalism rejects. A capitalist world system in which "development" and "progress" are conditional on the nation-state makes nationhood this subjectivity's political expression. The colonialist specificity of the imperative to nationhood is universalized in the postcolonial world, while the specificities of former colonies become difference in the universal world of nations. Hence, "[postcolonial nationalism] reasons within a framework of knowledge whose representational structure corresponds to the very structure of power nationalist thought seeks to repudiate" (1986, 38).

One should be cautious of the homogenizing tendencies latent in the term "postcolonial" (McClintock 1992, Shohat 1992). The conquest of

Latin America took the form of "settler colonialism," which meant that early ninteenth century nationalists did not consider themselves different *in kind* from the colonizers they fought against. *Criollos* claimed a territorial right to rule in the Americas. They legitimated it by their relationship to the land, forged in the colonial "fatality of trans-Atlantic birth" (Anderson 1991, 57) rather than inherent in a distinct essence. This was only the first formulation of the "national question" that has preoccupied Guatemalan pundits ever since a sovereign Guatemala was first imagined, one which continually metamorphoses into the "Indian question," for Guatemalan nationalism is formulated as the problem of incorporating Guatemala's majority Indian population into the nation. Attempts at resolving the problem, however, must draw their legitimacy from different sources in the late twentieth century, when capitalism's increasingly global functioning undermines the call to modernity and nationalism that once posed it.

Critiques of the concept of "ethnicity" in national and anthropological discourse frame the distinction between the universal and the particular as the problem of "race-making." In modern nations, categories of citizens identified with styles of appearance and behavior inconsistent with those institutionalized in civic life are labeled "ethnic" (B. Williams 1989, 412). Blood is the privileged trope of this difference. It maps categories of personhood onto the national history and landscape and produces racial categories that conflate time, space, and substance (Alonso 1994). Imagining a nation entails selecting a subjectivity that can accede to universality, and thus constructing internal difference, whether through exclusions or inclusions.

Authenticity intervenes in this project by reuniting the universal and the particular. It permanently joins essence to presence. This is authenticity's magic, the source of its power and its centrality to myths of nation and race. The force of the term, however, makes its meaning slippery. Critics (for example Adorno 1973) have seen "authenticity" as the quintessential modernist aesthetic problem, raised when alienation questions the immediacy of cultural experience. Postmodern theorists (such as Baudrillard 1983) seize on this discussion to prove the impossibility of authentic experience and culture in late capitalism. To pose the problem in ontological terms, however, dismisses questions of power, that is, how the authentic is authenticated, by whom, in what contexts, with what legitimacy, and so on (Bruner 1994). An authentic representation is one in which the relationship of form to content, of signifier to signified, is intrinsic and therefore eternal. But the very claim to authenticity recognizes the possibility of inauthenticity: some representations, it implies, are more intrinsic than others. Authenticity, thus, is always emergent and never more so than when the authentic representation is not an artifact, but a person, a producer of representations. The authentic sign must be per-

A final check.

formed, in that its meaning is negotiated and contextualized between the performer and the audience through evaluations of its form (Bauman & Briggs 1990). Performance structures the sign of authenticity and creates the intrinsic effect. It is authenticity's guilty secret, and the higher the stakes of constructs built on the foundation of authenticity, the more deeply concealed the secret must be.

Knowing the Indian: Guatemalan Nationalist Discourse

The current configuration of power in Guatemala places the military at the leading edge of the elite. Landowning, mostly coffee-growing elites, heirs to the *criollo* legacy, dominated politics from the late nineteenth century. In the early 1970s, the military, which had served the landowners as a quasi-private police force, began its ascendence over them. Two forces worked to undermine the oligarchy's authority. First, in conjunction with paramilitary groups, military governments developed and deployed the "process of terror" (Aguilera Peralta 1980), a systematic practice of disappearances, tortures, and massacres, to counter insurgency in Eastern Guatemala. Governance and war-making merged to an unprecedented extent. Second, indigenous people, who had maintained a certain autonomy in closed corporate communities since the coffee period (Wolf 1957), began to claim a voice in national debates, forming indigenous political parties, joining agricultural cooperatives, and protesting attacks on their land and people. Meanwhile, rifts within indigenous communities, between "traditional," Catholic Action, and radical sectors were developing to the point where certain community leaders called upon the state to intervene.

The combination of these forces resulted in an explosion of violence. The guerrilla movement, previously confined to the *ladino* East, was renewed in the late 1970s with indigenous support. Indigenous participation, motivated less by ideology than anger at army abuses (Davis 1988, 23) gave General Romeo Lucas García (head of state from 1978 to 1982) a pretext for declaring all Indians—and many *ladinos*—"subversives." The Lucas García regime alone destroyed some four hundred villages, with fifty thousand people killed, and one million more displaced (Manz 1988). The military High Command emerged stronger from this killing spree: officers seized massive landholdings in the agriculturally rich Zona Reina and made themselves millionaires at the price of Guatemala's condemnation for the worst human rights record in the Western Hemisphere.

New economic strength allowed the military to break with the civilian elite in the early 1980s over taxation. The oligarchy resented the military's pretensions to govern, while the military wanted the oligarchy to fund a new state project: the military's consolidation "as the central institution within the state, in a society whose central institution is to be, in turn, the state and not the private business community" (Anderson & Simon 1987, 12). The landowners lost their responsibility for the nation. Although the head of state has been civilian since 1985, the return to "legitimate" rule has, if anything, increased the military's political importance. Relieved of the theatrics of government, the army took charge of the concrete problems of administering populations. Officers from the military Zone of Cobán spoke freely about Guatemala's backwardness and her development through national integration—standard nationalist rhetoric. They saw themselves, however, as agents of progress toward the twenty-first century, and proposed to accomplish their task through a novel combination of repression and development. The military's Guatemala is "ideologically new." Its state and economic infrastructures are expanding to cover the entire national territory; its Indians, docile and subservient to the national interest, have been put in their place.

The mythical point of departure of military nation-building, its "classificatory moment of purification" (B. Williams 1989), is the Conquest. According to this myth, Europeans and Indians met and clashed, and Europeans proved superior. The next five hundred years have replayed this meeting of cultures and bloods, with everything that they index, in both individuals and society. Traces of *criollo* nationalism linger on, and some elites in Guatemala continue to define themselves as *criollos* (Casaus Arzú 1992). But their land-based claim is superseded by the blood-based claim of the Conquest tradition (Adams 1989); *criollos* lacking the requisite blood are liable to be defined out of the Guatemalan nation that this tradition shapes. The Indian is the nation's absolute point of reference, the basis for other's judgments about "us," but the criterion of nationhood is control over the Indian. Interpellated by the national "we," the Indian can never voice it. The Conquest myth certifies the military as the only party with both the substance and the will to build the nation.

Late twentieth-century Guatemalan nationalism positions itself as anti-colonial not by rejecting capital or Western rationality, but what it perceives as the ideology of the international community: accountability for human rights. It affirms that what we do with our Indians is our business. This statement does not argue that human rights are inappropriate in the Guatemalan case, but it denies that any violation of human rights is taking place. Instead, nationalists enlist human rights discourse to protect Guatemala's "national sovereignty" from *gringo* criticism (Schirmer 1993): they think they can tell us what to do because we are all Indians to them. The international community violates Guatemala's humanity by criticizing her internal affairs.

To keep itself pure Guatemalan nationalism must continually reinvent the Indian in a struggle that extracts national humanity from Indian animality, even if in animal fashion (Balibar 1990, 291). "Indian" is an evolutionary location: nationalism's aspiration to the rationality of the universal is also a racism, which transforms the subnational into the subhuman (Balibar 1990, 83). Although not overtly biological, complementary racist discourses that reduce culture to biology reproduce Indians' eternal objecthood. They have a charitable and a vicious aspect: the Indian is polite, soft-spoken, loyal, traditional, and makes beautiful and delicious things; but she is also lazy, dirty, smelly, suspicious, subversive, ungrateful, and primitive. Condescended to or reviled, the Indian is "good to think" for the national sense of self.

The difficulty lies in how to think the Indian. In the Conquest myth, everyone has at least a little Indian blood, so race cannot be an absolute difference. What distinguishes the Indian is her purity, an ineffable quality indexed in "*la forma de vestir y la forma de hablar*" (the way of dressing and the way of talking). This oft-cited guideline for knowing Indians refers to their distinctive handwoven clothing, the *traje típico*, and their alleged lack of fluency in Spanish. It is shorthand for saying that Indians are the same as the objects they produce and that they do not have language.

The confusion of Indian substance with Indian production makes it necessary to remind Indian culture connoisseurs that there is a person inside the clothes (Pettersen 1976, 11). Indian weaving, especially the women's *traje*, is, in the words of a tourist pamphlet, "a door of access to Maya culture," standing for all the rest of Indianness. Moreover, the objects Indians make replace their faculty of speech: they express themselves in the woven patterns of the "traditional symbolism of their history and ancient gods" (Pettersen 1976, 11). When they try to speak Spanish, they supposedly distort it, replacing all final consonants with "e" and using archaic words. An age-old Guatemalan joke genre relies on "Indian" mispronunciations of Spanish words to make puns. Also, Indians cannot make speeches: an articulate Indian speaker is a contradiction in terms, and if one presents herself, she can only be parroting someone else's words. Thus, members of the elite debate whether Rigoberta Menchú, the indigenous Guatemalan Nobel Prize winner, is really *inteligente* [intelligent] or merely *lista* [clever]. Lacking true speech, Indians cannot be fully cultural. Like their sweat, their culture simply comes out of their pores. Indeed, one term for Indians is *naturales* [naturals]: they are their earth, their corn, their past. Doomed always to repeat themselves, their substance cannot generate anything new. The punch line of a joke, "How did Rigoberta applaud when she heard about the Nobel Prize?" has the joke teller mimic Rigoberta slapping her hands together as if making corn *tortillas*, the indigenous staple food.

The prototypical Indian is a woman, for women do hand-weaving, are more likely than men to wear *traje*, and less likely to have intercourse, in all senses, with the outer world. Smith (1992) argues that an "anti-modern" ideology of the links between race, class, and gender defines Indian women's role in Guatemala. They agree to maintain their parochialism within the community, marked by dress and unilingualism in the local language, and embodied in their "modest demeanor" and shyness toward strangers. In return, they are offered autonomy within the community and "a certain personal security" (1992, 8), which the national, "modern," ideology of gender relations refuses women. She cites in support of her thesis the rate of Maya endogamy, which, at "90-95 percent in communities now averaging about 10,000 individuals, [is] one of the highest rates of community in-marriage in the world" (1992,14). Closure is the most salient ideological attribute of both Maya femininity and Maya community.

The emphasis on closure hints that reproduction is considered different in kind in Indian communities. The distinctiveness of Indian women regulates the reproduction of Indians, while the congress of unmarked, "modern" men and women secures the reproduction of the nation. Schneider (1969) notes the correspondence of United States ideologies of kinship to United States ideologies of nationalism, and argues it may indicate a more general isomorphism between the two. The homologies of accounts of gender relations in Indian communities with the nationalist account of primordial Indian difference—both anchored in the markers of dress and language—expose the desire that motivates knowledge of the Indian.

Indian women are subjected to intense speculation, to a gaze that recoils in horror when it uncovers what it seeks. Not simply desexualized, Indian women's sexuality is considered only to be denigrated. One afternoon, a young *ladino* man who had spent three years in the United States saw me sitting in a plaza and came over to chat. As he had experienced United States racism against Latinos, he recognized discrimination, but said that he could still not bring himself to flirt with a woman identified as indigenous for fear of the town's disgust. Similarly, Menchú (1983) describes working as a maid in Guatemala City for a *ladino* family. Her coworker, also indigenous but ladinized, was fired because she refused to sexually initiate the sons of the house. The mistress does not ask Rigoberta to serve in this capacity, and Rigoberta realizes she is simply too dirty—read, too Indian—for the mistress to risk her sons' sexuality with. Indian women's bodies cannot stand alone because their femininity is scandalous, contaminated. They must be securely wrapped in their *trajes* or expose themselves to contempt.[1]

The Rabín Ahau

Elections for indigenous queens were held for decades at town fairs—the first *India Bonita Cobanera* (Pretty Cobán Indian), for example, was elected in 1931—but the national contest began in 1971. A "hook" for tourists, it was intended to boost attendance at the National Folkloric Festival. The impulse on which the festival was founded in 1968 was both indigenous and nationalist. Local eminences wanted to provide a forum for folkloric craftspeople and performers (by definition indigenous people) to display and sell their arts. By assembling Guatemala's folkloric richness, the festival would put on display her "purest and most autochthonous values." Folklore is the fetish of Guatemalan-ness: The festival was to be a source of national pride, as well as a tool to make Cobán a city of national importance, instead of the backwater it had always been. However, the Festival alone was of insufficient interest to the desired audience, tourists and *capitalinos* (people from the capital). The organizers' solution was to embody folklore in the Rabín Ahau's womanly form. By 1972, according to the program for that year, queens from twenty *municipios* in different parts of Guatemala were competing for the title and the audience had grown.

As it became more important, the pageant's organizational structure changed. The founder left under accusations of embezzling, and more military-minded folklorists took control. The Cobán-born wife of General Kjell Laugerud (head of state from 1974-1978), was a promoter of local "culture." She added a presidential speech to the pageant, which turned out to be an embarrassment because Kjell tended to get stagger-ingly drunk. When Lucas García, a major Cobán landowner, came to power, he paid the entire budget (25,000 quetzals [$25,000 US] a year) out of his pocket, and continued to give a presidential address. The Rabín Ahau became truly "national," well attended by *capitalinos*, and broadcast on national television. After the return to a civilian presidency, the event survived on corporate sponsorship (from Guatemalan companies, as well as Pepsi-Cola and Crush), and TV and entrance revenues. The pageant was institutionalized, such that the head of the Events Section of the National Tourist Institute of Guatemala (Inguat) could describe it to me as "one among the many indigenous ceremonies of Guatemala."

Nineteen ninety-one was the pageant's largest and most spectacular year, but in 1992 it was almost canceled because of disorganization and a cholera epidemic. The sobered organizers of the 1993 pageant wanted to return it to its indigenist roots, away from its military connections. For the first time, the head of the organizing committee was himself indige-nous. Yet, the event's prestige is waning. The president, a civilian and for-mer ombudsperson for the United Nations instated after a constitutional upheaval in June 1993, did not attend. He had a Central American sum-mit to go to that day, but people thought he would not have come, to mark his distance from the Rabín Ahau's military associations. Bad organization kept the usual media and high-prestige guests from attending, and fewer candidates were presented than in preceding years. The Rabín Ahau is en-tering a new phase.

The 1993 jury was chosen in keeping with the pageant's newfound se-riousness. Its five members included the curator of the Inguat's collection of *trajes*, a right-wing indigenous politician who founded the first indi-genist political party, an anthropologist from the Universidad del Valle in Guatemala City, and two bilingual professors from the Academy of Mayan Languages. Rumors circulate that in previous years jurors were either un-qualified to pass judgment or had accepted bribes; those pageants' reputa-tions suffer in consequence. In 1993 jurors were chosen for their "exper-tise" in various folkloric fields, so their judgments about authenticity were considered particularly authoritative. To ensure immunity to bribes, their identities were kept secret until the pageant itself.

Elected in local contests, the candidates had to be sponsored at the national pageant by an entity considered "responsible" in their communi-ty, whether the mayor's office, a *cofradía* (indigenous lay religious order), or a local business. While not unrepresentative of Guatemalan indigenous womanhood, they were a particularly docile population. The fifty-four queens, who had to be single and between the ages of fifteen and twenty-two to compete, tended toward the younger end of this range: only eleven were twenty years of age or older. They had a higher level of education than average, with, generally, between six and eight years of schooling. There were some university students among them—extraordinary, given that the illiteracy rate among indigenous women is over ninety percent in Guatemala—and several teachers or bilingual secretaries, but others had only one or two years of school, and the most common profession given was "domestic services," (in other words maid). Their class position was difficult to determine except by inference, but their families did everything from selling *atol* (a corn beverage) to owning a sandal factory, although most farmed. All were Catholic, and some daughters of *cofrades*, in a context of increasing indigenous conversion to Protestantism. Finally, certain departments—Quetzaltenango, Suchitepéquez, Sololá, Alta Verapaz, and Guatemala—were much better represented than others, among them the Quiché and Huehuetenango, departments particularly badly hit by the civil violence.

Although the organizers wanted to shorten the usually epic length of the pageant, it began two hours late. One factor contributing to the delay was the organizing committee's ineptitude, but more importantly, the queens went on strike. They had two complaints: one, they had not been reimbursed for their bus fare to Cobán; and two, the organizing committee, to save time, had threatened to make the speeches rehearsed the night before count for the jury's ruling. A compromise was eventually reached that allowed the queens to speak and the pageant to proceed.

The lights went out and the pageant began. In the darkness of the gymnasium, a voice intoned the opening passage of the Fondo de Cultura Económica edition (1947) of the *Popol Vuh*, the chronicle of Quiché cosmology and history. The passage describes the creation of the world. When the announcer got to the moment when the creators say *"Tierra"* (Earth), and the earth comes into existence, the lights went on to expose the stage. The set was a pre-Columbian pyramid-like structure with a huge Maya head made of Styrofoam.

The announcer left myth-time to greet the audience:

> Welcome, everyone, to Tezulutlán (the pre-Colombian name for the Verapaz) on this night when the different cultures of the land of eternal spring come together. Languages, dances, *trajes*, customs, and traditions are united in this twenty-fifth National Folkloric Festival to say to the world: This is Guatemala!

The mayor, the head of the organizing committee, and the queens of both Cobán and the department spoke. Endless folkloric dances, performed by the Inguat's all-*ladino* dance troupe, delayed the rest of the contestants' arrival. When at last they came on stage, the queens had been instructed not to dance, to save time, and there was no runway. They spoke one-and-a-half minutes each (a significant reduction from years past), in their in-

Dancing the *son*.

digenous language and in Spanish. The speeches in Spanish were the crowning moment of the candidates' appearances: photographed and cheered as they spoke, close attention was paid to them. Certain speeches, delivered with oratorical mastery and enthusiasm, tending to such subjects as land claims, women's rights, and *ladino* racism, were thunderously appreciated, and punctuated the evening with bursts of excitement.

When everyone was done, the candidates danced a *son* en masse. Fifty-four candidates jostling each other to get to get upstage made a mockery of subtle regional distinctions. Sololá,[2] whose *son* is particularly *brincadito* (jumpy), tried to attract attention by flinging herself to her knees and bowing to the four cardinal points. While the jury deliberated, the committee took the opportunity to thank the media and corporate sponsors. Televisiete (a Guatemala City television station), Pollo Campero (a Guatemalan fast-food chain), and Pepsi-Cola got the biggest applause of the evening, far bigger than any of the queens.

The ten finalists had to speak again, answering questions like: "What is the role of the Maya woman/Maya youth in Guatemala today?" "What does your *traje* mean?" or "What can you do for your community?" When the announcer came up to the microphone after the jury returned, the audience's desire for a decision after five hours was palpable. The contestants, however, had to dance the *son* again, and only then were the winners announced and the jury's identity revealed. Totonicapán was the runner-up, to no one's surprise; a school teacher, she gave excellent and articulate speeches to much applause. When San Pedro Soloma won, however, it occasioned some surprise. I, and to judge by its response, the audience, had expected Tactic to take the title. Her speech had driven the crowd into a frenzy, while Soloma's was unremarkable except for its polish. The outgoing Rabín Ahau came out tearful, made-up, and teetering on four-inch heels (to universal disapproval) and relinquished the silver-and-jade crown to Soloma. Soloma's rather pointed prize, a Spanish dictionary, was presented to her by the master of ceremonies. The committee thanked the audience and media, spectators hurried home or to parties, and most of the queens were taken back to their lodgings. The new Rabín Ahau and a few other candidates got locked into the gymnasium by accident and had to make the five-mile trip back on foot at four in the morning.

Discussion

Several elements emerge from the experience of the pageant: the centrality of the speeches to its progression; the relative unimportance of the other points of authenticity (*traje típico*, *son*, race); and certain incongruous details (the strike, the locked-in winner). The principle that connects these elements and makes the pageant coherent is systematic denial of the pageant's performativity. It privileges the form of the performance at the expense both of the performers and of the audience's participation. Denying performance is the condition of possibility of the authentic Maya Queen. However, in the competitive world of the pageant, achievement, not ascription, counts. Moreover, a pageant that refused spectators the opportunity to respond to what they were witnessing would be truly tedious. For the pageant to accomplish anything, it must animate the form of the Maya Queen without fleshing her out.

This is the jury's sacred trust. The audience is allowed, even encouraged to move with the pageant. The jury, however, keeps a clear head in order to recognize the "intrinsic qualities," as one juror called them, that make up authenticity. The five points given in the program name authenticity's attributes, but the jury's ruling ultimately refers to the success with which a queen presents herself as a coherent, immediately apprehensible sign, erasing all traces of the process of signification.

Authenticity of race means no mix of Spanish blood, visible in an aquiline nose, slanted eyes, and dark skin. However, in a former organizer's words, "there are very few authentic Maya people," and the real difference between a Maya and a non-Maya, thus, lies in the *traje*. The authentic *traje típico* is an arcane object, invented by *ladino* folklorists: it is supposed to be the ceremonial *traje* rather than the everyday one, and must conform to specimens collected thirty to fifty years ago, despite the shifts in fashion which indigenous weaving has undergone. New queens often learn about the "authentic" *traje* from outgoing queens, but non-conformance to its standards is not considered a failure in transmission of knowledge, and still less a sign of creativity, but a racial corruption.

Similarly, good expression in the indigenous language (or *lengua* [tongue], as it is pejoratively called) and dancing the *son* are properties of a candidate's racial constitution. To speak *lengua* well, a candidate must talk for a certain length of time without using too many Spanish words. Although all the jurors spoke at least one indigenous language, no one spoke more than two or three; few members of the audience spoke even one. Speeches in *lengua*, therefore, were not heard and responded to as speeches *per se*, but rather as a "speaking in tongues," issuing forth from the pre-Columbian past and finding its medium in the candidates. The *son* is a marimba rhythm; the marimba is Guatemala's "native" instrument. *Sones* are the most mournful of marimba songs, and their names often refer to indigenous women. The correct way for a woman to dance the *son* is to lower her head, and, with her hands behind her back, hop back and forth from one foot to the other. It is the artful expression of what is considered Indian demeanor. Ideally, *son*, *lengua*, and *traje* are fused together into a powerful symbol of race.

The speeches in Spanish are an anomaly, which has made them a point of contention from the beginning of the Rabín Ahau. One observer notes in 1972:

> Personally, what impressed us most about that magnificent event was the confidence, grace and eloquence, with which, before the jury and before an audience estimated at more than three thousand spectators, the young and beautiful indigenous women who were competing for the coveted prize handled themselves.

However, approbation was not universal. Another reviewer argues:

> The speeches given by the participating Indians on the night of the election and which were probably written by the parish or by the town schoolteacher, were nothing more than a sorry brainwashing....It was truly painful to see how the election went on for four long hours that night....I say poor Indians and poor audience, the first for participating in a Miss World-type contest without knowing why or for what, and the others for applauding and thus "participating" in a fake event without knowing why either.

This debate (conducted by *capitalino* journalists) highlights the speeches' disruptive potential. For Indians to speak the national language is for them to enter the nation, which is impossible in nationalist discourse.

Consequently, the speeches have the ambiguous reputation of being "political" even during the most repressive military regimes. One informant told me about a Rabín Ahau who, during the regime of Lucas García, said that Guatemala was *last* among the countries of Latin America because it did not respect the rights of indigenous people. Although this story is likely apocryphal, it is indicative of the trouble the speeches are feared to cause. Even in 1993, with a much looser political climate, the program warned the candidates to confine their remarks to "culture" and leave "politics" alone.

Unvoiced in this warning is tension over the authorship of the speeches. The candidates are expected to speak impromptu, and the finalist speech measures their ability to do so. This is an unrealistic expectation, because it is standard pageant practice to memorize speeches. In the Rabín Ahau, however, great fear is attached to scripting. If the speeches are written in advance, reasoning goes, it is not by the queen. Who knows whose subversive agendas she might voice? Any reference external to the pageant is suspicious.

The candidates' presence as living, historical beings is, consequently, unwelcome. Forgetting the Rabín Ahau in a locked gymnasium, and failing to reimburse the queens' families for a substantial outlay in transportation costs—which provoked them to strike—are elements in this program of exclusion. Although these incidents seem trivial, they are continuous with the Rabín Ahau's long history of abusing its candidates and their entourages. In years past, rumor has it, participants were forced to camp in the central plaza, and make *tortillas* while tourists watched; similar stories of neglect and casual ill-treatment abound. The term "politics" indexes the suppressed fact of the queens' presence. The speeches are "political" because in them this fact emerges.

Although the quality of the speeches varied, the point they had to make did not: We are Maya, we represent what is best about Guatemala, and we have rights. There were several clever little phrases that made this point succinctly: Patzún said "We should say Guate*maya*, not Guatemala"; and Totonicapán asked that Guatemalans "put theory to practice" regarding indigenous people. Quetzaltenango argued for indigenous land rights, citing legal justifications, and said it was not enough to go on about the *son* and the *traje*. Most candidates, however, made their point by doing just this. But even the strongest formulations of the basic message were not political unspeakables *per se*, although they might have been at recent points in Guatemalan history. Their political danger does not lie in their threat to surprise dignitaries by listing horrors but in their threat to expose the construction of authenticity.

An identifiable genre shapes the speeches. Performative mastery of its poetics assimilates the speech in Spanish to the other attributes of authenticity, making the representation live in the audience's eyes. Remarkable consistency of style from the worst to the best speeches makes them audibly different from standard *ladino* rhetorical style as well as the speech style of *ladina* beauty queens. Textual coherence in the speeches derives from features of "Maya style" (Hanks 1989), including rhythmic intonations which meter phrases and create the effect of repetition between phrases, and standards of Maya ritual speech like repeating couplets and triplets. In addition, the queens use "Mayan-izing" vocabulary and intertextual references, often from the *Popol Vuh*. By manipulating these generic features, they speak to be heard as Indians in this least Indian of the pageant's moments. Maintaining stylistic consistency, they maintain authenticity's integrity, but if they slip they expose their performance and thus their "politics." The speeches are the pivot which turns performance into essence and keeps authenticity's secret safe.

Soloma's victory proves that authenticity is coherent style. Tactic's speech roused the crowd to screams that often drown out her voice in my recording. She spoke quickly and with great emotion, often swept away by the flow of her own words, but usually able to recover herself and her listeners. Soloma's speech, on the other hand, was less moving but more perfect. She maintained a smooth, mesmeric tone, repeating key words and creating a kind of poetry out of her banal answer to the question, "What is the role of Maya women today?" Tactic lost, audience and jurors agreed, because she was "too political." At a critical point in her finalist speech, her mastery deserted her. She was trying to speak about the existence of Guatemalans, "*del otro lado*" (from the other side), i.e. refugees, and her tongue became literally tied. Stammering and casting about for new beginnings, she had to reframe her comments with an injunction—*el pueblo unido jamás será vencido*—which is "political," but not outside the pageant's norm. Her importation of the material indigenous presence excluded by the pageant caused a failure in style, and this slippage rather than the content of her speech lost her the crown. The break in her speech revealed lurking suspicious others. Similarly, Soloma won not because of what she said but the seamlessness with which she said it. Her statement of presence, "I am here," was reinscribed by her voicing into an assertion of eternal Indian essence. Exposing nothing, she became everything she was already supposed to be.

The authentic Maya Queen lines up a series of tropes whereby she stands for her *traje*, which stands for her community, which stands for her blood, which stands for her culture, which stands for Guatemalan distinctiveness. If she throws off these pleasing correspondences, she sickens racism's desire, and is accused of "politics," an excess of body. If she keeps them ordered, however, she is a source of pleasure. The Rabín Ahau is a gorgeous sight, standing alone at the evening's end in her *traje* and silver

Tactic speaks.

crown, surrounded by thick incense smoke. She has transcended the real limits imposed on her by performing them to perfection; her display lifts us all into the really real.

Further Discussion

The meaning of the Rabín Ahau is intelligible to the queens as well as the audience; the strike would not have been an effective political tactic otherwise. Given the recognized limits of authenticity, why do candidates want to participate? One answer is *"para representar a su pueblo"* (to represent their town). This claim of representation is not to be taken lightly, even if it is ultimately reinscribed into nationalist logic. The Rabín Ahau offers indigenous people a space in the public sphere, which is rare in Guatemala. More intimately, however, what does this event offer those who participate? Candidates often said they came *"para conocer"* (to learn, to know).

Beauty, as I have said, is strictly *not* part of the Rabín Ahau. For a jury to elect a candidate simply because they find her physically attractive would violate everything the Rabín Ahau stands for. Physical appearance, people involved with the pageant repeated, was only pertinent to authenticity of race. Nor is the beauty of the *traje* supposed to take precedence over its authenticity. The queens and their mothers were no exception to these rules: when I asked about beauty, they looked blank or even offended. While I could not contain my exclamations of "*¡Qué LINDAS se ven todas!*" (How pretty everyone looks!), no one joined me. The exception was a discussion I had with a cousin of one of the queens. She told me that beauty lay in the capacities of a person—a standard response—but thought the Rabín Ahau had to be beautiful in order to "relate with people of another class." Furthermore, she thought the queens appreciated and admired the beauty of each other's *trajes*.

The objectless desire for knowledge that the queens invoke became a desire to know themselves through photography. Some candidates had brought parents or friends with cameras, but those who had not were willing to pay profiteers ten quetzals, an exorbitant sum, for photographs of their public appearances. This allowed me to establish an initial rapport with them. Having bought the cheapest functioning camera available at the local Quick Foto when I realized I ought to have a visual record of the pageant, I offered to photograph the queens for free. My services were instantly in demand.

Most of the pictures I took were standard shots of the candidates in their ceremonial *trajes*. The secret identity of the jury created a panoptic effect; never knowing when they might be watched, they always watched themselves. At one point, a rumor circulated that an organizer who had offered them chewing gum was testing them to see whether they would take it and, if so, how they would chew it. Queens who had accepted became anxious and ashamed, and those who had not looked smug. Even in unofficial contexts, therefore, their photographic demeanor and poses generally had a distinctly official air.

Over the four days the queens were in Cobán they were subjected to an endless round of activities—lectures, tours, parades, rehearsals—which left them entertained but exhausted. Organizers claim that one of the benefits of the pageant for candidates is this opportunity to get to know each other; indeed, this is one sense in which they wanted "to know." Exchanges of addresses and promises of future visits occupied much of their time. By the one free afternoon the queens had, just before the pageant, these girlish interactions had reached fever pitch.

The day was lovely and the candidates took their time to get ready: showering, combing out their hair, wandering around their dorms, and talking to one another. Some queens from the coast came over and asked me to photograph them. I noticed that they were only wearing their *cortes* (indigenous women's skirts) with T-shirts, and, hoping to save my film, assumed they meant I should wait until they were ready for the pageant. "*Pónganse bonitas*" (make yourselves pretty), I said, "and I'll take your picture." They insisted, however, that I photograph them as they were, and

Swapping trajes: Zacualpa an Chichicastenango and Chichicastenango as Zacualpa.

we went back to a grassy area. Looking over their shoulders at the camera and flipping their unbraided hair, they struck poses much like those of the official photos of candidates at *ladino* beauty pageants. They had "made themselves pretty," but not at all *authentic*, which I had meant them to do.

Learning that I was taking photographs, other queens came out dressed in each others' *trajes*. *Traje* is highly site-specific; the coherence of candidacy in the Rabín Ahau hinges on reading place automatically from dress. Moreover, the entire structure of the Rabín Ahau is founded on these platial building blocks, as the candidates' habit of identifying each other by community testifies. The simple act of swapping clothes radically shifts this structure. It separates the candidates' selves from their clothing, their presence from their obligation to represent.[3]

Menchú states that "for an Indian, taking a photo of him in the street is abusing his dignity, abusing him" (1983, 208). Photographs are prototypes of the objectifying gaze. What does it mean for Guatemalan indigenous women, surely among the most photographed of "natives," to solicit their own photographic images?

Their play asserts the irreducibility of performance. Enabled by girlish liminality, the queens tried on other versions of perfection than those required by the pageant for their own and the camera's evaluation. Practicing their relations with the "people of another class" I represented, and exploring the aesthetic possibilities of other *trajes*, the queens turned the technology of the gaze back on itself. This act is as "political" as the speeches. It incorporates the candidates' presence by inverting the aesthetic hierarchy that makes their exclusion possible. Acting like beauty queens, or like each other, they were inauthentic but not abject; for their play, their bodies were sufficient without falling into excess. Whether it (or their speeches) constituted "resistance" is moot; the appeal to beauty confounds nationalist discourse without overturning it. But it is not as dupes of racism and nationalism that the queens stake their participation in the pageant.

Conclusion

The Rabín Ahau is a complexly constituted representation whose strength resides in its apparent simplicity. By abstracting and motivating connections between disparate elements of indigenous being, the jury authenticates the Rabín Ahau for the delight of the audience and the nation. Seduced by the mirage of the really real, we convert from spectators to participants, and the Rabín Ahau defines our experience of reality. She restores symbolic order to Guatemala's paradoxical nationalism, specifying the juncture of nation and race by making authenticity the only appropriate appearance for Indian women.

Of course, the Rabín Ahau is a flimsy knot to tie together such weighty matters. The harmless pleasures of witnessing the pageant do not compare with marching in a civil defense patrol. Nevertheless, such pleasures provide a transparent medium for transmitting ideas about the deepest nature of the world. The "really real" goes to the heart of social being. Authenticity has often served as a source of empowerment and its availability mutually to tactics of resistance and strategies of power shows it should not be laughed off. Without detracting from critical struggles that base themselves in authenticity, however, the structures which generate the authentic should be recognized. They lay its burden only on certain shoulders and transform the inauthentic into the corrupt. This is a false opposition, constraining possibilities for action in the world. "Politics" in all senses must triangulate authenticity's coherence if these constraints are to be loosened.

Notes

This essay is based upon work supported under a National Science Foundation Graduate Fellowship. I am also grateful for the support of the Comins Fund of the Department of Anthropology at the University of Arizona, and for the helpful comments of Kamran Ali, Jason Antrosio, Elizabeth Ferry, and Richard Wilk.

1. Omitted here is the prototype of the "Indian-as-whore" (see Nelson 1993 for a discussion of this prototype in relation to the ones I have discussed). The existence of this

sexualized image of Indian woman might seem to contradict what I propose, but I would argue that, as an image of corruption, it is simply the corollary of the authentic Indian woman.

2. I am following the candidates' usage in referring to them by the names of the communities they represent.

3. Kay Warren informs me (personal communication) that professional Indian women also wear *traje* from different communities and give each other gifts of *traje* from their own communities. This is another possible identity which the queens may be playing with/practicing for, which, like the Rabín Ahau, involves a simultaneous disruption of and reification of an authentic Indianness.

8

Contestants in a Contested Domain
Staging Identities in the British Virgin Islands

Colleen Ballerino Cohen

Introduction

Summer is Festival season in the British Virgin Islands (BVI), a British Dependent Territory in the eastern Caribbean. In preparation for this annual event commemorating the August 1, 1834 emancipation of slaves in the British West Indies, people throughout the BVI[1] organize parade troupes, parties, and family reunions; calypsonians compose songs to perform in Festival competitions; and various private and civic groups step up their preparations for the beauty and talent contests that proliferate during Festival. Throughout the Caribbean, festivals provide rich occasions for performances and symbolic representations that reflect and comment on issues of widespread concern (Abrahams 1983; Manning 1977, 1978; Miller 1994; Stewart 1986). In the BVI, Festival's events—and occasional crises—are key arenas for articulating and negotiating the complexities of life in a country engaged in constituting itself as a national community with its own distinctive culture and identity.[2] In what follows, I look at some of the ways that beauty contests held during BVI Festival are engaged in the project to construct BVI national identity as well as to raise challenges to this project.

Following a review of the historical background to present-day concerns with BVI identity, I present a brief description of three beauty contests held during Festival 1991. While these contests were quite similar in structure and affect, my description focuses on differences between them. Not only did BVI residents devote a good deal of attention to such a comparison, but also the distinctive characteristics of each contest reflect the different cultural systems and fields of power within which constructions of BVI identity—and claims to it—are being undertaken. In the body of the paper I look in detail at a contest sponsored for Festival by the BVI Ministry of Education and Culture, the Ms. Glamorous, and Mr. Personality Contest. Gender differences highlighted in this contest make clear the different norms shaping men's and women's practices as members of a national community. And the entire event—from its performative content to its outcome—brings to light cultural knowledge and practices structuring competing claims to belong to the BVI national community. I conclude with some thoughts on why beauty pageants assume the importance they do in BVI life, particularly in the present period of nation-building.

THE BVI AS A NATION AND A PEOPLE
Overview

The British Virgin Islands is a British Dependent Territory consisting of over fifty-two islands, rocks, and cays located sixty miles east of Puerto Rico in the Lesser Antilles chain. In 1991 the BVI population stood at just under eighteen thousand (Development Planning Unit 1991). Until 1965, however, BVI population seldom exceeded eight thousand, with an average of six-thousand-five-hundred throughout most of the colonial period (Dookhan 1975; Harrigan and Varlack 1988). The dramatic increase in BVI population over the past thirty years is the result of a remarkable pattern of economic growth, stemming in large part from the development of the BVI as a favored destination for elite tourists, and in particular yacht chartering vacationers from North America (Cohen 1994; Cohen and Mascia-Lees 1993; O'Neal 1983). Historically one of the poorest, most scantily populated, and least economically developed of all the British West Indian colonies, the BVI presently generates a per capita income among the highest in the Caribbean. In 1992 the government reported a GDP of $105.7 million (Development Planning Unit, 1992). Of the current BVI population half are non-citizens from other Caribbean nations, most of whom migrated to the BVI during the early years of the decade 1980-1990 to work in the rapidly growing BVI tourist economy (BVI Beacon 1994). British Virgin Islanders (BVIslanders) who would have migrated temporarily or permanently prior to the recent period of economic prosperity are staying put (or going away for education or training, then returning), and BVIslanders who once left are returning.

In the BVI today the question of BVI identity—"what does it mean to *be* the BVI and *of* the BVI?"—is raised continually and in all sectors of the population. Although seldom posed explicitly, it is a question that is at the base of debates over, for example, labor practices and land ownership, the direction of economic development and the allocation of its profits. The question informs people's responses to governmental policies about citizenship and the status of the BVI *vis-a-vis* its colonial past, as well as people's daily responses to each other, as they sort out their different histories and the personal, social, and economic relations ensuing from their differences.

These concerns with national and personal status and identity arise in some measure from the restructuring of key relations and institutions accompanying de-federation. With the 1956 dissolution of the British Colonial administrative unit governing BVI affairs from 1871-1956[3] and 1967 constitutional reforms establishing the BVI as a British Dependent Territory with a locally-elected legislature and chief minister, the BVI assumed greater autonomy in handling its internal affairs, and institutions were put in place to consolidate it as a political entity. As legislative changes enhanced BVI political autonomy and consolidation, improved transportation and communication between far-flung BVI islands and communities made possible such things as centralized education and banking. Meanwhile, initiatives promoting "national" culture were at work to mute longstanding distinctions between different communities of BVIslanders: the establishment in 1952 of Festival as an official national holiday, in 1976 of a national beauty contest, in 1979 of a national folk dance troupe, and in 1982 of a Culture Officer provided a new basis for the people inhabiting the BVI to think of themselves and their relations to each other.

While this restructuring of colonial relations, institutions, and networks laid the groundwork for conceptualizations of the BVI as a distinct and bounded entity, present-day conflicts and concerns over membership in this entity—and claims to its resources—are related directly to recent economic prosperity and the demographic complexity ensuing from it. And one of the places where such conflicting claims are most seriously asserted and contested is the cultural arena, where people engage in constituting and representing identities.

National Culture and the Cultural Politics of Identity

Possessing and participating in a national culture is a means by which a heterogeneous collection of people constitutes itself as a homogeneous nation "of own kind" (Williams 1993, 153; see also Dominguez 1989; Fox 1990; Herzfeld 1986; Lofgren 1988; Verdery 1990; Williams 1990). Simultaneously, it is a means of excluding others from this collectivity (Foster 1991; Handler 1988; Williams 1991). Indeed, one of the reasons that identity assumes such importance and is so hotly contested is that what one can claim and legitimate as an identity has very much to do with what material and political resources one can also lay claim to; "identities," as Papanek has recently put it, "also represent entitlements" (1994, 42). Thus, the prosperity of the BVI tourist economy that is a source of pride to many BVI citizens is also a key factor in moves to further consolidate historically disparate communities of BVIslanders, and thus to distinguish them from communities of non-BVIslanders swelling the BVI population. In the same way, nationals from other parts of the Caribbean who may be singled out as "different" in order to ground constructions of a distinctively BVI identity also represent a source of competing claims to the country's resources.

By law, only BVI citizens have the unrestricted right to buy and hold land, and BVI citizens are usually given preference in hiring and in the awarding of trade licenses, college scholarships, and low-interest development bank loans. Following provisions of the 1981 British Nationality Act and of the BVI Constitution, BVI citizenship is acquired in one of two ways: one may be made a citizen or born a citizen. One is made a citizen by being granted "Belonger" status. This is usually a long and complicated process preceded by long-term residence (and prior legal "Residence" status), and requiring demonstration of moral integrity and productivity. More commonly, one is born a citizen through birth to parents in a legal marriage union, when one of the parents is a BVIslander, or through birth, legitimate or otherwise, to a BVI woman. A child born outside of a legal marriage union to a non-BVI woman and a BVI man is not automatically a citizen.

In terms of daily practice and local knowledge, however, a "Belonger" may also be marked literally by who one "belongs to": by what family and part of the BVI one comes from, and even by one's physical and behavioral characteristics. While it is conventional to carry the surname of one's father (except in instances where the father refuses to acknowledge paternity), one is assumed to "belong" to the lines of both father and mother. In this sense, "belonging" means being *of* the BVI, nation of birth or nationality of mother notwithstanding. For example, individuals born on the nearby United States Virgin Island of St. Thomas, and holding a United States passport, but of BVI parentage, will use "I from here" or "I belong here" to mark their sense that they "belong" to the BVI, through family name and the connection to a particular BVI place that is presumed to follow from this.

In contrast, children born in the BVI of non-citizen parents might signal their sense of equality with their BVI peers by claiming "I born here." This assertion that all births upon BVI soil are equal has some cultural merit, given both the questionable claims to "belong" to the BVI made by individuals holding citizenship elsewhere and the complications introduced by children born outside of marriage, in the BVI, of a non-citizen mother, but carrying the name of their BVI father. While having no grounding in any current or pending citizenship legislation, the claim "I born here" nonetheless points up contradictions in claims to cultural citizenship, where a person *of* the BVI may not necessarily *be* a BVIslander.

That the ostensibly different groups of people raising such competing claims to "belong" to the BVI are linked through a shared history of migration, colonial domination, and shifting political boundaries complicates and destabilizes efforts to constitute the BVI—and its people—as a bounded entity with a distinctive identity. What, for example, is to be made of the claims of recent immigrants from Santo Domingo who are attempting to "repatriate," to the BVI through reference to their BVI parentage or grand parentage?[4] These sorts of complications to the project of constituting identities prevail throughout the Caribbean where, Stuart Hall notes, "dif-ference...persists—in and alongside continuity," in a way that, for example, "positions Martiniquans and Jamaicans as *both* the same *and* different" (1992, 225-26, Hall's emphasis). In the BVI, as throughout the Caribbean, these sorts of complications turn the sites where identity claims are formu-lated, challenged, and contained into important political arenas.

BEAUTY CONTESTS AND NATIONAL IDENTITY
Representing and Enacting Identity

Three beauty contests held within an eight-day period in July 1991 to co-incide with Festival were key occasions for enacting the ambiguities and complications in constituting a sense of being and belonging to the BVI. Two of these contests—Miss World BVI and Miss BVI—selected queens to represent the BVI in international competitions; one contest—Ms. Glamorous and Mr. Personality—selected a queen and king to represent the BVI in regional competitions. As venues for the selection of "nation-al" representatives these contests showcased local standards of beauty, so-cial and moral deportment, citizenship, talent, and intelligence. Each con-test followed the same general format, with an introductory sequence in which contestants performed a dance number and then individually intro-duced themselves, followed by the modeling of fashions in a number of categories, such as casual wear, sports wear, and evening wear. These fash-ions—and the costume and props for a talent demonstration, if one was given—were purchased through the financial sponsorship of local busi-nesses, whose names were prominently displayed on banners worn by the contestants in the initial and final sequences of the contest. Toward the end of each contest, contestants were asked to respond to questions about current events and contemporary issues. While points were tabulated to determine the winner of the contest, contestants were brought back on stage in their evening wear, to be serenaded by a male singer. Interspersed between contestant displays and demonstrations were musical and dance performances by non-contestant entertainers.

Structured as contests, these events were promoted and referred to in daily conversation as "queen shows" or simply "shows." While each con-test was broadcast over BVI radio, its value as a "show" was assessed in terms of its success as a form of entertainment in which one participated directly: as a member of an audience *watching* and *judging* a performance, as a member of an audience *making* a performance in interaction with staged enactments, as *on stage* oneself, participating in what was considered one of the very few occasions annually on which one could really "get dressed up." In this sense, the contests operated like the baroque theater, as described by Schivelbusch:

> ...the baroque theatre was more of a social, festive centre than a true auditorium. The audience gathered there not to concentrate on what was happening on the stage but to participate in a double production. The performance on the stage was matched by one put on by the audience...there was no clear dividing line between actors and audience. (1988, 204)

In the baroque theater the elision of audience and stage was achieved by the homogeneous lighting in the auditorium, and resulted in making "everything...a game of entanglement and resolution" (Schivelbusch 1988, 204). A similar effect was achieved in the BVI auditorium, where fixed cement bleachers running the full length of both sides of the main floor directed audience attention to the action within the audience itself as much as to what was happening on stage. Within the BVI auditorium during the "show," audience members scrutinized (and frequently commented loudly upon) each other's dress, each other's company, each other's responses to the action on the stage. In this manner they enacted the diverse positions and perspectives taken up in the BVI community at large.

The Miss World BVI Contest: Local vs. Cosmopolitan Allure

The Miss World BVI contest was only in its second year in 1991, but was heralded in radio advertisements and newspaper articles for weeks before Festival as "a night of excitement, a gala of stars, a truly captivating event...like no other" (*Island Sun* 1991a, 12). A contest selecting a woman to represent the BVI in the Miss World Pageant, Miss World BVI was organized by a local entertainment concern and was sponsored by one locally-owned and one internationally-owned business. Promotions for this contest targeted audiences in the United States Virgin Islands (USVI) as well as the BVI, and underplayed its local content in favor of its cosmopolitan "sophistication," as embodied in the international media stars serving as its judges and commentators. Thus, for example, a full-page newspaper article promoting the 1991 Miss World BVI contest featured 3"x5" photos of its local contestants, and was headlined "Miss World BVI 1991 Contestants," yet its opening paragraph focused exclusively on the pageant's "cosmopolitan" offerings:

> Appearing on the Miss World BVI 1991 show are Miss America 1990 Debby Turner, Tonya Williams (Dr. Olivia Barber—Actress from the Young and the Restless), Lawrence Childers (Director

A "Glamorous" Miss BVI contestant parading for a fully engaged audience.
Photo by © Catherine Sebastian

IMG Models New York), Miss American Virgin Islands, Sandy
Shatkin. People of the British and U.S. Virgin Islands get ready
for a night to remember. (*Island Sun* 1991b, 24)

This rhetorical occlusion of the contestants in the Miss World BVI
Contest mirrors a tension within the BVI between an allegiance to local
economies and interests and a desire for items and experiences associated
with the metropolis, a tension that was also reflected in debate over the
pageant's two-tiered price structure. While the Miss World BVI Pageant
ticket price of $20.00 was higher than the ticket prices for either of the
other two pageants being held during Festival, it was considered in keeping with its offerings of international TV and beauty stars as judges.
Meanwhile, its $30.00 VIP ticket guaranteeing reserved non-bleacher
seating and a champagne toast at intermission was ridiculed and dismissed
as out of line.[5] The same tension was at the heart of one of the major crises
of BVI Festival 1991, a standoff over Festival's carnival ride concession between the committee in charge of Festival and a local entrepreneur. I summarized this crisis in a descriptive write-up of Festival 1991:

"Coney Island" rides brought into the British Virgin Islands from
the United States Virgin Island of St. Croix were lit and running,
night after night, but could take no riders until what was dubbed
"the Coney Island controversy" was resolved. The Coney Island
had been contracted for by the Festival Committee "because the

local funland was not large enough"; yet, as the British Virgin Islands owners of the local funland protested to Government, "Festival was going to be 40 to 50 percent of our business. We made financial commitments to the bank based on Festival season and now all those are in jeopardy...It is an effort, conscious or unconscious, to kill the business...A government must look out for its own growth" (BVI Beacon, August 1, 1991, 1, 13). While Festivalgoers were almost unanimous in their expressions of pleasure and pride at "finally" having a "real" Coney Island for Festival, the second-place calypso song, "Buy Local," received greater air-play on the local radio station than any of its counterparts.

The Miss BVI Contest: Festival Politics and International Entanglements

From 1976 until 1990, when the first Miss World BVI contest was held, the only forum for selecting a national beauty Queen was the Miss BVI contest. The Miss BVI contest is a franchise of the Miss Universe pageant and is sponsored by the Festival Committee, a private corporation of citizens responsible for planning and carrying out of all official Festival events and competitions. Until recently, the Miss BVI contest was the premier social event of Festival, with its participants and audience members alike repairing to Festival Village at its conclusion to meet friends and walk around in their Festival finery. Because of its central place in the Festival calendar of events, and its status as the first such event to send a BVI representative to an international competition, the Miss BVI contest is still considered the legitimate forum for the selection of a national beauty queen. Nevertheless, public opinion held that this legitimacy was seriously challenged in 1991 by the popularity of the Miss World BVI contest.

The $15 admission charge for the Miss BVI contest was the traditional rate for this "show," but ticket sales to the Miss BVI contest were slow and it failed to achieve the subscriptions of the much ballyhooed Miss World BVI contest. In the context of the standing-room-only crowd that had attended the Miss World BVI contest a week earlier, the poor turnout for the Miss BVI contest was a commentary not just on the perceived quality of the "show" but also on the Festival Committee itself—its degree of sophistication, its organizational and leadership ability, its right to the control it wielded over all of Festival. Mirroring public and political debate about how Festival should be organized, who should be in charge of Festival, and whether or not Festival should be developed as a tourist event, the commentary surrounding the Miss BVI pageant was also a commentary on the status of the BVI in a larger world, in which the localized content and concerns of a small-island festival could seem awfully parochial.

This concern with relative degrees of sophistication of BVI "queen shows" is not unlike the concern with respectability documented throughout the Caribbean and "rooted in the metropolitan-oriented colonial system of social stratification based on class, colour, wealth and Eurocentric culture, life style and education" (Besson 1993, 16; see also Miller 1994; Wilson 1973). In the BVI, the present-day impulse to continual self-assessment on the basis of (not necessarily local) standards that are presumed to be normative and superior, is also a consequence of living in a community whose economic well-being is keyed to its success at anticipating and serving the tastes and desires of elite Western tourists. At the same time, the concern with BVI sophistication and status expressed in debate over the relative merits of two beauty contests was indicative of quite tangible entanglements that were very much on the minds of BVI residents in the summer of 1991. Another excerpt from my write-up of Festival explains this:

> The floats sharing first prize for Festival 1991 parade represented protests against a recent British mandate that all dependent territories abolish the death penalty. Their signs, symbols, and dramatical performances enacted the sentiments expressed by a British Virgin Islands local:

> England doesn't have the same taste in our mouth like it used to be. Whether we go independent or not, we don't care. We want both worlds: America's flair, good economic prosperity, progress and economic development and British Law and Order. Now England has pulled the rug out from under the law and order. Manners, values, traditions are OK, but they're not gonna stop the criminal element that is becoming so close with the drugs and all. But now we got no status with Britain. We don't even have the British passport and rights that colonies had and French and American territories have even today. So we say to England: How we got no status and you still making laws for us?

The Ms. Glamorous and Mr. Personality Contest: Local Knowledge and Citizenship

In contrast to both the Miss World BVI contest and the Miss BVI contest, which selected women to represent the BVI in the Miss World and Miss Universe pageants respectively, the Ms. Glamorous and Mr. Personality contest was a low-budget affair selecting representatives for talent and fashion contests held throughout the year in various parts of the Caribbean. Sponsored by the Ministry of Education and Culture, the Ms. Glamorous and Mr. Personality contest was promoted in mimeographed leaflets as a cultural event put on for local family enjoyment. While the $12 admission charge for the Ms. Glamorous and Mr. Personality contest was considered in line with its local and unexceptional offerings, public enthusiasm for the show—which was being resuscitated as a Festival offering after a ten-year hiatus—was minimal. It was the most sparsely attended of the three. Yet post-contest reviews were wildly enthusiastic, and everyone who knew I had attended it engaged me in excited and intense discussion about all of the elements of what public commentary deemed "a great show."

In content and disposition the Ms. Glamorous and Mr. Personality contest was above all about local knowledge. Like the other two contests in respect to its structure, the sponsoring of contestants, and the seriousness with which its contestants undertook the competition, the entertainment value of the Ms. Glamorous and Mr. Personality contest seems to have resided in its audience—which was made up almost entirely of women and children—not taking it as seriously as the other contests. Indeed, the play between seriousness and frivolity that most distinguished this contest from the other two created a highly charged space where notions of an "official" aesthetic and legitimacy were in constant and complicated interaction with challenges to any singular standard of judgment.

THE MS. GLAMOROUS AND MR. PERSONALITY CONTEST: GENDERED IDENTITY AND NATIONAL LEGITIMACY

Normative Gender "Style"

Held on the Friday night immediately preceding the Saturday night Miss World BVI contest, the Mr. Personality and Ms. Glamorous contest was referred to by one informant as "a frivolous bit of additional entertainment put on for Festival," and as being in a different league from the more "intellectual" Miss World BVI contest. In another description—this one by one of its contestants—the Ms. Glamorous and Mr. Personality contest was placed on a par with the other contests. In her reckoning this contest was different only in its featuring men and women. In fact, while all the contestants in the Ms. Glamorous and Mr. Personality contest were expected to give standard introductory presentations, and all competed in casual wear and evening wear, certain of their competitive events differed. Where Ms. Glamorous contestants competed against each other in modeling sports wear and business wear, the Mr. Personality contestants competed against each other in talent demonstration and bathing suit modeling.

These differences in the men's and women's competition mirror gender differences in behavior, roles, and goals in BVI social and economic life. Thus the focus in the women's competition on modeling business wear reflected both the high proportion of women in clerical and mid-level positions in banking and tourism, and the high social status that is marked by wearing pantyhose, pumps, and well-matched suits or separates.[6] Moreover, insofar as these positions tend to be occupied by "Belongers," in highlighting women's business wear the Ms. Glamorous competition made explicit an important marker of class differentiation as it intersects with gender and national difference alike. For men on the other hand, a salaried position in banking or tourism carries less status than a higher-level political or supervisory position or success as an entrepreneur, to which male aspirations tend to be directed. Here, the focus is upon individual ability, drive, and power—attributes highlighted in the exclusively male talent and bathing suit competitions. Thus, the gender-marked titles—Ms. Glamorous and Mr. Personality—not only signaled that this event was a male and female competition, but also made manifest differences contributing to notions of distinctive gender "style." Most indicative of a successful Ms. Glamorous was the demonstration of ability to "put together" a glamorous look; most indicative of a successful Mr. Personality was the ability to perform or "put on" a powerful persona.

Ms. Glamorous: The Fashionable and Connected Woman

The four women contestants for the title of Ms. Glamorous differed widely in body type, skin shade, and stage presence, with the extremes of variation represented by a short, stocky, dark brown-skinned woman, and a tall, stick-thin, light-skinned[7] woman who moved like a professional runway model. Audience assessments of the qualities of all the Ms. Glamorous contestants employed a number of conflicting aesthetic standards, but placed greatest emphasis on evidence of an ability to "glamorize," to show off to greatest advantage one's attributes by "putting together" a good look. For example, while the first appearance on stage of the short, stocky contestant was greeted by loud calls and guffaws, these turned immediately to approving comments upon this contestant's alluding directly to her body shape, and strolling deliberately and confidently around the stage. Audience approval of this contestant—encapsulated by a comment, "she do good with the audience, she do good with what she got"—was sustained throughout the show by this contestant's choice of fashions that, in line and color, worked to "glamorize" her stocky frame.

The ability to "glamorize" was itself taken as evidence of a second highly valued contestant attribute—"having someone behind her," literally working with her to "put together" a good look. Alluding to the importance in women's lives of local family connections and support, audience approval of this attribute pointed to a key cultural basis of women's legitimacy in the larger community. Thus, for example, while the light complexion and model-like bearing of the one contestant were acknowledged as probably to her benefit, her Guyanese nationality, her mixed racial heritage, and her cool demeanor were taken as evidence of her *not* having "someone behind her," and were presumed to be working against her in the competition. In contrast, the audience favorite was a local woman whose dramatic fashion choices and cocky stage presence were received with comments such as, "See, she have someone behind her. That's good."

Another frequently heard comment, "The audience like who they know," speaks to the favoritism shown by the audience toward local contestants. Combined with the phrase "someone behind her" the phrase "The audience like who they know" reveals the intimate awareness that the audience had of backstage doings, including the amount of work done and money spent in preparation for the event. Audience judgments of and responses to the contestants consistently took such "backstage" knowledge into consideration. In this sense, they mirrored the operation of a national politics which, still deeply embedded in family ties and local allegiances, are negotiated extensively on the basis of local knowledge of "behind-the-scenes" dealings. Indeed, the Ms. Glamorous and Mr. Personality contest opened a public space for its largely female audience to demonstrate political knowledge and local savvy. Such demonstrations may have been especially charged experiences for non-BVI members of the audience. For their heady enactments of cultural competence (through assertions of knowing what was going on backstage) and passionate support of local candidates was in marked contrast to their political "illegitimacy," as nationals from other islands.

Simultaneously, the Ms. Glamorous contest is a venue where women can compete outside of the normative constructs of femininity enacted in the Miss BVI and Miss World BVI contests, and thus enact constructs more congruent with local knowledge and practice. For example, women wishing to compete for the Ms. Glamorous crown need not necessarily meet the standards of Western-style beauty that are so conscientiously upheld in the other contests. Thus, the audience approval of the stocky contestant that underscored the local importance of fashion style also contested an aesthetic idealizing thin bodies and white skin.

Mr. Personality: The Stylized and Self-Fashioned Man

The appearance of the Mr. Personality contestants in bathing suits was the high point of the Ms. Glamorous and Mr. Personality contest, and was greeted with wild shouts and applause. This audience response was due in part to the fact that the male modeling of bathing suits was an unantici-pated offering of the contest, in part because of the obvious reversal of tra-ditional beauty contest practice. Inspiring the loudest and most boisterous audience response, however, was the overplayed sexual provocativeness of the contestants as they paraded up and down the stage in skimpy bikinis. The stylistic impact of these displays of male sexuality was enhanced by what the audience and Mistress of Ceremonies alike speculated to be stuffing placed strategically in the men's bikini fronts. The performances throughout the bathing suit competition laid stress on simulated sexual power and stylized prowess. Hence, in stark contrast to the enthusiastic response to the simulations of male sexuality in the front-stuffed bikinis was the wholesale distaste expressed by the audience to hair that could on occasion be seen rising from the pubis to the navel. In every such case, contestants displaying the offending hair were chastised loudly from the audience for not having properly applied concealing foundation make-up.

The emphasis on stylized prowess was underscored in other fashion segments of the Mr. Personality competition, which accentuated individ-ual creativity and self-fashioning. Men's fashion selections were more highly stylized than were the women's and were frequently designed by the wearer. While the women's fashions were for the most part elegant and sophisticated versions of daily wear, the men's fashions simulated flashy MTV style, and many were direct take-offs on the lines and colors of costumes from the film, *Dick Tracy*. The Mistress of Ceremony's com-mentary and audience response alike stressed the visual *impact* of the men's outfits and the individual thought and effort that went into select-ing the various pieces of any given outfit. Indeed, so controlling was the stress upon the self-fashioned man of individual impact that at one point during the talent portion of the contest the Mistress of Ceremonies mis-takenly attributed authorship of a well-known popular musical standard to the contestant singing it. A letter of thanks titled "Dignity and Determination are Strong Points" and written by the winner of the 1991 Mr. Personality crown to his "many loyal admirers and fans for their gen-eral support" articulated in dramatic prose this emphasis on individual im-pact and self-fashioning:

> As a young and talented individual I do say the scope of destiny lies strong within the walls of determination to go on and start from here…and to further capitalize greatly and spread my wings of confidence, determination, and potential far beyond the imag-ination. And to cast the golden opportunity of making it in life in my desirous field. In the direction of fame and loyalty. To be ambitious and straight forward makes of course a better charac-ter of you.

The newly crowned Mr. Personality 1991. Photo by © Catherine Sebastian

As the reference to having "people behind them" mirrored a constitutive feature of the normative BVI woman, so the emphasis on stylistic prowess and self-fashioning was expressive of what is generally understood to be desirable in the BVI man—individual style and entrepreneurial drive. Likewise, as women's demonstrations emphasized the higher social status of women holding office and management positions, so men's performances fit a local cultural system in which a man whose salaried income exceeds $25,000 dollars a year experiences himself as "poor" because he "works for someone else."

Gender Performance and Contesting National Identity

Scholars looking at the link between sexuality and nationalism point out that all national identities are distinctively gendered, and moreover, that taken as natural, these national gender distinctions ground constructions of the nation—and membership in it—as natural (Hall 1993; McClintock 1993. See also Parker et al. 1992; Yuval-Davis and Anthias 1989). In providing a stage for its contestants to perform prevailing norms of femininity and masculinity, the Ms. Glamorous and Mr. Personality contest buttressed the nation as it is constituted of a distinctive set of cultural practices and knowledges, and simultaneously reinforced the "naturalness" of it. Yet even as it provided a space for performances of gendered BVI identities, the Ms. Glamorous and Mr. Personality contest opened an arena for contesting knowledges and practices structuring BVI identity, and hence for contesting conceptualizations of the BVI as a distinctive and bounded entity.

For example, from the perspective of its contestants, the Ms. Glamorous and Mr. Personality contest was also a means of self-improvement or self-schooling (learning how to walk, learning to speak in public, learning self-confidence), and a steppingstone to certain careers—for women, careers in management and modeling, for men, careers in modeling and entertainment. In this respect, women contestants were enacting a form of entrepreneurial drive similar to that explicitly highlighted in men's performances. Simply by participating in the contest, they called into question the gender differences in interest and proclivity marked by the contest's separate categories of performance. In like manner, while the bathing suit competition was one of several representations of gender norms, it may also have served as an occasion for subverting them: revealing through parody the constructed nature of gender, it showed the "real" to be "a certain kind of naturalized gender mime" (Butler 1991, 23). Finally, as respects the expressed purposes of women and men contestants alike, in highlighting their desire for upward mobility contestants drew attention to internal differentiation based upon class, and thus called into question representations of the BVI nation as a homogeneous grouping of "own kind."

A "Great Show": Legitimacy Up for Grabs

What most distinguished the Ms. Glamorous and Mr. Personality contest—what made it a "good" show—was that even as it put on stage the cultural knowledge and practices constitutive of local "fitness" as a BVI woman or man, it opened for challenge the very notion of normative "style." But post-contest reviews of the Ms. Glamorous and Mr. Personality contest declared emphatically that it was a "great show." Constitutive of its spectacular success, what made it a "great show," was a finale that put all claims to legitimacy up for grabs.

At the conclusion of the evening wear portion of the Ms. Glamorous and Mr. Personality competition, all contestants were gathered on stage to await the decision of the judges. Audience commentary at this point focused spiritedly on who was "supposed" to win. In the case of Mr. Personality, audience commentary favored a local man whose consistently "professional" modeling and talent performances and serious attention to fashion and style were cited as evidence of his drive to succeed and hence of his solid chances of winning region-wide competitions. In contrast, audience speculation about who should win the Ms. Glamorous crown revealed a confusion over what standards the judges would apply in determining a winner. When the first runner-up title was awarded to the local woman whose dramatic fashion choices and stage presence had been taken as evidence that she had people "behind her" this confusion was cleared up: the audience understood that "contestant number three"—the thin, light-skinned, model-like contestant—would win the crown. Thus, when the Chairman of the Festival Committee announced that the winner was "contestant number one"—the short and stocky contestant—the audience erupted, expressing in loud and highly charged commentary a sense simultaneously of the absurdity of the choice and its appropriateness, for as one audience member commented, "She deserve it, she do a good job."

Such commentary turned instantly to fury when the audience realized that the judges were signaling to the Festival Committee Chairman that he had made a mistake. As some individuals in the audience shouted abusive comments in the direction of the Chairman of Festival Committee, and others speculated that perhaps he had done this whole thing in order to "make it a better show," most members of the audience began arguing amongst themselves over the appropriate response to what everyone acknowledged was an untenable situation.

For meanwhile, contestant number one had been escorted by the reigning Miss BVI to her throne and had been crowned with the Ms. Glamorous crown, even as contestant number three was being seated in a third chair that someone had slipped in between the two original thrones. At this point, Miss BVI, now standing behind two seated "winners," removed her own crown and placed it on the head of contestant number three. As the audience digested this move, the Chairman of Festival Committee recovered his composure enough to announce the second and first runner-ups to Mr. Personality. With the audience attention shifted to this event, contestant number one slipped off her crown (which Miss BVI put on—she was then wearing the Ms. Glamorous crown, and Ms. Glamorous was wearing the Miss BVI crown) and moved to stand back in place. The announcement of the winner of Mr. Personality served as a sort of closure to this event, and the audience—still arguing about the debacle, but at a much reduced pitch—began to disperse.

In terms of problematics put in play throughout the show itself, this mess-up at its end served to articulate, without resolving, tensions embodied in the "two crowned" (as the two Ms. Glamorouses were thereafter referred to): the "good job" done by a local woman in the context of Western standards of beauty and physicality entirely inappropriate to her skin shade and body type and the "natural" fitness to those same standards of a light-skinned woman with no local connections of note. But what seems to have made this show's finale especially satisfying was that its "two crowned"—each with "legitimate" claims to a title—were so precisely representative of contemporary BVI national experience. In one sense, this is because, to paraphrase a BVI local, it wouldn't be the BVI without confusion over ownership of single plots of land. Confusion and disputes over land ownership are embedded in a long and complicated BVI history of family inheritance and migration patterns,[8] and their illumination through the incident of the "two crowned" thus had special significance to native BVIslanders. Superseding these disputes over BVI family land, however, are contemporary disagreements over BVI "nativeness" and the rights and privileges accruing to this status. These disputes involve BVIslanders and non-BVIslanders alike, and with equal intensity. It was these confrontations over identities and their related privileges and perquisites that made the mess-up at the end of the Ms. Glamorous and Mr. Personality contest so significant and satisfying, and that made the contest a "great show." For the "two-crowned" mirrored the contradictions and ambiguities of claims and counterclaims to rights to "belong" to the BVI, while the passions their crowning unleashed pointed to the importance of the stakes.

Conclusion

The question of who should and should not be able to claim "Belonger" rights was the focus of the winning song in the 1991 Festival Calypso contest, "Where We Born is Where We From." Composed and performed by a St. Kitts national, the song was written, according to its author, Benji V, "to reach the ears of certain people who made the laws" (*Island Sun* 1991c, 2). In the song Benji V assumes the voice of a native-born BVI male, and thus reiterates performatively the claim he makes in the text of the song itself:

> They say if me girlfriend gets her baby in my country
> The baby can't have the same rights like me.
> How come when anybody go to Rock City [St. Thomas, USVI] to
>   get their baby
> Their baby could have the same rights like a Tomi? [St. Thomian]
> Where a baby first see sun, that country must be their own,
> They must have the rights like anybody born in the same region.
> So if mother born in Antigua and she children born in Tortola
>   [BVI]
> Where we born is where we from…

Like BVI beauty contests, the BVI calypso contest is a highly competitive event whose frequently controversial outcome and always relevant content spark widespread interest and debate. For individuals competing in either of these types of contests, winning can have important and far-reaching consequences with respect to social status and occupational mobility. On the other hand, the payoff for the majority of the public attending these contests is the opportunity to reflect on, comment on, and engage each other over issues of local political and cultural consequence.

One of the many skits dramatizing BVI life "long time" ago.
Photo by © Catherine Sebastian

Thus, as Miller (1994) points out for Trinidadian calypso contests, it is the content and sentiments of a given calypso—and not the reputation or fame of the singer performing it—that most influences what contestant an audience will support. In the five years that I have been observing contests put on in association with Festival in the BVI (1990-1994), a majority of beauty contestants' talent skits have dramatized differences between contemporary life and life from "long time," with a recurring theme being one that stresses the "loss" of "traditional" culture and the ravages of drugs. In their answers to interview questions, BVI beauty contestants make explicit their positions on current debates—including debates over citizenship and rights. Meanwhile audience responses to these skits and interviews are a key component of the appeal of "queen shows" and simultaneously provide a good indication of trends in public opinion.

As the BVI continues in its efforts to articulate and promote a sense of what the BVI is, its beauty contests also emerge as forums for expressions of an "official" BVI identity. In making note of the special character attributes that make them the preferred representative for their county, for example, BVI beauty contestants give expression to ideals and values shaping constructions of the BVI as a distinct entity. BVI beauty queens' participation in competitions abroad—the details of which are recorded in local newspaper articles—provide a similar opportunity. Thus, the comments of Miss BVI 1990 upon her return from the Miss Universe competition underscored the link between BVI national identity and its tourist economy, as well as highlighted features predominating in BVI promotions of itself as a tourist destination:

> Although I did not reach the top ten, I am happy to have sold tourism for the BVI. My sash indicated my place of origin and allowed me to explain the Territory's geographical location and the natural beauty it possesses. (*Island Sun* 1991d, 1)

In like manner, the comments of the BVI winner of a regional Miss Caribbean Talented Teen pageant mirrored the sense of national pride and regional preeminence that has accompanied recent BVI economic prosperity: "What's so great about [being selected over contestants from nine other Caribbean countries] is that we were the smallest islands there" (BVI Beacon 1991: 1).

Even as BVI beauty contestants are under pressure to conform to local aesthetic and social standards, they are also evaluated in terms of an international aesthetic. This is especially the case when the beauty contest is also a venue for selecting an individual to represent the BVI in contests abroad. As we have seen, the tension between these two "communities" of interest is a particularly salient one for BVI beauty contest-goers who, like most residents of the BVI, are implicated through family ties, migration histories, consumer practices, and electronic communication systems in diverse and far-ranging systems of values, networks of interests, and structures of power. The intersecting but frequently contradictory influences of these various connections are seldom consolidated or resolved by the selection of a beauty queen; indeed, the final decision of the judges is almost always disputed in heated public debate that goes on for weeks after each contest. But the seriousness and intensity with which people engage in theorizing about what happened in a beauty contest and why, is an indication of just how much attention is given to studying the workings of the various systems and structures in which they are involved. Besides presenting good opportunities to practice, demonstrate, and refine the knowledge that comes of such study, BVI beauty contests also seem to offer a temporary respite from the dissonance of the competing interests and values they bring to light, by constituting a common ground of "national interest." This is what is suggested by a newspaper account of the response of one Miss BVI to conflicting standards of beauty:

> Commenting on beauty, [Miss BVI 1990] pointed out that beauty is difficult to judge and it is seen differently in different parts of the world. "Not winning Miss Universe should not deter one's spirit, participation in the pageant is important to self and country as an ambassador." (*Island Sun* 1991a, 1)

Of course, not all residents of the BVI have the same stake in its interests and future, and so not all will be equally convinced by the sentiments underlying Miss BVI's remarks. But this is, I think, precisely why beauty contests assume such importance in BVI life: Affording an ideal stage on which to display the BVI that is emerging in the contemporary Caribbean context—and all the conventions attendant to identification with its project and trajectory—the beauty contests at the same time provide rich and varied materials and opportunities to contest this display. To borrow from Stuart Hall's (1992) insights into Caribbean identities and Caribbean cinema—beauty contests are important not because they invite demonstrations that stabilize and normalize experience but because, in putting into play the complexities and contradictions of BVI experiences and affiliations, they foreclose any such possibility. If beauty contests are sites for constituting identities at all, these are the identities that emerge from the interplay of the differences and similarities of their participants, identities "defined not by essence or purity, but by the recognition of a necessary heterogeneity," identities that "are constantly producing and reproducing themselves anew...allowing [people] to see and recognize different parts and histories of [them]selves...to constitute [themselves] as new kinds of subjects...." (Hall 1992, 234–36)

Notes

An early version of this essay was presented in November 1991 at the Annual Meeting of the American Anthropological Association, and short portions on BVI history and tourism are drawn from Cohen 1995 and Cohen and Mascia-Lees 1993. Special thanks to Rick Wilk for his always helpful comments and conversation; to tireless ethnographic photographer and queen show-goer Catherine Sebastian, whose photographs appear in this article and on the cover of this book; to Bill Maurer, who was with me in the field in 1991 and who provided important insights into BVI citizenship and land disputes; and to the H.L. Stoutt Community College, BVI Government, the BVI Festival Committee, and my many friends in the BVI for their support and cooperation. This paper draws on fieldwork in the BVI (1990-present) focused on national identity, national culture, and tourism development, and supported by Vassar College Faculty Research Grants, and Ford and Dana Fellowships for undergraduate research.

1. Local usage prefers "BVI" to the longer British Virgin Islands; "BVIslander" is used more frequently than "British Virgin Islander" to designate a native of the BVI. In deference to these conventions, I use BVI and BVIslander throughout this paper.

2. The notion of the BVI as a national community derives from Anderson's (1982) demonstration that nations are not the natural outcome of a sociological or political progression, but are the product of the collective imaginations of the people inhabiting them. However, my discussion of BVI national identity follows more closely Chatterjee's (1989, 1993) corrective of Anderson. A key problem for nations emerging out of the colonial experience is how to imagine forms of community that are not, as Chatterjee puts it, simply "'modular' forms of the national society propagated by the

modern West" (1993, 5; see also Chatterjee 1989). For Chatterjee, what distinguishes the nationalisms of these emerging nations from the historical nationalisms of Western Europe, the Americas and Russia is that while their political institutions may be modeled on liberal-democratic ideals underpinning the modern state—their national cultures, while "'modern,'...[are]...nevertheless not Western." (Chatterjee 1993, 6). For these nations, then, national culture is not just where the nation as an imagined community comes into being, it is where possibilities for sovereignty lie, even though the state may be in the hands of a colonial power.

3. The British Virgin Islands, together with the islands of St. Kitts, Nevis, and Anguilla had been formed into a single British Colony earlier, in 1816 (Dookhan 1975; Harrigan and Varlack 1988). Today, St. Kitts and Nevis are independent states, and Anguilla is a British Dependent Territory like the BVI.

4. The notion that one might "repatriate" to a nation that one has never in fact even been physically connected to, is an instance of a form of patriotism, that works to problematize "the hyphen between the nation and the state" (Appadurai 1993, 427), and to call our attention to the fact—particularly pertinent to the BVI case—that "while nations might continue to exist, the steady erosion of the capabilities of the nation-state to monopolize loyalty will encourage the spread of national forms that are largely divorced from territorial states" (1993, 421).

5. Indeed, in light of the peculiar arrangement of auditorium seating, consensus held that the best seats for observing the whole show (referring in particular to the show in the audience) were the $20 bleacher seats.

6. Freeman (1993) provides an especially illuminating analysis of the link between clothing and status in Barbados.

7. Caribbean color terms distinguish among a wide range of shadings. While there is no agreed-upon terminology for categories of skin color in the Caribbean, skin color is generally correlated throughout the region with social status (Mintz 1984; Segal 1991).

8. Following emancipation, BVI land was held in common by families or communities, and land is still frequently allotted to members of an extended family group for building a house or for a provision ground, without the formality of deed or sale or even the approval of all individuals with claims to it. While a Cadastral survey in the 1960s was intended to resolve land boundary and ownership disputes, the allocation and ownership of family land remains a vexing problem. See Maurer 1994 for a history of these disputes.

9

Carrying the Queen
Identity and Nationalism in a Liberian Queen Rally

Mary H. Moran

Introduction: Liberia and Liberian Queen Rallies

Since early 1990, the small West African nation of Liberia has been literally torn apart by civil war, ethnic massacres, the dissolution of the central
government, occupation by foreign troops, and increasing fragmentation
of the contesting armed parties. Carried on in the shadow of better known
conflicts such as those in Bosnia, Kuwait, Somalia, and Rwanda, the
Liberian tragedy has been largely ignored by the rest of the world. While
not surprising, given its small size and lack of strategic importance to the
major powers, the fact that *Liberia* has been the site of such complete dissolution has come as a shock to researchers concerned with the region. As
the oldest independent republic in Africa, with 133 years of ostensibly
"democratic" tradition and no obvious longstanding "ethnic" tensions of
the kind purported for Bosnia or Rwanda, Liberia seems an unlikely candidate for catastrophic political turmoil. In a recent article, Anna Simons
has raised the question of why anthropologists seem unable to come to
terms with the problem of state dissolution, even as more and more of us
find our field sites consumed by this process (1994, 818, 822). This essay
is part of a broader attempt to confront this question.

With the clarity of hindsight, one can see that the signs of Liberia's im-
pending disaster were everywhere in the early 1980s, even in the seemingly
ubiquitous beauty contests or "queen rallies," which were so much a part of
both rural and urban life. Indeed, although the nation, prior to the civil war,
participated in international pageants like the Miss World competition, the
majority of Liberians experienced beauty contests in this form.

A queen rally is a subset of the category of events known as rallies, or
public, competitive fund-raising programs similar to the American
telethon. While the specific history of these events is unknown, Lawrence
Breitborde's informants in the mid-1970s reported that they had been
popular for more than the last ten years (1977, 234). Although also em-

ployed by churches for the support of their own activities, most rallies, even when sponsored by private organizations, are explicitly nationalist events because the money they raise is earmarked for local and national "development"; usually infrastructure like roads, schools, libraries, public buildings, and so on. One of the largest public marketplaces in Monrovia is called the "Rally Time" market because the funds which built it were raised in this manner. Of course, by some accounts, tax-paying citizens should have such public infrastructure provided for them by the state without being solicited for private donations. "Development rallies" are therefore an odd commentary on the failure of the central government to fulfill its part of the bargain for local allegiance.

This observation is not meant to imply that centralized tax collection is either the best or most efficient means of allocating resources to such projects. Liberian citizens, like those of many postcolonial states, however, found themselves both taxed *and* exhorted by their national governments to provide for their own local development needs without expecting the state to "do everything for them." As we shall see in the following examples, the tension between the ideal of "development" as a collaborative, integrative project incorporating the locality and the nation and the actual unwillingness of many postcolonial states to direct resources to rural areas emerges quite definitively in the Liberian queen rallies.

While the support of public works, national celebrations, and social services through private donations did not originate in Liberia (the Reagan and Bush inaugurals and the "thousand points of light" provide familiar examples), Liberians have turned this practice into a form of public entertainment. Little wonder then, that the grafting of the beauty contest format onto the rally should prove so popular. The contestants, or "queens," represent specific local constituencies, and are displayed briefly to the audience before being seated at a long table. Before each is a bowl to hold donations; the audience members pass in a line along the table, placing money in each bowl with the largest amount going to their favorite. The queen who generates the highest total is the winner and is crowned and paraded through the streets by her supporters.

On the superficial level, the queen rally does resemble a beauty contest; the language of the introduction emphasizes the beauty of the queens and the fineness of their clothes. They usually walk back and forth before the audience so everyone can get a good look at them before taking their seats behind the table. Such promenades also take place between "rounds" of giving, on the premise that the beauty of a particular woman may cause some to change their minds and switch allegiance at the last moment. Yet, in another sense, the Liberian version inverts the standard form of the international beauty pageant, in which women move and perform before a seated audience and (usually) male judges. In this instance, it is the sponsoring constituencies which are "on stage," demonstrating their wealth, prestige, and organizational skills. The women are essentially passive tokens; they *represent* the competing groups without actually competing themselves.

In fact, a close analysis makes clear that a woman's age or physical appearance usually has little or nothing to do with her following. Breitborde, in his linguistic analysis of a series of queen rallies from Monrovia, reports that one church youth group entered a woman in her fifties as their queen (1977, 236). The exception would perhaps be very small scale queen rallies held by church groups or between competing high school classes, which may turn on differences in the locally defined attractiveness or popularity of the queens themselves. So widespread is this form of fund raising, by the way, that I have seen mixed-sex groups of young children playing queen rally; setting up a row of little girls, placing stones, representing coins, in tin cans, crowning the winner with a bit of tin foil and parading her around the neighborhood in a wheelbarrow.

Theoretical Considerations

How can the widespread but essentially local practices described above shed light on the ultimate failure of the Liberian nation state? In a recent review of the literature, Robert Foster has noted that the latest anthropological work on "national cultures" appears to divide into two broad sets of concerns: (1) the processes by which local and national elites seek to demarcate, privilege, or compel a particular and distinctive identity for all citizens and (2) the confrontation of both elites and non-elites with the "interconnectedness of cultures brought about by global flows of images, objects, and people" (1991, 235–36). That these two projects may, as is readily apparent, work against each other is of obvious concern to the practitioners of nation-building worldwide. "That is, does the global diffusion of cultural forms threaten or enhance the means that enable the imagination of the nation as a bounded, sovereign, and essentially distinctive community?" (Foster 1991, 249). Among the internationally available forms by which both distinctiveness and membership in the "family of nations" can be simultaneously signaled, Foster mentions folk festivals, theme parks, worlds' fairs, sports competitions, and beauty contests (Ibid. 1991, 249).

But what happens when the *form* of the beauty contest is assimilated on the local level, as in Liberia, without obvious nationalist or internationalist agendas to drive it? One possibility is that homogenized Western standards of beauty will be ignored or displaced in favor of local aesthetics. Such contests may even become points of resistance against the nationalist project and its disembodied, decontextualized aesthetic while celebrating the interwoven relationships of small scale communities (see Lavenda 1988). In another scenario, the female participants may be reduced even further to anonymous ciphers while the real competition goes on between local factions, classes, or ethnic groups and their sponsors or enemies on the national level. In such a situation, one must ask the question: Why retain the *form* of the beauty pageant at all? What is it about the privileging of a particular kind of female physical appearance that serves as such a highly charged point of articulation between local and national discourses?

In the following analysis of a series of events from Liberia in the 1980s, I will argue that beauty contests have come to be linked inextricably with notions of progress and "development." Beauty contests operate internationally and cross-culturally within a discourse of evolutionary change that includes a hierarchical understanding of the relationship between center and periphery. This implicit evolutionary model assumes that economic and infrastructural alterations in the countryside will inevitably result in lifestyle changes bringing rural populations into contact with national and global cultural practices. For a small locality, far from the national capital, the act of sponsoring beauty pageants signals the acceptance of a number of "foreign" but recognizably "developed," "advanced," or "modern" ideas, including putting women on public display, which may contradict local sentiments. It is an enactment of the aspirations of local elites, usually men, and may therefore provide a site of contest for differing notions of nationalism and national identity. Displacing these highly charged contests onto something which is both, as Lavenda (1988) notes, "deadly serious" and, simultaneously, utterly trivial, means that none of the real competitors has to take a dangerous stand in opposition to state power. Using women's bodies as camouflage, local elites and their national allies can literally experiment with different combinations of class and ethnic blocks, exposing lines of cleavage in the community and deliberately pitting them against each other. But in the end, the winners and losers are only powerless young women, obviously no threat to anyone.

Since Liberian queen rallies are not defined as "political" events (and continued throughout the early 1980s ban on "political activities" issued by the military government), they usually allow any semi-organized collectivity to enter and compete on an equal basis. In the contrast between successive years, discussed below, we see the implications of limiting participation to groups representing only one kind of social identity, specifically, ethnicity. It is here that some of the earliest warning signs of the coming Liberian tragedy are to be found.

Case Studies: Harper City, 1982 and 1983

The following analysis will consider two queen rallies from consecutive years, 1982 and 1983, which took place in the Maryland County capital of

Harper in southeastern Liberia. Both rallies were held as part of the celebration of former President William V.S. Tubman's birthday, a national
holiday. The southeastern counties of Liberia are the poorest and least in-
tegrated into the national economy of all Liberia's regions. Although only
a few hundred miles from Monrovia, lack of all-weather roads makes the
overland trip between the national capital and Harper a grueling two days.
With an indigenous population speaking languages of the Kwa family, the
southeast is distinguished from the more stratified and ethnographically
better known Mande-speaking areas of the north and west by the absence
of universal secret initiatory societies and the relatively recent transition
to agriculture from forest hunting and gathering (d'Azevedo 1962).

Maryland County and the city of Harper were products of the same
contradictory nineteenth-century forces which gave rise to Liberia itself.
In the United States, moral opposition to slavery combined with an in-
ability to imagine a multi-racial society in which ex-slaves could live as
equals gave rise to the colonization movement, which sought to "return"
free African-Americans to their "homeland." The settlement at Harper
originated as an act of the Maryland state legislature in 1832 and reflected Maryland's position as a border state with the largest population of
"free people of color" in the country (Martin 1968, 55). Arriving in 1833,
a small group of immigrants settled at Cape Palmas, a strategic point on
the West African trade routes. At various times they were both in conflict
and alliance with the indigenous Glebo already occupying the Cape and
with surrounding peoples to the interior and along the coast. The settlement had a brief existence as an independent state, Maryland in Liberia,
between 1854 and 1857, when it was incorporated into the Republic of
Liberia as Maryland County (Martin 1968, 192–201).

The city of Harper, like the other Liberian coastal towns which began
as settler enclaves, became over time a multi-ethnic service center for the
surrounding county. The dominant economic and political class consisted
of descendants of the American settlers and a few highly educated professionals of indigenous Glebo origin who were recognized as "civilized" (see
Moran 1990). Most import-export trade and local retailing was controlled
by a few hundred Lebanese citizens, some of whom had lived in Harper
for most of their lives. Barred from citizenship by the Liberian constitution (which limits naturalization to those of at least one-eighth African descent), they could play no official political role but held considerable economic power. The majority of Harper's population was drawn from the
southeastern Liberian ethnic groups, with a small number of Muslim
traders from the north, and another group of resident aliens, the Fanti
people of Ghana, who specialized in off-shore fishing. The population in
1982-83 was estimated at between ten and twelve thousand people, not including the surrounding Glebo towns and villages (Moran 1990, 74).

W.V.S. Tubman, the national hero whose birthday was being cele-brated, was born in Harper and was the first non-Monrovian to become President of the Republic of Liberia. The descendant of freed slaves from Georgia, Tubman ruled Liberia from 1944 until his death in office in 1971 as President and head of the single political party, the True Whig Party. His hometown benefited from his generosity, receiving a great deal of in-frastructure and impressive public buildings. Much of this was eroded under the administration of his successor, William Tolbert, when power was transferred back into the hands of the Monrovia-based settler fami-lies. Since Tubman had presided over a period of unprecedented growth in the Liberian economy and was associated with popular reforms such as the enfranchisement of the indigenous population, his birthday, November 29, continued to be celebrated as a national holiday after his death. The military coup of 1980, while ostensibly directed against the en-trenched power of the True Whig Party, never challenged the mystique and affection surrounding Tubman's memory. Although, since the coup, political authority in Harper and elsewhere had been transferred to young army officers of local indigenous origin, Tubman's birthday remained a national holiday and was celebrated in Harper with an especially elaborate three-day program of events.

In 1982, still in the first months of fieldwork with the Glebo people of the indigenous towns surrounding Harper, I first heard the upcoming "Birthday Queen Rally" being discussed by the city market women. The "chief" of the market women, herself an important city official and mem-ber of the military mayor's advisory board, was exhorting the other mar-keteers to "support our queen." Another market seller, a member of one of the Islamic ethnic groups who are resident aliens in the southeast, told me that she was "looking for a little girl" to be a queen and trying to raise money among her compatriots "for the clothes." From these conversa-tions, I came to understand that a queen rally was an annual part of "the Birthday" celebrations and that it required a great deal of preparation. It was also clear that women, while they may be almost invisible at the actu-al public event, were important organizers and actors in the behind-the-scenes management of major queen rallies.

The rally was held in the evening at Harper City Hall, an elaborate product of the Tubman era. My estimate of the size of the crowd was something over seven hundred people, packed into a large ballroom on the second floor. A local brass band played at the rear of the room and a "cultural troupe" performed an idealized version of local indigenous dances. A Master of Ceremonies introduced the three queens who had been formally entered in the contest: a very young girl (perhaps twelve years old) representing the Lebanese business community, a young woman in a blue evening gown representing Harper City, and a queen for

"Marylanders Outside of Maryland." This woman, a member of a local Glebo family who was now stationed with the national police in a distant, northwestern county of Liberia, was herself a "Marylander outside of Maryland" who had come to visit her family for the holiday. Her support came from a group of government officials, including a few Cabinet Ministers, who were originally from the Harper area and had also come "home" to celebrate. They included the Minister of Youth and Sports, the Minister of Rural Development, both members of local indigenous groups, as well as military officers, university students, and others who had "come for the Birthday." The Minister of Justice, a member of the illustrious Tubman family, was also in attendance. It is important to note that the "Marylanders Outside of Maryland" did not constitute a permanent organized group, but had formed from the random "homecomers" specifically for the purposes of the queen rally.

The Master of Ceremonies called on three other non-local resident constituencies, the Fullah and Mandingo (both Islamic groups who are traders) and the Fanti to put forth queens. Finding no organized response, the M.C. simply asked for volunteers. Three women representing these "stranger" groups were prevailed upon to enter the contest. The audience was repeatedly reminded that they were chosen at the last moment and so had not come "prepared to sit" (that is, elaborately dressed). An additional queen was entered by a soccer team made up of more expatriate Marylanders, mostly university students living in Monrovia. This brought the number of queens in the rally to seven, representing the Lebanese, Harper City, the Marylanders Outside of Maryland, the Fullah, the Mandingo, the Fanti, and the soccer team. The chief of the market women arranged bolts of beautiful and expensive cloth, symbolizing wealth and royalty, over the backs of the chairs on which the queens were seated and on the floor in front of the table. The M.C. announced that there would be three fifteen-minute "rounds" during which contributions to the bowls in front of each queen could be made. The band struck up, and the rally began.

The contributors who approached the queens in the first round were primarily the important visitors from Monrovia, local officials, and business people, including the Lebanese shopowners and prominent market women. The hundreds of people crowding the back of the hall looked on with interest, but did not offer cash. At the end of the first round, proceeds were counted and the Lebanese queen was ahead with over $100, followed by the expatriate Marylanders and the Harper city queen. The partisans of each queen were exhorted to "bring money" for the second round. The band played as contributors literally danced across the platform before the queens. As the competition heightened, the contributors became exclusively men.

In the second round, the expatriate Maryland contingent made a stronger showing. With support from the three cabinet ministers, the policewoman moved into first place, passing the Lebanese queen. The Harper City queen lagged far behind, in spite of backing from local Harper officials, the County Superintendent, and the market women. The third and final round was shaping up as a battle between the local Lebanese business community and the national government officials from Monrovia.

Indeed, during the last round, both the crowd and the participants seemed gripped by a frenzy of excitement. Young men of the Lebanese community pulled packets of bills from their pockets, waved them dramatically in the air, and slammed them on the table before their queen. The Monrovia contingent followed suit. Since United States currency is used in Liberia and there are few large denominations in circulation, substantial contributions were made in thick wads of one, five, and ten dollar bills. The sheer abundance of currency on the table seemed to whip up the crowd as they stamped and cheered with each new contribution. The Maryland County Superintendent made a valiant effort to generate support for the Harper queen, but attention was riveted elsewhere.

The Minister of Youth and Sports announced that the expatriate Marylanders intended to "carry the queen" and challenged the crowd by offering to double any amount given to the Harper queen in the next ten minutes. He was wildly cheered, but no one took him up on his offer. The last round ended and the M.C. and the queens began counting the money. The room was tense as people speculated about who had won.

The Minister of Youth and Sports was to announce the winner, but first he delivered a lecture, criticizing the local people for not participating, just sitting back and letting the "Monrovia people" do everything for them. Tubman was dead, he reminded them, and they couldn't look to him for help anymore. They should take the Lebanese community, the Minister continued, as an example; they were, after all, "strangers," yet they had done their part for the "development" of Maryland County. With that, he announced that the expatriate Marylanders had won, beating the Lebanese by just ten dollars (which no one, especially the Lebanese, really believed). The total amount raised was $2,910; the expatriate Maryland queen bringing in $1,089, The Lebanese queen $1,079, the Harper queen $400, and the soccer team queen, the Fanti, Fullah, and Mandingo queens garnering $100 or less apiece.

The winning queen was crowned with a gold paper crown. She commented that she would take the crown back with her to Nimba County and tell all the Marylanders there what had happened. She added that she hoped that next year the crown would stay in Maryland. The County Superintendent reminded the visiting ministers that the lack of participation was not due to "deficiencies in spirit, but in means." In his travels around the country, he had noted that recent declines in the national economy seemed to have hit the southeast more severely than anywhere else and he emphasized the necessity of help from Monrovia. He then collected the evenings proceeds, announced that it would be put to use on some as yet undisclosed development project, and the queen rally was over. Note that simply by invoking the theme of "development," the Superintendent was able to both link the event that had just transpired to the nationalist project *and* avoid specifying the use to which the money would be put.

Exactly one year later, many of the same participants were gathered in the same hall for the 1983 Tubman Birthday Queen Rally. There were, however, notable exceptions and significant changes from the previous year. The Lebanese community, convinced that they had been the victims of a deliberate miscount, declined to put forward a queen. The queen rally was now in combination with a fashion show, sponsored by the "Women of Harper." Glebo informants referred to these women as "the married women in town," meaning "respectable," "civilized," middle class, and wealthy women, primarily of settler background, although the "barely civilized" young wife of the Superintendent was prominently listed. This year, an admission fee was charged at the door, perhaps to discourage the large crowd of non-participants from the year before.

There had been much anticipation that Samuel K. Doe, the military Head of State, would appear at the queen rally; he was in Harper for the holiday and had participated in a development rally just that morning, in which he had personally pledged $12,000. Apparently, one rally a day was enough for the Head of State, but the Deputy Vice Head of State, the Speaker for the military government, and several other military and civilian cabinet members were in attendance. The most significant change was in the constituencies represented by the queens. They were now identified with officially recognized Liberian "tribes"—Kru, Grebo,[1] Bassa, Krahn (the group to which the Head of State belonged), Fanti, and a "Muslim queen" for the Fullah and Mandingo combined. The Master of Ceremonies explained that the queens represented "some of the tribes in Liberia and two from outside," meaning the Fanti and the "Muslims." The attire of the queens ranged from evening gowns and bouffant wigs to a modified version of the white paint and minimal clothing of a Sande bush school initiate. The latter was apparently an effort to incorporate a "tribal" understanding of feminine beauty, but was strangely misplaced since the Sande secret society does not exist in the southeast.

After the first round, in which all the queens averaged about sixty dollars, the Fanti queen was leading. In between rounds, the fashion show, with clothing modeled by prominent Harper women, drew more attention than the queens. In fact, it was the fashion show which most relentlessly followed the Western model of a beauty contest, since the women modeled a number of revealing outfits, including shorts and bathing suits, which were considered quite daring in a provincial community like Harper. In the second round there was a pronounced lack of enthusiasm, demonstrated by the fact the queens only averaged about ten or eleven dollars each from the round. A local official appealed to the crowd, pleading that the Grebo queen (representing the local population) *must* "carry the crown"; they must not lose to "foreigners." Those in the crowd murmured that if they had not been charged admission at the door, there would be more for the queens.

The third round was a bit more spirited and larger amounts of cash began to appear on the table. It was clear that many had been "holding back" for the last round. In the end, the Grebo queen won the round but not the rally; the Fanti "carried the queen" with a little over $300. After the queen was crowned, one of the cabinet ministers made a speech warning, ironically, against "tribalism and sectionalism." The event ended with the Fanti literally carrying their queen in triumph through the streets of Harper for most of the night. I learned later that they had coordinated their efforts, pooling money from many small contributions and holding it back until the last round in a concerted effort to win.

Analysis and Conclusions

What accounts for the differences between these two consecutive queen rallies? In neither case was the sponsoring locality successful in winning the competition, but is winning, after all, the objective of holding a queen rally? The goal of the rally, from the perspective of the organizers, is to raise money; money that is destined to link the locality to the national project of "development." In the 1982 rally, the three primary competing groups represented essentially *class interests*. The expatriate Marylanders were the new national elite; people with roots and loyalties in the rural, indigenous sector, but who had only recently gained access to all the resources of the state. The local elite, those who lined up in support of the Harper queen, had fewer resources to command. Their salaries, positions, and lifestyle, as well as their ability to carry out their jobs were dependent upon a continuing flow of cash and services from Monrovia. Even the market women, while less directly dependent on government salaries, must respond to the constraints of the local economy. If the contributions made by visiting national elites, both in such structured events as rallies and on a more informal basis in the form of gifts, remittances to local kin, and purchases made on trips "home" are considered part of the local economy, it was in the interest of local elites at the 1982 rally to promote competition between the expatriates and the Lebanese, even at the expense of local pride. The Lebanese were in a vulnerable position as resident aliens, who could not transform their considerable economic power into overt political clout. Once the limit to competitive giving had been reached and someone had to win, local elites had more to lose by offending the Monrovia officials than the Lebanese business community. The Lebanese perception that they had been cheated was probably correct.

During the intervening year between November of 1982 and 1983, the Liberian economy continued to slide downward. Harper City infrastructure deteriorated even further, with electrical power only a distant memory and the provision of purified water at public taps sporadic at best. Popular support for the military government, still relatively high in 1982, was on the wane a year later. An attempted coup, just a few weeks before the Birthday celebration, had shaken the country and produced some amazement that the Head of State would risk leaving the capital for a trip to Maryland County. To ensure his security, large numbers of soldiers and military equipment had accompanied him to Harper, giving the town the appearance of a siege. Unnerved by the coup attempt, the soldiers were edgy and continually harassed the local population, destroying the holiday mood for everyone.

Another factor was the "feminization" of the queen rally from 1982 to 1983. In 1982, although there were other rallies associated with particular projects held during the Tubman Birthday holiday, the City Hall queen rally was the major fund-raising event for local development. Although the women represented various constituencies, the 1982 rally was clearly and obviously the primary arena for male prestige competition (excluding the organized sports) of the holiday events. In 1983, in connection with the Head of State's visit, a major development rally was held during the day (possibly for security reasons, to avoid traveling after dark) that combined speeches by local leaders and an address by Doe. Individual pledges were announced by local business leaders and officials and Marylanders in government and the military in amounts ranging from ten dollars to $2,000. With the Head of State's personal pledge of $12,000, something over $30,000, at least in pledges, had been raised for Maryland development that morning, with ample opportunity for all to demonstrate their wealth and generosity. There was not much cash or inclination for a second rally that night.

In addition, the fashion show and sponsoring group organizing the 1983 queen rally stamped it as a "woman's event." There were many more women in attendance than had been at the morning development rally and, having less access to cash than men, they had less to give. The class identity of the women organizers had also changed from 1982 to 1983. The market women had been specifically recruited by the military mayor of Harper in 1982; in 1983 it was "civilized" women who were asked to take charge of the event. While civilized women, as the consorts of powerful men, have considerably higher status than the "native" market women, they also, ironically, have less right to allocate cash, even in relatively wealthy households (see Moran 1990). While the role of the market women had been tacitly acknowledged in 1982, their relative invisibility in the actual performance marked the queen rally as a prestigious "civic" event. In contrast, the explicit visibility of women as organizers and sponsors (and as fashion models) in the 1983 queen rally emphasized its lack of prestige in the overall Birthday celebration.

The organization of the queens by ethnic group was probably designed to extract a large sum from the Head of State in support of "his" Krahn queen. Without his presence, there was not enough ethnic competition to generate anything like the excitement of the previous year. The restriction on competing groups to represent themselves only as "tribes" eliminated the possibility of last minute entries, like the soccer team queen, which had lent excitement the year before. This strategy also enforced a homogenized, inclusive ethnicity which had little relevance to the actual soci-political realities of southeastern Liberia, as in the conflation of ethnic groups to produce a "Muslim queen" and the loading together of many competing local identities onto the queen representing the "Grebo" (see McEvoy 1977 on southeastern "ethnic realities"). The cabinet members who were present seemed much less willing to identify themselves with these so-called ethnic groups than they had along class lines the year before. The only appeal which seemed to move the crowd was a defensive one against "foreigners" (the Fanti). In the end, no one seemed very upset when the Fanti "carried the queen."

In practical terms, the admission fee charged for the 1983 queen rally may have made up for the low donations collected during the rally itself. I do not wish to speculate about what actually happened to the proceeds from rallies like these; certainly, Maryland County and Harper city infrastructure seemed to see little of it. It is important to view such events as not just reflective of local politics, however, but as structured in crucial ways by national events and the relationships national leaders have with those still in their communities of origin. Deeply held Liberian values concerning loyalty to a patrilineally defined "home," the generosity expected of the wealthy, and the ties of personal obligation were all enacted in the queen rallies and constrained individual choices about giving and not giving. Furthermore, the 1982 rally came at a time when new elites of indigenous background, both national and local, could still see themselves as having finally come into their own after generations of subordination to the settler minority. Education, class position, and connections to the new leadership really did seem to be what mattered most in the newly opened field of opportunities created by the 1980 coup.

More than the settler group which preceded them, the new inheritors of state power were directly confronted with the paradox delineated by Foster; how to be "modern," nationalistic, and even developed while still celebrating and defending the local ties and aspirations which had provided the moral authority for the coup? How to choose, out of that vast, circulating repertoire of "global" cultural practices those idioms and performances which could best "enable the imagination of the nation as a bounded, sovereign, and essentially distinctive community?" (Foster 1991, 249).

Under settler hegemony, simply being of "tribal" origin was the important distinguishing factor; membership in a particular group was not considered important in terms of socio-economic mobility. Fearful of ambitious young soldiers like himself, Samuel Doe began the systematic purge of all but members of his own ethnic group from the ranks of the elite military forces and strategic government posts. While the original post-coup cabinet had been truly multiethnic, even including prominent settlers like Justice Minister Tubman, by 1983 a Krahn power block was emerging which owed its existence and its allegiance to Doe alone. Only two years later, in 1985, Doe would retaliate against the already dead leader of an unsuccessful coup by massacring about four-hundred random members of his ethno-linguistic group. This brutality prompted the formation of ethnically defined resistance groups, with no political ideology beyond opposition to Doe and led by men whose sole ambition was to gain control of the apparatus of the state. The Western media, when they have bothered to report on it at all, have reduced this complex situation to "ancient tribal hatreds," suddenly and irrationally unleashed (see Moran 1995). At the present writing and tens of thousands of deaths later, Liberia remains mired in chaos, with the warlords of at least five major armed factions unable to agree on the conditions for a cease-fire, let alone a power-sharing arrangement which would allow for eventual elections and the return to civilian rule.

With the benefit of hindsight, it is tempting to view the switch from class to "tribal" identification for the Harper queens as an ominous portent of what was to come. While the local officials who organized the rallies may have been merely trying to extract the largest possible donations, as I have suggested, they were also certainly aware of the prevailing trends in Monrovia. Although the national officials delivered their clichéd warnings about "tribalism," they were themselves complicit, along with the local elites, in the manufacture of ethnicity as an overriding category of identification. The queen rallies may thus be read as a public discourse about political and economic power, national ideology, and personal identity as these are negotiated between the central government and the locality, often by individuals with ties in both places. In the local context, such divisions could be highlighted in a setting that was safely defined as apolitical, slightly frivolous, and "women's business." In this sense, the queen rallies provided a forum for expression and competition that was simply unavailable elsewhere. Translated into national policy, however, these newly fabricated "tribal hatreds" could not be contained by mapping them onto the bodies of young women. In such a contest, beauty was the last thing on anyone's mind.

Notes

This essay is based on fifteen months of fieldwork in southeastern Liberia in 1982-83, supported by a National Science Foundation Graduate Fellowship and a Hannum-Warner Alumnae Travel Grant from Mount Holyoke College. I am grateful to Colleen Ballerino Cohen, Richard Wilk, and Beverly Stoeltje for their helpful editorial comments and for the comments of several anonymous reviewers.

1. It is conventional among scholars of Liberia to use "Glebo" to refer to the people of the two coastal confederacies (*dakwe*) occupying the coast from Fishtown Point to the Cavalla River, including Cape Palmas. "Grebo" is used to refer to the language group which includes the Glebo and a large number of other individually named coastal and interior *dakwe*. As used by the national government, "Grebo" (like "Kru" and "Krahn") has come to be used as a "tribal" designation, but it implies a homogeneity and political solidarity that has no historical basis.

10

Miss Tibet, or Tibet Misrepresented?
The Trope of Woman-as-Nation in the Struggle
for Tibet

Carole McGranahan

The Tibetan nation debuted on stage December 1991 at the Lhasa
Holiday Inn as twenty-five women in "traditional" Tibetan costume competed for the title of "Miss Tibet." The first and only pageant to take
place thus far in Chinese-ruled Tibet, the "Miss Tibet" pageant introduces the trope of woman-as-nation to Tibet. Almost all the expected features of any Western pageant were present, yet the Chinese state via the
Communist Party left its distinctive trademark on the contest, resulting in
a pageant that resembled a stereotypical Chinese "minority nationality"
cultural show. Participation also diverged from the expected: workplaces
were ordered by the Chinese Communist Party (CCP) to enter their most
beautiful employees as contestants in the six and a half hour contest.
Orchestrated by Western expatriates, judged by Western and Chinese
(male) officials, and participated in by Tibetan (and, it was rumored,
Chinese) women, what was the event titled the "Miss Tibet" pageant? For
whom is Tibet represented as woman?

Beauty pageants can be read as attempts to circumscribe women's
worlds within that of the nation. The idea that women both physically and
culturally reproduce members of the nation, and are as well foci and symbols of ethnic and national identity is offered by Yuval-Davis and Anthias
(1989). However, an analysis of the gendering of nations, of the positioning of women in relation to the state, and of complexities of discursive
representations of women does not necessarily arrive at a universal locale
from which to theorize about women and the nation. We must question
the ease with which women have been made available as signs of the nation, and instead interrogate both discourses of gender, and discourses
that become gendered. Ortner (1990) writes of the need to examine discourses that both challenge and parallel dominant tropes of gender. In so
doing, essentialist tendencies linking women and the nation break down,
revealing the vagaries of specific constructs and contexts, and illuminat-

ing the very lack of clarity in which the discourses of gender and nation have been deployed as aligned. A growing body of interdisciplinary (and often feminist) literature that attempts to theorize the discursive relations between women and nation often begins with a link to nationalist projects.[1] Yet, it is important to differentiate between women's participation in nationalist projects and the representation of the nation as female. If nation-as-woman is presented as a dominant trope in beauty pageants, we must question who offers that formulation, who partakes of it, and how other discourses appear in response. Unrecorded meanings ascribed to the pageant by the contestants may be located within, outside, or parallel to Chinese- and Western-intended readings of the Miss Tibet pageant. As dominant Chinese discourse and infrastructure penetrate the political border of Tibet, the power of the Chinese state, while hegemonic in its formulation, fails to be exclusive or exclusively totalizing.

Inasmuch as the beauty pageant is about women and the relation of women to nation, it is also about relations between states and nations. In the Miss Tibet pageant, women are used as both an instrument in the debate over the Tibetan nation, and as representatives of the debate. Politics in Tibet strays far from the boundaries of nationalism and nationalist discourse. Debates over Tibet center on questions of history, of cultural and political identity, and of the power to represent and the condition of being represented. Thus the task of representing Tibet does not begin or end with "Miss Tibet." Instead it is a continuous process tied into plural notions of history, culture, and political agenda. The identity that China has crafted for Tibet rests in selected readings of history and culture. Chinese views seek to legitimate Chinese rule in Tibet to both international governments and monitoring agencies, and also to Tibetans and Chinese alike. As portrayed by the Lhasa Holiday Inn, Tibetan culture, and current tensions surrounding Chinese-Tibetan relations, are marketable commodities open to appropriation and consumption. What are the motives behind these definitions? What is their salience?

In this paper I will explore how the Miss Tibet pageant is a microcosm of larger issues at play in Chinese-ruled Tibet, and examine how women have come to stand for nation within the Miss Tibet pageant. The groups involved—Westerners,[2] Chinese, and Tibetans—occupy varied positions in complex political, social, and economic hierarchies in Tibet. Acting both with and for these groups are the pageant contestants: Miss Tibet's carefully scripted, yet selectively read, role in the mapping of the Tibetan and Chinese nations. My analysis will show the connections between the refraction of nation in representations of Tibetan women, and the interests of Chinese Communist Party officials and Lhasa Holiday Inn staff in sponsoring a beauty pageant in Tibet. Within the "Miss Tibet" pageant, an imagined and idealized Tibetan woman represents Tibet to foreigners, to the Chinese state, and to other Tibetans. How has the beauty pageant brought together Western and Chinese factions in their struggle to define Tibet? As the Chinese and the Westerners ostensibly collude in promoting this particularly gendered representation of nation, Tibetans appear to stand outside the contest as key players in a watchful position. Tibetan nationalism does not validate the cultural trope of woman-as-nation. How, and why then, have women become implicated in this struggle for nation?

STAGING THE PAGEANT: PLACE, POLITICS, PROBLEMS
"In the End, Beauty Triumphed Over Bureaucracy"

The Lhasa Holiday Inn (LHI), home of the Hard Yak Cafe, is one of a number of strangely liminal tourist hotels that hover on the outskirts of cities in China.[3] Middle- and upper-income foreign tourists tend to stay at the Holiday Inn, which is the only international-class hotel in Tibet. It was here that the Miss Tibet beauty pageant was held in December 1991.

The pageant was the kick-off event for the Tibet Autonomous Region's "1992 Golden Year of Tourism," celebrating the fortieth anniversary of China's "Peaceful Liberation of Tibet."[4] The idea for the pageant originated with Western staff at the Holiday Inn who presented it to the TAR branch of the Communist Party for approval. Initial plans were for the beauty contest to be a large-scale media affair. More than four hundred foreign film and television crews requested to participate. As the question of both political problems and potential reprimands from Beijing arose, local government enthusiasm began to wane. Foreign journalists renowned for their tendency to critique China's presence and policies in Tibet were the first to be eliminated. The Party's reshaping of the pageant was under way.

Under the orchestration of the CCP, the pageant resembled a specific genre of "minority" cultural production. Such productions focus on costume, song, and dance of China's "minorities" and are performed for both domestic and foreign tourists.[5] Pageant participants were instructed to model local fashions, and Tibetan cultural performers (as well as two yaks and a pony) joined the contestants on stage. Pageant promotional buttons ("I Love Miss Tibet") and posters were vetoed immediately. Posters were only allowed to be hung within the hotel itself. Even the name of the pageant was not immune to official scrutiny. Objections to the title "Miss Tibet" were raised, and the more innocuous "Miss Fashion Parade Evaluation" was suggested by the Chinese. However, the Westerners prevailed in this matter, and the pageant winner was crowned "Miss Tibet."

The CCP sent directives to local work units requiring participation of each unit's most beautiful women. Twenty-five women participated, a majority of whom were professional actresses, dancers, or singers. Among foreign judges and spectators, unconfirmed rumors circulated that Chinese women as well as Tibetans were participating. Pageant contestants were judged on general impressions, artistic qualities, poise, appearance, and interviewing skills. No interviews actually took place, however, and impromptu questions went unanswered. For each of the ten foreign judges, the CCP dictated that there would be two Chinese judges. As a result, there were five more judges than there were contestants. In addition to the judges, over one hundred spectators, mainly journalists from Hong Kong, flew into Lhasa to view what one journalist called the Miss Tibet "Forbidden Tour" (Woolrich 1992). Finally, the intended grand prize of a trip to Hong Kong (and thus, out of China) was vetoed by the CCP. Instead, a fur coat was awarded as first prize. The winner—a married Tibetan woman, a mother, and member of a Tibetan dance troupe—was escorted from the event in the sidecar of a police motorcycle. The front of her cart read "Holiday Inn, Lhasa—Miss Tibet."

The three groups competing to define Tibet do so from revolving positions of power, as the Miss Tibet pageant demonstrated. Packaged to fit specific (yet shifting) needs, Tibetan identity is simultaneously constructed in different ways by LHI staff and CCP officials. Collusion occurs in the presentation of the pageant as a tourist spectacle, yet breaks down in meanings ascribed to the pageant by the two groups. The staff at the LHI seek to frame Tibet in Western-defined humanitarian terms sensationalized by local political tensions; in opposition, CCP officials seek to circumscribe Tibet within Chinese terms of state and nation through historical and political rhetoric. Thus, as crafted by Western LHI staff to promote the authenticity of cultural experience available by staying at the LHI, and by the CCP as an occasion to legitimate continuing Chinese rule in Tibet, the pageant does not necessarily correspond to Tibetan constructs of cultural and political identity. Assumed by both the LHI and the CCP is an oppositional Tibetan stance: an independent Tibet that is remembered and recast by the Holiday Inn, and is patrolled and policed by the Chinese state.

Tibet vs. China: Constructs of Identity and History

In 1949, Chinese troops marched into eastern and northern Tibet, and by 1950 they had effectively gained control over the country. At this time, Tibet was an independent state. In 1951, the 17-Point Agreement was signed incorporating Tibet into the People's Republic of China. According to anthropologist Melvyn Goldstein,

> In the next few months, several thousand troops of the People's Liberation Army arrived in Lhasa; although the old system continued to exist in some form for another eight years, October

> 1951 marks the end of the de facto independent Lamaist state.
> (Goldstein 1989, 813)

His Holiness the Dalai Lama, the spiritual and temporal leader of Tibet, fled a suspected Chinese kidnap attempt on March 10, 1959. Many members of the Tibetan government, and thousands of other Tibetans from all areas of Tibet, joined him in escape to exile in India. They remain there and in countries around the world today. According to Shakya (1993), the fall of Lhasa to the Chinese was a pivotal point in the minds of the Tibetan people. Despite regional differences among Tibetans, Lhasa was the symbol of Tibet—"the center of their universe" (Shakya 1993, 10). With the Chinese invasion, life in Lhasa was disrupted as Tibetan scripts of history, identity, and nation were rewritten in Chinese characters.

Today, Lhasa is the capital of the Chinese-designated Tibet Autonomous Region (TAR). The population of Lhasa is over one-half Chinese.[6] Recent changes are reflected in the city's landscape. Architecturally, many of Lhasa's new buildings resemble those of a Chinese city, and in the fall of 1993, against the advice of UNESCO, a series of historic Tibetan houses in the Barkhor, the Tibetan quarter of Lhasa, were demolished under government order. Economically, opportunities abound for Han Chinese who come as government cadres and also as small business owners or laborers. Hui and Uighur entrepreneurs, among others, have also found their way to Lhasa's bazaars and market areas. However, amidst the hubbub of destruction and reconstruction Lhasa remains the center of the Tibetan Buddhist world, and a sacred space for Tibetans inside, and outside, the boundaries of Tibet.

With the consolidation of the People's Republic of China (PRC) in 1949, China viewed itself as a Han Chinese nation inclusive of other peoples as "minority nationalities" (see D. Norbu 1991). Together, the Han and these others form the Motherland, the People's Republic of China. The question of a Chinese national identity is necessarily tied to the state. It has been suggested that Sun Yat-Sen's creation of the "imagined" Han nationality, and subsequently the idea of China as comprised of the Han and four other nationalities (the Hui, Manchu, Mongolians, and Tibetans) "led to the invention and the legitimization of the Self" (Gladney 1991, 87).[7] Currently, some fifty-five non-Han Chinese groups—comprising eight percent of the PRC population, yet inhabiting over 60 percent of the PRC's total land mass—are recognized by the Chinese government as "minority nationalities" (Dreyer 1993, 358-9).[8] This number includes peoples who have been all but assimilated into Chinese culture, as well as groups who remain distinct from the Chinese. Current Chinese data reports approximately 4.6 million Tibetans within the PRC (Dreyer 1993, 363). Of this number, 2.08 million reside outside of the Chinese-designated Tibet Autonomous Region; an additional 100,000 live as refugees outside of

Tibet.

In Lhasa, and throughout Tibet, practices and beliefs of Tibetans are governed, legislated, and defined on Chinese terms through the programs of the Chinese Communist Party. Chinese state literature on Tibet typically emphasizes the national "unity" of the PRC.

> Ever since the Tibetans have overthrown once and for all invasions from imperialist powers, and within this great family of the motherland, where equal rights for nationalities are enjoyed, they have started marching forward along the promising path of unity. ("Exhibition of Reconstruction Achievements," 1991)

In Tibet, actions directed against Chinese rule are classified by the Chinese government as "splittist activities," including protests, the distributing of pamphlets, the forming of pro-independence organizations, possession of literature from the Tibetan Government in Exile, or any other activities perceived by the state as potentially "splittist." Such activities are portrayed by China as attempts to "divide the Motherland." Since the 1950s, a large number of Tibetans have been arrested, imprisoned, tortured, and killed for asserting their belief that China should free Tibet (See *Defying the Dragon* 1991). Mass protests rocked Lhasa from 1987 to 1989, and continue today, with recent unrest exploding in other Tibetan provinces as well. Today Tibetans continue to escape Tibet for a life in exile; those crossing the border into Nepal are on occasion forcefully repatriated by a Nepali government sympathetic to Chinese policies.

As a result of these tensions, the status of Tibet as a polity within China is wholly structured in political terms at the regional, prefectural, and county level. For example, the Tibet Autonomous Region's branch of the CCP, and not a local cultural organization, ordered contestants' participation in the Miss Tibet pageant. The limits of acceptable ethnic or cultural expression—such as that by the participants in the Miss Tibet pageant—are circumscribed by the state, and subsequently categorized as either harmonious or threatening. Under either pretense, the political overtones are clear—certain aspects of Tibetan (or "minority") culture are acceptable to the state in certain times and certain contexts, and the authority to decide when, what, and where rests with the state.[9] Within China, even the smallest organizations require the involvement of a CCP representative. The role of the party is not just to police behavior, but to circumscribe it within a very present notion of the state. According to Anagnost:

> The socialist realist text...projects utopian fiction onto the space of lived reality, and it does this not through the individuation of its characters, but through a different operation. It classifies characters into coded positions, representations that are moral exemplars, clusters of signs that must be made visible in order to cir-

culate throughout the social body and thereby produce the effects of power by making the party, in its turn, also supremely visible in a dazzling display of presence. (1994, 149-150)

Thus, the Chinese Communist Party, Chinese government structures, and organizations such as the Public Security Bureau and the People's Liberation Army order certain spheres of life within Tibet—dictating the limits of ethnic boundaries reconstructed as a single national boundary. In this way, Tibetan transgressions against Chinese rule in Tibet become not mere ethnic unrest, but violations of a shared identity located in a fictive history—that of members of the People's Republic of China.

In many ways the struggle over nation and identity in Tibet is a struggle over history. In terms of writing Tibet's history, the form and history of the state is contested. Tibetan histories emphasize Tibet's independence from China through the notion of separate states, and intersecting but separate histories (see T. Norbu and Turnbull 1968; Shakabpa 1967). Countering this are Chinese presentations of Tibetan history which consistently portray Tibet as a historical, inalienable part of China (see Wang and Suo 1984). In addition, Western political discourse currently reconfigures both Chinese and Tibetan concepts of history, nation, and state in line with specific liberal notions of how these categories are constituted. For example, political arenas such as the United Nations, diplomatic tables, and international legal bodies, demand an adaptation of history and politics to a specific Western framework.[10] On the relationship between history and national identity in China and India, Prasenjit Duara writes:

> [P]remodern political identifications do not necessarily or teleologically develop into the national identifications of modern times. A new vocabulary and a new political system—the world system of nation-states—select, adapt, reorganize, and even re-create these older identities…The real significance of the historical question lies in understanding how it is articulated within the contest over the meaning of the nation. (1993, 784)

In the struggle for Tibet, history, nation, identity, and politics necessarily intertwine. Different degrees of categorical inflection are manifest in varied representations of Tibet. As history and identity become entangled in the process of defining Tibet, it is important to note that they are neither separable nor singular entities.

THE DISPLAYED AND THE CONTESTED

Returning now to the pageant, foreign spectators and judges were supplied with letters from the Chinese government warning against activities "incompatible with the status of a tourist," i.e., the distribution of photos,

books, or videos that offer a version of Tibet different from state literature. The few foreign journalists who did manage to attend the pageant
were watched closely by the Public Security Bureau (PSB). An electricity
failure during the evening wear segment provided a photo opportunity for
the foreign media (the "hack pack") as both picture-takers and picture-
subjects.

> Up to this point, the hack pack had been reasonably well-behaved
> but en masse they now decided to get to work. Out came the cam-
> eras and enough flash power was emitted to light up the room
> again. The PSB had obviously been waiting for the moment it
> could catch the impostors red-handed, as they too whipped out
> powerful lenses and began taking pictures. The stand-off lasted
> about ten minutes with each side aiming its weaponry at the other,
> until one of the better-looking contestants appeared and the guns
> swung round and trained on her. (Woolrich 1992, 26)

The scene depicted here is not just that of the pageant, but a reading of the
political tension between China and Tibet, and subsequent Western and
Chinese claims to represent Tibet. As the pageant relies on the unstated
recognition of Tibetan resistance to Chinese rule in Tibet, it also inserts
Tibetan women into the male world of conflict. As such, they, and Tibetan
culture, are caught in the crossfire of Western and Chinese debates over
the Tibetan nation. Woolrich's weaponry metaphor is appropriate on two
levels: first, because Tibetan struggles against Chinese rule have been met
by armed resistance; and second, because the pageant contestants can be
read as silent signs of Tibetan nationalism, and thereby signify the potential for resistance. Control over this potential is exercised by both Chinese
and Western arms-bearing factions. Thus, as the "guns" turn to the
woman, she becomes not just a female on display but a figure in the drama
of constructing and contesting modern Tibet. I now turn to a discussion of
the "displayed and the contested"—first, the trope of woman as nation
within the beauty pageant; second, an exploration of Chinese and Western
contexts for the state/nation/woman debate in Tibet; and third, the place
of Tibet and Tibetan identity within the global realm.

The Beauty Pageant: Woman as Nation?

"Miss Tibet." Tibet as woman. Whose definition is this? Do nationalist
sentiments require an essentialized notion of female?[11] Or are women
merely an available vehicle for the banner of nation? Within the Miss
Tibet pageant, the trope of woman as nation is double: salient for Chinese
and Western interests, and not so for Tibetan interests. In addition, the
woman-nation-Tibet triad is specifically located within the current polit-

ical context that allows competing Chinese and Western factions to argue for—through the medium of the pageant—the inclusion of Tibet within their respective ideologies of state and nation.

While the pageant itself was contingent upon and informed by a nationalist Tibetan discourse in spirit, it did not require (nor allow) the participation of its representatives. Women's presence in the pageant follows the same dualistic logic found in the pageant structure. In the triad woman-nation-Tibet, the category of woman is empty insofar as it does not stem from identifiable Tibetan cultural or political traditions.[12] Tibetan formulations of national identity do not rely on an image of the nation that is gendered feminine.[13] In fact, Makley (1994, 22) argues that "the main repository of Tibetan culture/identity is *not* Woman, but male-dominated institutional Buddhism." And Klieger recognizes the Dalai Lama as the "biological and spiritual *father* of the Tibetan people" who embodies the patron/client dyad prevalent in notions of Tibetan identity (1992, 78, my emphasis). The pages of *Tibetan Review*, a journal published in India by exile Tibetans, reverberate with calls for the preservation of Tibetan culture and national identity through education: a project that is not gendered male or female in exile (see D. Norbu 1994; Phuntsog 1994; Shastri 1994). Yet, in regard to capitalist and communist promotions of Tibet, woman as bearer of nation is marketable to specific audiences and is therefore an externally valid category. In negotiating readings of the pageant, it is clear that while Tibetan Woman is the object upon which our gaze is focused, she is not the subject of the pageant. Instead, the Tibetan nation and the Tibetan state are the subjects under contention.[14] In struggling to define the Tibetan nation, how has a beauty pageant provided the stage for debate? Whose fantasy of nation does Miss Tibet fulfill?

In China, beauty pageants are one of the latest rages. As increasingly liberal economic policies open China's eastern provinces to the capitalist world, the number of beauty pageants skyrocketed to around forty-five during 1991 alone (Tefft 1993). In her article "Goodbye Mao Cap, Hello Tiara: Beauty Pageantry Sweeps China," Sheila Tefft focuses on the irony of beauty pageants in a country led by philosophies ranging from Confucianism to Communism. Interestingly, a majority of the pageants are held under the auspices of the local Communist Party, as was the case in Tibet. Contests in eastern China crowned "Miss Air Hostess," "Miss Etiquette," and "Miss International Coconut Festival" signaling the apolitical nature of these contests, and a continuity with the CCP's desire to crown a woman "Miss Fashion Parade Evaluation" rather than "Miss Tibet." Within China, despite the devaluing of minority nationality cultures as evolutionarily primitive, there is a romantic fetishization of (specifically women's) minority costumes and customs. Ethnic dance troupes perform for official state visitors. Minority women are popularly thought of as beautiful (and sexually liberal);[15] their pictures grace the pages of *Beijing Review* with surprising frequency. In many ways, the person, the culture, the people, are reduced to a visual representation manifest in women.

The spheres of discourse that pageant contestants enter are varied, and often it is images of women, rather than the women themselves that are important. The gaze that constitutes women as representative of nation, or as any form of fantasy, is necessarily external, and in the case of the Miss Tibet pageant, male. The "trope of nation-as-woman" is located within a "particular image of women as chaste, beautiful, daughterly or maternal," whereby nation can be "gendered feminine...despite or rather *because* of the actual experiences of their female populations" (Parker et al. 1992, 6). Nationalist projects are also involved in the definition of women's subjectivity at certain levels—"The very language of nationalism singles out women as the symbolic repository of group identity" (Kandiyoti 1994, 382). Yet, within the Miss Tibet beauty pageant, women are a vehicle, not a repository, for national and cultural identity in that they carry but do not embody the nation. Additionally, nationalism in the Miss Tibet pageant is not singular: multiple nationalisms as well as multiple constructs of Tibetan nationalism are present. Constructed images of women within the pageant do not require a correspondence to women's realities for legitimation. Thus, a privileged image of woman-as-nation within the spectacle of the beauty pageant links women to the nation in hypothetical or ideological senses only. As nations are "gendered feminine," the multiple groups declaring this relation seek to promote specific agendas (e.g., Chinese political legitimacy), and do so within well-established frameworks (such as Western beauty pageants). In the Miss Tibet pageant, space was not provided for the female contestants to declare their own relation to nation—be it Tibet or China. Instead they remain the Defined. The trope of woman-as-nation is thereby constituted as empty, a colonized sign, on the Tibetan side of the struggle.

Tibet and Tibetan Women in China: Representations, "Minorities," and the State

Why not "Miss Tibet?" Chinese government resistance to the pageant title is not surprising, for allowing a territorially-defined title might suggest a legitimately sovereign territory. As local CCP officials debated the pageant title, perhaps they envisioned Miss Tibet winning the Miss China title and ultimately representing the PRC at the Miss Universe pageant, resulting in a political media fiasco in which Miss China is referred to as *"Miss Tibet."* The potential legitimation of territory that is present in the pageant title debates brings us to the center of recent events in Tibet—the struggle for power, legitimate rule, and the authority to represent a people and a country.

Tibetan women in Lhasa necessarily operate within a number of realms, including that of a normalized gender established for women in communist China.[16] Recently, numerous authors have argued against essentialized notions of Chinese women and Chinese feminism (see Chow 1991a, 1991b; Rofel 1993; Barlow 1994). In contrast they espouse a more nuanced and complex view of women within the modern Chinese state. Yet, their arguments lack a recognition of the experiences of "minority nationality" women in China, which are similarly circumscribed within the rhetoric of the state to which they have a different relationship than Han Chinese women. How might the stories of these doubly peripheralized women force us to ask new questions of both state and nation in China? In post-1949 China, women received a new place in society in line with then current politics of state and nation.

> [T]he revolution resituated Chinese women inside the state under a Maoist inscription. Women could only be represented as women through the state's Women's Federation....[T]he socialist state in China...colonized and produced feminism. "National woman" became the only viable feminist under Maoist politics. She was a revolutionary, a "backbone cadre," who has reached an elevated status through commitment to class politics and wholehearted support for state policies. (Barlow quoted in Rofel 1993, 45)

Women's voices are regulated through the state. As individual Tibetan women conduct their lives within Chinese dictates, they and groups that represent them, such as the Tibet Women's Federation, become to an incomplete extent a part of the Chinese national project. The PRC construction of a national identity both involving and relying on "minority nationalities" is evident in Chinese government attempts to write minority women, and minorities in general, into the Chinese state. The beauty pageant is a method by which minorities in the PRC are placed as public adornment to Han culture—anachronistic peoples to be brought into temporal and spatial alignment with the Chinese world. In the beauty pageant, Tibetan women provide a template for the legitimation of this PRC project.

PRC state ideology is influenced by a Marxist framework that places Tibet within evolutionary stages of "feudal serfdom/class-based primitive exploitation" at the time of the Chinese "liberation" of Tibet.[17] Through this reductionism, Chinese histories of Tibet are "emptying" in that Tibetan history is fractured and fragmented in the process.[18] Chinese writings also tend to highlight certain aspects or events at the expense of larger historical or ethnographic records. One recurring example is a fixation on Chinese Princess Wen Cheng, married in 641 A.D. to the Tibetan King Songtsen Gampo.[19] Rarely is it mentioned that Songtsen Gampo was also married to a Nepali princess and had a healthy number of Tibetan wives as well. TAR Tourism officials suggest that tourists travel Wen Cheng's route from Xian to Lhasa, and the princess is often featured in Chinese tourist literature about Tibet (see *Xinhua* February 6, 1994). Diamond (1988) has suggested that this Chinese historiographic feature is used by the Chinese state with regard to all "minority nationalities."[20] In essence, what we are presented with is the writing of a "simplex history," socialist style.[21]

While the focus on Princess Wen Cheng is Chinese-selected, the focus on Miss Tibet is not a unilateral Chinese project. The image of the beauty queen is available through Western cultural constructs, approved (and reconstructed) by CCP government officials, and is carried by the Tibetan women contestants. Potential for conflict within the pageant was sufficiently diminished through Chinese government action—the choosing of judges, of contestants, and of pageant format and advertising. The power of the state to construct nation extends to the specific agents—in this case, Miss Tibet—that the state employs. Thus, although women are not immune to the ills of "splittist activities," their carefully rehearsed roles in the Miss Tibet pageant are claimed by the state as representative of, rather than threatening to, the nation of Tibet within the PRC.

Transnational Capital and Culture at the Holiday Inn

The site of the pageant, the Lhasa Holiday Inn, is a privileged space in Tibet. At issue with regard to the pageant is the LHI's manipulation of political tension as a tourist attraction, and a corresponding claim to present an authentic Tibet to tourists. In so doing, LHI staff presents the hotel as an actor, thereby minimizing the distance between their guests and the authentic cultural experience available by staying at the Holiday Inn. In 1991, the LHI was the only establishment in Lhasa managed by a Western staff. At the time, LHI staff included Italians, Americans, Belgians, and British employees among others. The hotel has a somewhat unstable history.[22] Opened in 1985 by the Chinese government, the hotel closed as a result of numerous complaints six months later. At the request of the Chinese government, the Holiday Inn was asked to take over hotel management. Original staff were both Westerners and Chinese employees from other Holiday Inns in the PRC. Gradually, Tibetans were trained to move into non-menial positions, and at the time of the pageant comprised the majority of the staff. Management, however, remained in the hands of the Westerners. Currently, the Holiday Inn has a ten-year contract, with all hotel proceeds returning to the Tibet Tourism Bureau, a government

agency. This arrangement places the hotel in a powerful economic position, according to former hotel manager Ernesto Barba, as seventy-five
percent of all foreign revenue in the Tibet Autonomous Region comes
from the LHI. Barba also stated,

> If I told them [the Chinese] I wanted a white elephant grazing in
> the garden, they'd let me do it. (Thurston 1992, 19)

The economic power that the LHI wields is evident to the CCP. Despite
Chinese attempts to avoid "Westernization," the LHI escapes full censorship because of the revenue that the hotel returns to the state. This collusion between state and hotel allows the pageant to take place, despite the
contestory nature of their individual messages.

The Lhasa Holiday Inn is Tibet's only international-class hotel, and
therefore host to package tourists, VIPs, and visiting human rights dele-
gations. The image of Tibet presented at the hotel is one steeped in
stereotypes, yet it hints strongly at discord beneath the surface. Consider
the following hotel literature:

> Khy Khy Club, the world's first Tibetan discotheque opened at
> the Holiday Inn Lhasa on April 17th. Guest of honor, Mr.
> Harrison Ford, the original Indiana Jones, joined in the celebra-
> tions as dancing at Tibet's most exclusive nightspot continued
> well into the early hours. Already being dubbed "the Club 54 of
> Lhasa" crowds have been gathering each night outside the Khy
> Khy Club in the hope of gaining entrance or of catching a
> glimpse of the exclusive clientele.
>
> The ribbon cutting ceremony was performed by Mr. Mao Ru
> Bai, the Vice Governor of Tibet, to the tune of a military drill dis-
> play by a local security force.
>
> Among the guests at the Khy Khy Club are Miss Tibet con-
> testants, tall Khampa beauties and local dignitaries who mix with
> the international jetset for fun-packed evenings of intrigue and
> possibly subversive activities.
>
> The music is nostalgic "Mao Tse Tung Swing" by the live
> band, mixed with the latest international nightclub hits spun on
> the turntable by the Khy Khy Club's South American disc jockey.
> (Holiday Inn document in English, 1992)

With liberal poetic license, Western staff at the Holiday Inn create for
Tibet a role in a world whose boundaries are easily (and superficially)
transcended by the "jetset" crowd. The "possibly subversive activities" in
effect involve two groups—those represented by "Miss Tibet contestants," of which there were perhaps some "tall Khampa beauties," and the
"local dignitaries" who represent one end of the political spectrum. By

linking and inherently juxtaposing the Tibetan women and the "local" (most likely both Chinese and Tibetan) political representatives of the CCP, Holiday Inn literature places Miss Tibet at the opposite end of the spectrum, as the antithesis to Chinese rule. In the Western cultural world of beauty pageants, writ large in spheres like the Miss Universe pageant, is the notion of women as representative of nation. It is this same notion that the Holiday Inn is suggesting here.

Self-positioning is also prevalent in hotel literature for reasons of legitimacy. The hotel's tourist audience requires reassurance that their experiences are not just authentic but unique; the hotel makes every attempt to provide this. Subversiveness then can be seen as a mark of authenticity. In this manner, claims in Holiday Inn literature replicate standard tourist industry writings in sheer exaggeration and exoticizing of culture (see Crick 1989; Rossel 1988; Smith 1978). The appearance of Harrison Ford demonstrates this. His presence in promotional literature lends credence to the Holiday Inn's ability to authentically package Tibet. As Indiana Jones, as a movie star, and as a supporter of the Free Tibet movement, Harrison Ford embodies the role that the LHI has claimed for itself: an authoritative presenter of culture and navigator of political undercurrents. Ford is perfectly positioned to be associated with glamorous Miss Tibet contestants, and therefore to bring an international aura to the jet-setting tourist experience one may have at the Holiday Inn. According to one journalist, "Tibet was *the* chic place to go" for Italian tourists during the summer of 1992 (Thurston 1992, 18).

When the Holiday Inn arranged for an Italian fashion show to take place in Lhasa, the foreign press exploded. Special behind-the-scene privileges were offered by the LHI to the Italian group such as visits to monasteries usually off limits, and a luncheon at the site of Lhasa's sky burial grounds. The occasion at hand was the opening of a pool in the shape of Tibet at the LHI.[23] The opening was to coincide with the annual Tibetan bathing festival. An editorial in *The Observer*, a London-based newspaper, accused the LHI of blasphemy in the form of "fashion shows in front of the Dalai Lama's palace, photo opportunities where the Living God once meditated, luncheon next to Lhasa's most sacred burial site" (quoted in Thurston 1992, 18). The Holiday Inn denied the charges, and the event went on. Their actions, however, have not gone unnoticed.

On November 20, 1993, a boycott of the Lhasa Holiday Inn was announced by the London-based Tibet Support Group.[24] The organization accuses the Holiday Inn of "cultural insensitivity," and makes specific reference to the "Miss Tibet" pageant held at the hotel. In response, an England-based spokesperson for the Holiday Inn stated that the Lhasa hotel is "particularly sensitive politically, and the hotel monitors the local situation very closely," and that the hotel employs "a significantly high proportion of Tibetans." (Bennett 1993). This last comment appears to be a response to a 1992 criticism of the hotel by the Tibet Information Network, also based in London, for

> insensitivity to local culture and its close relations with the (Chinese) regime. For one period during the last four years, the hotel was staffed by Chinese people dressed as Tibetans and wearing Tibetan name badges. (TIN news release, May 27, 1992)

The LHI's manipulation of the local political situation is in a sense protected by a strong economic position. In terms of power, the Holiday Inn claims multiple spheres, yet ultimately is only operating in Tibet at the invitation of the Chinese government.

The addition of the Western contingency in claiming to offer a version of Tibetan culture factors into the state-nation struggle between China and Tibet. As the Chinese population of Lhasa grows, and ties between Tibet and the global Tibetan diaspora strengthen in some areas, the foreign staff at the Holiday Inn simultaneously seek to incorporate a vision of Tibet into its transnational worldview. What is the vision of Tibet that the LHI is assuming? Is it a vision of Tibet that recognizes the Tibet Government-in-Exile and the more than 100,000 Tibetans in exile, or one that limits its definition to the Tibet of the Tibet Autonomous Region? It appears to be simultaneously neither and both. The LHI orchestrated a "Miss Tibet" pageant not a "Miss T.A.R." or even a "Miss Lhasa" pageant. The Tibet that the Holiday Inn speaks of is the pre-1959 Tibet, not the geographic area currently bounded by Chinese political claims. The commodification of Tibet for tourism, and the appropriation of political tensions, is presented alongside conflicting Chinese state dialogue regarding Tibet. By doing so, the LHI invalidates the state's monopoly on representations of nation.

> Commercial interests, too, engage in objectification, promoting festivals of authentic folk culture, national-historical theme parks, world's fairs, beauty contests, and international sports competitions. All of these national-cultural forms can be found throughout the world. (Foster 1991, 249)

The political nature of many of these representations must be addressed. While the Chinese state undoubtedly has political motives as well as commercial interests in Tibet, does the Holiday Inn seek merely economic gain? Or is there more at stake in their hosting of the Miss Tibet pageant?

Analyses of transnational interventions into national culture can be read in terms of power struggles. For Dirlik (1994), the power to represent others is itself an issue of contention at many levels:

Managers of this world situation themselves concede that they (or their organizations) now have the power to appropriate the local for the global, to admit different cultures into the realm of capital (only to break them down and remake them in accordance with the requirements of production and consumption). (1994, 351)

Through this lens, the Holiday Inn can be seen as appropriating local events for global consumption, inserting Tibetan culture, Tibetan women, and the Tibetan nation into the realm of transnational capital and onto the global stage.

Extending the Gaze: Tibet and the Global Realm

The woman who won the Miss Tibet pageant recently toured the United States as a member of a Tibetan cultural dance troupe from Lhasa. Sponsored by the Chinese government, the troupe's performances were boycotted by Tibetans and Tibet supporters. For these protesters the Tibetan nation was not represented, but desecrated by Chinese support of the performances. What definitions of Tibet form in the transnational realm?

Beyond the borders of the Tibet Autonomous Region exists a larger Tibet. It is this Tibet, potentially the referent of the title "Miss Tibet," that the Chinese government seeks to delegitimate. The Tibetan Government-in-Exile, thousands of Tibetans living in exile, and numerous supporters of their cause around the world contest Chinese representations of Tibet. Foreign governments are also involved. During the early years of the Chinese occupation, the CIA trained Tibetans in Colorado to fight against the Chinese. In 1993, the U.S. Congress attached conditions requiring human rights improvements in Tibet to Most Favored Nation trading status with China. Diasporic Tibet reaches into Tibet. Identities crafted in exile are imported to Tibet through travelers, radio broadcasts, publications, and word of mouth. For example, a Lhasan woman who was arrested for shouting "Long live Independent Tibet" and "May all people be free," had the following dialogue with the police:

"How many relatives do you have in India?"
"All Tibetans in India are my relatives."
(quoted in Devine 1993, 63)

In Lhasa, while definitions of Tibet embraced by Tibetans arise from within a larger Tibetan community, in many ways Tibet also exists as seen (and presented) by the Chinese government and the expatriate staff of the Holiday Inn. Chinese rule in Tibet has caused a Tibetan identity of unity to be privileged, shifted, recovered, and rethought. In this transnational context—from Tibet to the diaspora and back—a national identity takes hold. The answer to the question of who partakes of this identity varies both inside and outside of Tibet.

Portrayals of the Miss Tibet pageant in the foreign media picked up on the potential threat within the pageant by highlighting both the irony of the contest and the unease of the contestants. Articles by male journalists also emphasized that the Tibetan participants were not familiar with the concept of a beauty pageant:

> not one of them ["the girls"] had the faintest idea of what a beauty contest was and…had never heard of Miss World.

Nonetheless, they report that the pageant winner embraced the idea wholeheartedly, stating:

> Now that I've won, I'd like to go on and be Miss World and try to help people. (Woolrich 1992).

Thus, these women, assumed by Western journalists to be unfamiliar with worlds beyond Lhasa, are exposed to Western values through the pageant. A Western view of Tibet as an isolated Shangri-la becomes transformed into a new modern Tibet.[25] However, the fact that this was the first beauty pageant in Tibet does not necessarily lead to similar conclusions. Despite the actual extent of contestants' knowledge of the Miss World pageant, Lhasa residents are undoubtedly familiar with a "modern" world—both Western and Asian.

Modernity travels to Lhasa through other venues as well. In their publicity literature, the LHI claims that their Khy Khy Club, opening in April, 1992, will be Lhasa's first disco. However, at the time of the pageant, there were at least four discos in Lhasa. Run by Tibetans, Chinese from Sichuan, and also Chinese security forces, these discos were gathering spots for the hip young of Lhasa—visiting Tibetans from India, local Tibetans, Chinese newcomers, and children of high-placed cadres dressed in the latest Hong Kong fashions and carrying cellular phones. In many ways Hong Kong appears in Lhasa as the merger of Asia and the West. Foreign judges were flown in from Hong Kong, the winner was originally to travel to Hong Kong, and Hong Kong fashions and music predominate in the disco scene beyond the Holiday Inn. At the same time, influence seeps in from India as Tibetans living in exile in South Asia return to Lhasa with twists on modern Tibetan culture shaped under a different national tradition.[26]

In the Chinese press, modernity is often presented within the realm of traditional "Tibetan" culture. Women are shown to be modern through changes in fashion, a further example of the selective focus on non-controversial aspects of "minority" culture discussed previously. Articles appear in Xinhua News Service and *China Daily* with titles like "Lhasa Sees Rebirth of Traditional Fashion," "Nomadic Tibetan Women Take to Modern Life," and "Tibetans Take to Puffed Sleeves." According to one article, women's notions of their bodies, and of fashion have changed in recent years through the wearing of new "bright and lively" clothing:

> One Tibetan girl explained that she never before thought she could become so slim and so confident, but that her thinking changed after wearing a new style Tibetan robe.

In addition to the jump to a Chinese modernity, the women are able to retain their ethnic identity, according to a Xinhua article:

> Zhouma, a Tibetan primary-school teacher, said: "I can still easily be identified as a Tibetan girl in this kind of fashion, which is both stylish and easy to wear.

These developments fit well into PRC plans—encouraging a modernity compatible with Chinese characteristics—and indeed are the very aspects of Tibetan culture that the Holiday Inn does not highlight.

Control over access to the outside world, and therefore outside ideas, recently slipped from the hands of the state with the advent of satellite television in Lhasa. To rectify this situation, in early March 1994, the TAR government banned the Holiday Inn and other establishments from "receiving and relaying programmes from...outside Tibet" for, among other reasons, "poor censorship of programmes" ("Tibet," March 9, 1994). The directive specifically mentioned the BBC, the Chinese Channel, and Star TV as stations televising programs at odds with state ideology. Modernity is to arrive in Tibet only through the channels of the state, or is not to arrive at all.

This modernity with which China seeks to infuse Tibet and Tibetan culture is a modernity with Chinese characteristics.[27] This project in every way seeks to legitimate Chinese rule in Tibet as it highlights the political, social, and economic progress made by Tibetans since their "peaceful liberation" and incorporation into the PRC. Schwartz states this project has backfired on the Chinese:

> The Chinese would have the Tibetans see them as modernizers rather than oppressors. But Tibetans identify their own national aspirations with "modernity" in the global sense, a point of view that further highlights the deficiencies of Chinese rule in Tibet. (1991, 13)

A different tactic is employed by the Holiday Inn to claim legitimacy in Tibet. By focusing on the "real" aspects of Tibetan culture, and on the potentially explosive political situation, the LHI frames Tibet within Western modernity—beauty pageants, fashion shows, international tourism, and jet-setters mingling with local officials and glamorous Tibetan women. As a result of these two varied approaches, different commentaries are present in the Miss Tibet pageant regarding Tibet, representations of Tibet, and on the role of women as markers of Tibetanness. In the beauty pageant, the representation of Tibet is located at the intersection of multiple issues—the multiple definitions offered of Tibetan identity; the interplay of Westerners, Chinese and Tibetans in Lhasa; and the spheres participated in by women within and outside the context of a beauty pageant.

CONCLUSION: STATES, NATIONS, AND BEAUTY QUEENS

It is tempting to conclude that the local branch of the CCP allowed the Miss Tibet pageant to take place because they viewed women as non-threatening political actors. However, Tibetan women in Lhasa have long been central in the resistance to Chinese rule. The anniversary of a major women's protest in Lhasa on March 12, 1959, following the Dalai Lama's flight to India is honored each year in exile. Both nuns and laywomen participate in anti-Chinese movements through protests, signed petitions, and political songs.[28] The Chinese state's awareness of women's participation in Tibetan independence activities is certain. The attempt to present the pageant as non-political relied on a revision of the pageant structure to constitute an acceptable forum for the spectacle of "minority nationality" culture. In changing pageant structure to resemble a cultural arts program, the government directs focus towards the women (as symbolic or cultural, not as political), and through them to the Chinese state. The potential viewing of Tibet as separate from China is challenged through the inclusion of songs that inevitably praise Mao, the PRC, and the Chinese Communist Party. This deflection would only be recognizable to Tibetan and Chinese present at the pageant, and not to the majority of Western spectators and LHI employees who spoke little or no Tibetan or Chinese.

As China imagines a state that includes the Tibetan nation, Tibetans recall not only two nations, but two separate states. Thus, Anderson's definition of the nation as "an imagined political community—and imagined as both inherently limited and sovereign" is salient at very different points for China and Tibet (1991[1983], 6). The power of the Chinese state takes hold in the form of a "national-cultural imperialism," an extension of Anderson's concept of "official nationalism" in which nation is stretched over empire (Chen 1992). In this form, nationalism protects the interests of the state.

> The most intriguing "official nationalism" of its kind—since it has a strong appeal among the Chinese people even today—finds its expression in the military and religious suppression of "national

minorities" such as the Tibetans, Uighurs, and Mongolians, with the justification of "national territorial integrity." This is an example of what I call national-cultural imperialism by which a Third World country such as China can legitimate and exercise its own central, imperial hegemony over regional or ethnic groups in all spheres. (Chen 1992, 709)

China's central hegemony is thus dependent on non-Chinese others.[29] The position of non-Han cultures within the Chinese state is delineated by the PRC's self-definition as a state composed of many nationalities (but led by the Han) (Chen 1992). State appropriation of local cultural symbols is often a means of constructing an inclusive PRC state and nation (see Mueggler 1991). Such actions are evident in Tibet in PRC claims of credit for the reconstruction of Buddhist monasteries destroyed during the Cultural Revolution. However, much rebuilding is financed by local Tibetan communities, not by the state. The Chinese state defines the Chinese nation, and includes Tibet in the definition. The discourse surrounding claims to define and represent the Tibetan nation is shifting as a result of the many participants—Tibetan, Chinese, and Western, among others. Yet, while the Tibetan nation remains, the struggle for state continues.

In representing Tibet, "Miss Tibet" does not merely assume an identity crafted by Westerners, approved by the Chinese, and judged by both. As much as she is Miss Tibet, representative of a nation, this is also a misrepresentation. In certain circles in Lhasa, people know exactly who Miss Tibet is. In others, the term and the title remain foreign. Thus, the question to be asked is not are woman bearers of nation, but how do both women and men navigate the available definitions of Tibet, of nation, that intersect with their lives, and perhaps clash with their own definitions? While subscribing to one view of "Tibetan," at times it may be expedient for Tibetans in Lhasa to adhere to other definitions. In this way, the trope of woman as nation is double in the Miss Tibet pageant: it is both simultaneously empty of and laden with meaning.

Miss Tibet's identity was in part written by male judges and journalists, thereby transculturally implicating gender in the modern locale of the beauty pageant. Further, her position has been saturated with Chinese political propaganda through the various restrictions placed on the pageant by the CCP, and the cultural performances included in the program. The script prepared for the twenty-five women who competed for the pageant title was co-authored by the Chinese and the Western hosts. Once prepared, the script was open to revision at the hands of the pageant contestants, whose voices remain to be heard amidst the raucous crowd of the thirty judges, the organizers, and the media who gathered to dictate the boundaries of nation, to present a suitably exotic and subversive yet sanitized Tibet, and to photograph women on display. Unanswered interview questions, and her parting comments—"I want to help the world"—notwithstanding, Miss Tibet still has not spoken.

My argument here is not that Tibetans are not active agents in the construction of Tibetan nationalism. However, those who do participate in nationalist activities are classified by the current government as "splittists" and therefore left out of certain public discussions of Tibetanness such as the "Miss Tibet" pageant. Although the Holiday Inn acknowledged "possibly subversive activities," this serves not to bring Tibetan nationalists into the discussion, but diffuses their power and reiterates their absence. Through the forum of the "Miss Tibet" pageant, Tibetan nationalism (present as an underlying potentiality) and Chinese power are negotiated in a setting familiar to a Western audience: woman as representative of country. This gendered depiction of Tibetan identity may be economically salient for the expatriate management at the Holiday Inn, or rhetorically recognizable for "minority" women in China, Tibetans, however, are absent from this particular discussion of the nation. They do not need to speak, they are spoken for.

Postscript

In the midst of writing this paper, I returned to Lhasa. At the Holiday Inn I was told that the Miss Tibet file had been "canceled." There were no Western staff remaining who worked at the hotel at the time of the pageant. The only managerial level employee available was a Tibetan who told me that the pageant was a "success." During my stay in Lhasa, week-long festivities to celebrate the reconstruction of the Potala Palace, the former home and monastery of His Holiness the Dalai Lama, had been arranged by the government to coincide with the Tibetan festival of Shodon. The nearby monasteries of Drepung and Sera, as well as the monastery at the Potala, had been instructed by the government to display their giant thangkas (Tibetan Buddhist religious paintings) during the festival. It was the first time since the Dalai Lama fled Tibet in 1959 that the thangkas were displayed. I attempted to schedule a meeting with Miss Tibet,[30] but to no avail. I was told repeatedly that she was too busy for interviews. She was performing for Chinese government officials on the roof of the Potala and at other events around Lhasa.

Notes

I wish to thank the following people for offering advice and criticisms on early drafts—John Ackerly, Colleen Ballerino Cohen, Val Daniel, Norma Diamond, Ann

Forbes, Laura Kunreuther, Bill Lockwood, Char Makley, Sherry Ortner, Warren Smith, and especially Crisca Bierwert, Beth Drexler, Maureen Feeney, and Javier Morillo-Alicea for their patience in not only reading and commenting on successive drafts, but for challenging me to fully develop my argument. Thanks also to Mary Moran, who suggested that I write this essay in the first place, and to Robbie Barnett for providing crucial references. I regret that for political reasons I cannot name the many people who helped me with my research in Lhasa. Information about the pageant was obtained from the following sources: Thurston (1992), Tierney (1991), and Woolrich (1992); and was supplemented by research conducted in Lhasa during September through November 1991, and August 1994. My research was supported by the Thomas Watson Foundation, the National Science Foundation, and the International Institute of the University of Michigan.

1. See Barlow (1994); Chatterjee (1993); Jayawardena (1986); Kandiyouti (1994); Liu (1994); Natarajan (1994); Radakrishnan (1992); Skurski (1994); Yuval-Davis and Anthias (1989).

2. Within the context of the beauty pageant, I use the term "Westerners" to refer to those non-Chinese, non-Tibetan, primarily European and American spectators and organizers of the pageant.

3. The quote in the header above is from Tierney (1991).

4. The political boundaries of Tibet differ between Chinese and Tibetan rule. The current "Tibet Autonomous Region" is a political entity created by the Chinese state, and does not include a number of regions that were governed by the Tibetan Central Government in Lhasa prior to the Chinese occupation of Tibet. Areas outside the T.A.R. include Tibetan Autonomous Prefectures and Counties in Qinghai, Gansu, Sichuan, and Yunnan Provinces.

5. Blum (1992) suggests that the mythologization of "the Other" in China occurs on two levels—an ideal romanticization paired with an exaggeration of perceived negative aspects of non-Han cultures. The Other is seen as both different and subservient to the Chinese. Wenhua, "culture," is inherently judgmental implying of the "national minorities" either a "low" or "high" level of culture, or no culture at all (Diamond 1993, 75). As a result, Chinese culture is often portrayed as a gift to be given to the culturally backward "minority" peoples. Examples of this view are often present in magazines intended for a foreign audience, such as *Beijing Review* and *China Reconstructs.* Consider this excerpt from an autobiographical article of Tibetan singer Tseten Dolma:

   > In 1956, I was lucky enough to be chosen to visit other parts of China with a group of young Tibetans. ... I visited a number of provinces and prefectures, and saw a way of life that I had never imagined before. For the first time I felt what an honorable thing it was to be Chinese, and I longed from the bottom of my heart to sing about it. (Dolma 1989, 14-15)

   As presented for Western eyes, ethnic minorities of the PRC aspire to be Chinese as an honorable goal. Their voices and stories are channeled to the outside world through the Chinese Communist Party-guided media apparatus.

6. The question of Chinese migration to Tibet is a difficult one. The International Campaign for Tibet (October 1994) recently revealed as national policy the Central Committee of the Communist Party's policy of "helping Chinese move to Tibet as part of an economic development program to counter the region's separatist movement." Chinese settlers in the Tibet Autonomous Region include Communist Party officials, security personnel, and Chinese entrepreneurs from all parts of China among others. See J. Norbu (1989) and Sun (1994) for a review of Chinese migration to Lhasa.

7. Contributors to debates over the construct of Chinese national identity include Blum (1992); Cannon (1990); Diamond (1993); Dikotter (1992); Dreyer (1976); Gladney (1991); Samuel and Dittmer (1993); and Wu (1991) among others.

8. Importantly, many "minority nationality" groups occupy the politically strategic frontier areas along the Indian and former Soviet borders.

9. In the Amdo area of Tibet, official cultural policies have to some extent recently allowed for a temporary revival of Tibetan culture and religious practices. According to *Beijing Review*, traditional theater is "flourishing" in Tibet (May 25-31 1992: 32-33). However, the flourishing of "culture" is contingent on current trends in policy. During the summer of 1993, six Tibetan officials, students and cultural figures, including a famous comic, a writer, and other Tibetans involved in official work on the Tibetan language were arrested prior to Jiang Zemin, China's Communist Party Secretary's visit to Amdo. This was the first time that cultural activists had been arrested in Tibet (Barnett 1993).

10. See van Walt (1987) for a reading of the case of Tibet within international law.

11. Or male, as the case may be?

12. What I am suggesting here is that women have not been equated with nation in Tibet. This is not to say that Tibetan gender ideologies regarding women are not implicated in the structure of Tibetan culture or society, or in women's experiences within established structures. The collection *Feminine Ground: Essays on Women and Tibet* (Willis, ed., 1987), and specifically the articles by Janet Gyatso and Barbara Nimri Aziz, as well as Charlene Makley (n.d.) contribute significantly to an understanding of the role of gender in Tibetan culture and Buddhism.

13. Klieger has suggested that Tibetan national identity is negotiated between a "perceived western mythology [regarding Tibet] and indigenous historical reality" (1992, 149). He further states, "The image of Tibet which modern exiles often choose to present to the world is rooted in quasi-mythical Buddhist realm of Emperor Ashoka, and modified over the centuries through interactive experience with T'ang, Mongol, Manchu, and various western agents of patronage: Tibet, a land so sacred that even the mighty emperors of China saw fit to pay religious homage; a people intent on preserving the Complete Transmission of Buddha's teachings for the benefit of the world" (1992, 149).

14. I make this point to highlight the supposed focus of the beauty pageant on women rather than the nation. While beauty pageants may separate these two realms, actual production of both nations and states is often contingent upon specific gender (and other) ideologies. The work of Ann Stoler (1989a; 1989b; 1991) has been important in revealing this link.

15. Han Chinese stereotypes of ethnic minority women are explored by Diamond (1988).

16. Contributions towards the cultural theorizing of women and gender in Tibet is offered by Barbara Aziz (1987) and Charlene Makley (n.d.).

17. For examples of Chinese writings on ethnic minorities within the PRC, see the works of Fei Xiaotong (1979; 1981a; 1981b), and Yan (1984) for a discussion of "inequality" between "nationalities" in the PRC.

18. In neighboring India, claims by a foreign power to rule and to write Indian history were dependent on both the categorization of Indian society in European historical stages, and on "an emptying out of all [Indian] history" (Pandey 1990, 94).

19. See Chodag (1988), Heyu (1988), and Wang and Suo (1984) for examples.

20. Swain (1990) offers a reading of the "commodification" of non-Han Chinese ethnicity through tourism in southwest China.

21. See Daniel (in press) for elaboration on the concept of "simplex history"—a single-minded project that implies a form of "cultivated selectivity."

22. For further information about the Lhasa Holiday Inn, see Forbes and McGranahan (1992).
23. The question of borders arises at this point. What is the shape of Tibet, and thus of the hotel's pool? Pre-Chinese rule boundaries, ethnic Tibet borders, or those of the Tibet Autonomous Region?
24. For further information on the Holiday Inn boycott, see *Working With the Dragon: Holiday Inn and China in Tibet* (1993).
25. For critiques of Western romanticizations of Tibet, see Bishop (1989) and Lopez (1994).
26. Two independent Tibetan publications present exile perspectives on Tibet: the English-language *Tibetan Review* published in Delhi, and the Tibetan-language *Mang-Tso* ("Democracy") published in Dharamsala.
27. For a detailed discussion of modernity and alternative modernities in China, see Xudong Zhang (1994).
28. See Goldstein (1982) for an analysis of Tibetan political satire songs in pre-1959 Tibet.
29. In this sense China can be viewed as not just an imperial power, but a colonial one. As Ann Stoler has demonstrated for twentieth-century colonial cultures in Southeast Asia, the power of the colonists is exerted not just in the ruling of another, but as a means of engaging in self-definition through this Other.
30. Although her name is public knowledge, and the "real" woman holding the title is not unimportant, I have chosen not to use her name. To do so in the context of this paper would locate the problematic discussed not in the category of "Miss Tibet," but rather with the individual title holder. I am arguing that the representations of nation-as-woman, in the context of this pageant, were controlled largely by non-Tibetan people, and not by the pageant contestants.

11

The Miss Heilala Beauty Pageant
Where Beauty Is More than Skin Deep

Jehanne Teilhet-Fisk

Introduction

When I went to the Kingdom of Tonga in Western Polynesia in June of 1981, it was to study *ngatu*, tapa cloth. But the excitement surrounding the Heilala Festival preempted the women's attention, and mine as well.[1] Tonga is a constitutional monarchy, an independent kingdom protected by England that struggles against growing pluralism to maintain a stratified society where the chiefly and/or noble (*'eiki*) ranks are socially differentiated from commoners (*tu'a*).[2] As Campbell and others have noted, this struggle is manifested in tensions "arising between the new economy and the old social order, just as they have arisen between the new economy and the old political order" (Campbell 1992, 227). These tensions in turn are articulated in the debate over "beauty" that emerges in the Miss Heilala Beauty Pageant.

I started my study of the Miss Heilala Beauty Pageant with the premise that I was studying ethno-aesthetic systems. I soon realized, however, that the Miss Heilala Beauty Pageant is vested with multiple political and cultural meanings that are put into play around different perceptions of beauty. In the Miss Heilala Beauty Pageant, I discovered, beauty is more than skin deep.

THE MISS HEILALA BEAUTY PAGEANT
"Beauty" and Tongan Identity

The beauty pageant is a focal point of the Heilala Festival that is held annually from late June through early July in Nuku' alofa, the capital of Tonga. The Heilala Festival week is a recent invention filled with cultural events, craft competition, church pageantry, spectator sports, parades, nightclub revelry, and ancient dances. The Festival, a cultural tribute to the king Taufa'ahau Tupou IV, was also designed to promote tourism and instill pride in "the Tongan way." The Festival is timed to coincide with His Majesty's birthday on July 4th, which is proclaimed a public holiday. Thus the Festival, its beauty pageant, and the king's birthday (an occasion entrenched in cultural protocol) are complementary events. While his Majesty is the symbolic keystone of the Heilala Festival—which, according to local sources, was named in 1979 after "the flower of our royal family"—younger members of the royal family also legitimize and sanction the beauty pageant.

An outgrowth of a beauty pageant organized as a charity fund raiser in the 1950s by a member of the royal family, today's Miss Heilala pageant is the official forum for selecting a woman to represent Tonga against other Polynesians at the Miss South Pacific Pageant, before going on to the Miss World or Miss Universe competitions. In addition to representing a Tongan identity in international competitions, the Miss Heilala Pageant is a popular way of maintaining links with the many Tongans living abroad. Roughly 60,000 Tongans live abroad, compared to the 100,000 who live in Tonga (Campbell 1992; 223).[3] Thus, the Miss Heilala Beauty Pageant represents an important means of sustaining a "Tongan" community, one that agrees on certain values that can be put into public practice when all its diasporic segments return once a year. At the same time, however, the organizational structure of international beauty pageants imposes on the Miss Heilala Beauty Pageant practices and ideas that run counter to Tongan identity. For example, the inclusion of an internationally-mandated bathing suit competition compromises traditional avoidance *tapus* (taboos) that prohibit men from gazing upon any portion of their sister's body that would normally be clothed.

These tensions between local and global standards of behavior are most evident in the conflict between Tongan identity as it is defined and enacted in Tonga, and as it is defined and enacted by the expatriates or "Tongan Nationals" who return to Tonga for this pageant.[4] The local and expatriate Tongan perspectives ultimately run counter to each other. This contradiction functions at the levels of language, the economy, the political order, and national ideology, and leads directly into the most personal, private, and powerful features of identity: kinship, family, body, sexuality, and relations between the sexes. These contradictions, tensions, and conflicts become most clear in simple questions about what constitutes "beauty."

The local Tongan community has its own perception of beauty, *faka' ofo' ofa*, that goes far beyond the surface of physical attributes and is deeply entrenched in social and moral values that uphold and emphasize the family, kinship, church, and a nationalist ideology based on constitutional monarchy. Tongan expatriates, especially those born abroad, have a different and narrower definition of beauty, one not embedded in Tongan cultural values. The expatriates' ideas about beauty can also differ depending on whether they come from the United States, Australia, or New

Zealand. These expatriate ideals are affected by global notions of beauty that are less culture-specific, but are based generally upon Euro-American preferences. The Miss Heilala Beauty Pageant is a key site where these different aesthetics articulate and conflict.

THE 1993 MISS HEILALA FESTIVAL

All agree that the 1993 Heilala Festival was exceptional—it had more of everything including an all-time record of nineteen pageant contestants, more than half of them from overseas. Everyone wanted to make the 1993 event a special celebration for the King's seventy-fifth birthday, the Silver Jubilee of their Majesty's coronation, and the installation of two nobles. It lasted fifteen days and nights, and Tongans of all ages came from other islands and from overseas to participate as audience, congregation, performers, or contestants in a panoply of events.

In a Tonga caught in a transition era "in which the indigenous and the foreign are unequally and unevenly blended" (Campbell 1992, 228), the Heilala Festival instills a sense of allegiance, community, and social interdependence, by bringing the indigenous and the foreign together. The band concerts, children's talent shows, spectator sports, float parade, gay beauty pageant, and the nightly events of the Miss Heilala Beauty Pageant tend to incorporate and express changing attitudes toward modernization, the new economy, formal education, and authority. Other occasions are culturally indigenous and promulgate the old social and political order with gala affairs that pay tribute to the *'eiki* class. These events include elaborate dances performed by entire villages, contrapuntal singing groups contending for honors, lavish invitational (birthday and jubilee) feasts, regal installations of nobles, and handicraft competitions designed to maintain the quality and integrity of ancient media.

The interaction of these events distributed all over Nuku' alofa, produces new relationships and dialogues that can either pit older values against contemporary ones or bind them together. This process is especially visible in the beauty pageant—a modern vehicle that is not Tongan, but that nonetheless helps to define, communicate, and package Tongan culture, identity, and pride.[5]

A Tongan Perspective on Beauty Pageant Practices

The 1993 Miss Heilala Beauty Pageant had five separate judging events for all contestants. Four of these events—Miss Talent Quest, Miss Tau'olunga, Miss South Pacific, and Miss Heilala Ball—were open to the public, who purchased separate tickets for each. The fifth event, the Tongan-English interview, took place in private at a special luncheon attended by contestants and judges. Although the five events are evenly weighted in final marks, the prizes differ, with the largest prize of 2,000 *pa'anga* (exchanged at a little less than the United States dollar) and a round-trip ticket to the United States of America and London going to the winner of the coveted Miss Heilala title. Contestants must be part Tongan (as one informant put it, "one-quarter, one-half—any part"), single, and between the ages of eighteen and twenty-four.

In spite of the impressive awards and the broad entry criteria, local women are hesitant to enter the Miss Heilala competition. Indeed, all of the Tongan contestants I interviewed in 1993 reported being "talked into" entering by their mother, aunt, or girlfriend. One of the reasons they gave for their hesitancy was that it is "un-Tongan" to put oneself on public view. This rationale is grounded in normative gender practice in which women tend to avoid public exposure, "preferring instead spectator or humble positions" (Marcus 1978a, 242).

It is difficult to generalize about Tongan women because their individual ranks and social roles differ in their positions as sisters, aunts, wives, and/or queens. Whereas houses, land, titles, and secular powers are passed down through men, honor, mystical knowledge, abstract power, and political veto rights are passed down through women. Sisters therefore have powers and rights that they lack as wives. Even a commoner woman has more influence as a sister than as a wife. The influence wielded by Tongan sisters is bolstered by brother-sister avoidance practices.

In Tonga, sisters command respect and avoidance from their brothers, a practice embedded in a descent system where the father's side outranks the mother's, but where sisters outrank brothers, thus giving the father's sister and her children the highest rank. The father's sister has ritual or mystical powers and material rights over her brother's children (Goldman 1970; Rogers 1977; Marcus 1978a, 1978b; Bott 1981; Biersack 1982; James 1983, 1988). The father's eldest sister has the highest rank and is called *mehekitanga*. She is usually the *fahu* or the woman "who is ceremonially or ritually superior in a particular social context." (Rogers 1977, 167). Although the practice is now less common, brothers tend to defer to the superior status of their female siblings by according them *faka'apa'apa*, respect and honor. Out of respect for their sisters, brothers are under pressure to avoid situations that might compromise their sister's and classificatory sister's honor.

The Miss Heilala Beauty Pageant as a Reflection of Social Hierarchy

The Miss Heilala Beauty Pageant is structured to reflect the Tongan social order. The zenith of the social hierarchy is represented by the H.R.H.

Crown Prince Tupouto'a, who is the official patron of the festival and installs Miss Heilala. His sister, H.R.H. Princess Salote Mafile'o Pilolevu Tuita, promotes the Miss Tonga/San Francisco Beauty Pageant in the United States and brings the winner(s) back to compete in the Miss Heilala Pageant. Without the royal family's approval, there would be no Miss Heilala contest for, as Kaeppler has observed, "innovation in Tonga takes place downward from the top of stratified society" (1993, 95). All official Festival events are honored by the appearance of the royal and noble families and various "VIPs." Their presence gives honor to the contestants and valorizes their role as representatives of the Kingdom at local, national, and international events. The royal family's presence also assures the allegiance of the local participants and community at large and helps prevent the use of the Festival as a platform for oppositional or anti-royal views.

The more educated middle-class Tongans and nobles often act as judges. Tongan judges must bridge the social order, while balancing their place within the Tongan social order and professional community. Therefore, their social obligations and relationships influence their judgments and sway their votes. Should a patron or judge of higher social rank indicate that a particular contestant (maybe his sister's daughter or girlfriend) must place first in a certain event, then the other judges and/or those tallying the votes will obey out of respect. Independent auditors, computer systems, and Euro-American judges are slowly being introduced to bring an element of "objectivity" and change into "the Tongan way" but the final tallies for the winner of the different titles are never made public, so modernization usually loses to Tongan protocol.[6]

The winner of the pageant is never crowned "Queen" or "Princess," as in American pageants, nor would a noble's daughter enter such a contest.[7] Many of the contestants are from the *tu'a* class (commoners and/or rising middle class). These commoners are, in some sense, more elevated in the local hierarchy than expatriate contestants, Tongan, or part-Tongan nationals. These non-local Tongans frequently enter the pageant without understanding or even thinking about their social class or place in the local social structure. From their perspective, they might also be considered as being outside the social structure altogether.

Indeed, these Tongan expatriates conventionally come to the Miss Heilala competition with Euro-American egalitarian and individualistic ideology (see Stoeltje, this volume), believing that they will be judged on the basis of beauty and talent. In 1993, several of the non-local Tongan contestants I interviewed were convinced that they would win the title or at least place as first runner-up, particularly because Miss Tonga/New Zealand had won the Miss Heilala title in 1992. But this did not happen.

"BEAUTY" AT THE LOCAL AND GLOBAL JUNCTURE

Although it includes several practices that conflict with local Tongan norms and social arrangements, the Miss Heilala Pageant does not pose a direct threat to the old political order. It does, however, rearrange social relations, and thus furnishes an entry into modern reforms that question social hierarchy and hereditary privilege. It is also a place where many kinds of unresolved tensions come to a head at the local and global juncture.

One kind of tension between local and global standards in the pageant is created by the inequality in financial assistance given by the sponsors. In its early years, the pageant was sponsored by the *'eiki* class and the heads of extended families, but that has given way to sponsorship by corporations like Benson & Hedges and Royal Beer, who want the contestants to promote their products.[8] In 1993 some of the locals complained that the Tongan expatriates got the "richest" sponsors, and that without better sponsorship the locals could not keep up with the new styles.[9] This inequality also pitted the Tongan expatriates against each other (i.e., Miss Tonga/San Francisco and the other women from California, Miss New Zealand Tonga Tourist Association, Miss Australia Tongan Tourist Association) and against the local contestants from the main island (Tongatapu), as well as against the other island candidates (Ha'apai and Vavau), and this in turn kindled regional factionalism.

Factionalism at the local, global, and regional level was also apparent when the California-Tongan contestants were constantly singled out and taunted by the audience for the way they dressed and the way they spoke Tongan. The Californians were not prepared for the old ways; as one contestant from California explained in a personal interview, "I brought my shorts and pants and then, well, I was told, 'We don't want you wearing shorts, not even around the hotel.' I was amazed because even though I am part Tongan, I was not born here, and I wasn't raised knowing their culture, knowing how strictly conservative they are" (Tongan-American, June 30, 1994). Californians were also charged, more than any other expatriate group, with being "snobs" and propagating American attitudes and change. While local Tongans will frequently allude to tourists (and Euro-American videos, television shows, and movies) as undesirably "other," they tend to tolerate casual dress and "progressive ways" without adopting them. There is a grave problem, however, when non-local Tongan contestants "return" with the same dress styles and values as tourists. Local adolescents and children become confused: since these expatriates are Tongan, not *papālangi* (European), they don't understand why their parents are opposed to their adopting American fashions.

Diasporic Tongans are thus caught in a double-bind. The only venue in the entire festival that is readily open to their participation is the pageant. Yet when an expatriate wins the Miss Heilala title (which has happened on several occasions lately; in 1990, 1992, and 1994), local Tongans are less than pleased. As they put it to me, they do not want Tonga represented locally or abroad by an expatriate who they perceive as being more *papālangi* than Tongan. It sends a confused signal to the local Tongan youth about Tongan identity.

Factionalism and Cultural Unity

Global standards and the inclusion of expatriates in the Miss Heilala Beauty Contest has generated local discontent and factionalism, but has also promoted cultural unity and the essentialization of a Tongan identity overseas. When Princess Pilolevu moved to San Francisco, California with her husband to open the Tongan Consulate, she became more aware of these complex issues of identity and Tonganness; one result was the first official "Miss Tonga/San Francisco Pageant" in 1993.[10]

I interviewed some former Miss Heilala contestants who were attending the Miss Tonga/San Francisco Pageant in 1994. They all affirmed that the 1993 Miss Heilala pageant had a profound affect on their sense of identity and cultural pride in being Tongan. Within the pageantry, amid the subtle plays of status rivalry and conspicuous consumption, there lies an affirmation and even celebration of ethnic identity and national pride in being Tongan—indigenous or expatriate—in a global world. When the Tongans from abroad return for the Heilala Festival they may not share the values of the local Tongan community, but they do share in the value of being Tongan. As an older expatriate from New Zealand explained to me, "When you are Tongan you always know who you are. You are never to be anything less than the very best. The constitution of Tonga is Tonga, King, God and my heritage, so that's always implanted in a Tongan's heart." After a pause this expatriate added, "though in this generation, here and overseas, it kind of got lost somewhere."

Miss Tau'olunga: The Retention of Tongan Culture

To keep the "Tongan way" from getting lost, the Heilala Festival and Beauty Pageant uses categories that reaffirm and strengthen Tongan ethnic identity, cultural pride, and language. The judges "assess the contestant's knowledge of both the Tongan and English languages, of Tongan culture and their general knowledge" (*Heilala '93* 1993, 9). The beauty pageant also has the unique Tongan category of Miss *Tau'olunga*, which has the most sub-categories and awards the most prizes.

The official Festival booklet *Heilala '93* explains that "while all events rank equally for marks towards the award of the title, the one aspect of this

Michelle Niu performing the *tau'olunga* in a costume made from fresh leaves. July 1993. Miss Niu is from *Nuku'alofa* and she won Miss Heilala.

pageant which is unique to Tonga, and which distinguishes this pageant from other beauty contests, is the Miss *Tau'olunga* evening." The *Tau'olunga* is the classic solo dance of Tonga culture, traditionally performed by the daughters of the royal family and nobility.[11] Every aspect of the presentation—the costume, the set-piece movements, the grace and art of their execution, the charm and beauty of the dancer—are strictly marked. The *Tau'olunga* is more than a dance; "it is an expression of the essence of Tongan culture, combining beauty, skill, respect and modesty…" (Heilala '93 1993, 8).

The Miss *Tau'olunga* evening is the cultural highlight of the Miss Heilala Pageant and always has been. The likelihood that this event would ever be performed in an international setting is very doubtful as its definition of beauty is expressly Tongan. This is the event where the local women excel, with grace and dignity. A Tongan friend explained, "We believe everyone has a double that only comes out when you dance. Your double is pure, ethereal, really perfect, it goes into the core of Tongan culture which is trying to bring out the best in people, and the *Tau'olunga* epitomizes this cultural affect. It is always a family's pride, a village's pride, so if Miss Ha'apai wins then the whole of the Ha'apai island wins."

The *Tau'olunga* is the only event that is judged solely by Tongans in the Tongan language and with Tongan aesthetics. Judges look for beauty, chiefly motions, facial expression, and body-foot coordination, while allowing room for creativity, intent, and the ability to invoke feeling (Heilala Festival Week Program, 1985, 17). Miss Tonga/New Zealand thought that the expatriates had difficulty performing the *Tau'olunga* "properly, the real Tongan way, as it is the most difficult dance in all the South Pacific." A former judge confirmed that "overseas girls have trouble winning this section: they don't grow up knowing how to dance it."

Local Tongans believe that expatriate contestants in the *Tau'olunga* event are given too much leeway, and often ridicule their awkward performances. Her Royal Highness explained: "There aren't enough teachers of Tongan dance for them to be able to understand the movements and like it. Hula and Tahitian is very popular, you can look in the telephone book and find a hula teacher in Foster City [California] who was born in Hawaii. So they dance the hula to show their pride in being Polynesian." Many of these women will perform a Polynesian dance for the contest as a way of saving face for not being able to execute the *Tau'olunga* as well as the local contestants.

In former years, the *Tau'olunga* was always accompanied by a small, often spontaneous group of men and/or women who would share the stage, their exaggerated movements and jovial antics drawing attention to the dancers' beauty, grace, and skill. This is called *tulafale* and is one of the ways that Tongans express their pleasure with the beauty of a dancer's movements. When the Tongan Tourist Association assumed greater control over the Miss Heilala Beauty Pageant in 1980, this part of the *Tau'olunga* was eventually cut from the program because, I was told, it was "distracting" and "lacked a sense of professionalism." Another way of expressing pleasure is by shouting words of praise, *māile*, or making a *fakapale*, placing paper money or presents upon the dancer. *Fakapale* is the customary way to raise money for charitable funds, and it has been retained as part of the *Tau'olunga* event.

In 1993, the committee added a new element to the *Tau'olunga* competition, giving extra points for original dance compositions and original dance costumes. The goal, according to the director of the Tongan

'Ana M. 'Otufai, Miss Tonga-San Francisco, bringing a prestation of cloth to a dancer at the traditional entertainment for King Taufa'ahau Tupou IV, Mala'e Pangai.

National Center, is "to preserve and maintain Tongan traditions." These costumes are made from vibrant colors of freshly picked leaves. The intricate patterns and the means and methods of making the ancient forms are cherished family secrets.[12]

Miss South Pacific: The Antithesis of Miss Tau'olunga, Or Whose Notion of Natural Beauty?

The high value placed on the Miss *Tau'olunga* event is reflected in the prizes awarded—the winner receives 500 *pa'anga*, and a trip to Honolulu—in contrast with the winner of the less valued Miss Talent Quest who only receives 250 and no trip. While local Tongans perceive Miss *Tau'olunga* as the personification of Tongan beauty and skill, Miss Talent Quest is seen as being caught in a transition, and Miss South Pacific is denounced as being anomalous and anti-Tongan. Indeed, Miss South Pacific is the event that causes the biggest rift between local Tongans, expatriate Tongans and the foreign audience at large. The conflict centers on the way "natural beauty" is interpreted and displayed in the "beach wear" section of the event, where contestants are judged in "Polynesian costume and beach wear" on "poise, natural beauty, modesty and figure" ("Briefing Papers for Miss Heilala Contestants" 1993).[13] The conundrum is whether the judges and contestants should make decisions based on Euro-American norms of body aesthetics that are the standard in international competitions, or repudiate these norms in deference to Tongan notions of beauty.

In Tonga, the body and the moral behavior associated with the body are not separate from ideals governing kin relations, relations between the sexes, brother-sister avoidance, and the social order at large. As among Polynesians, Tongans have always symbolically mapped potency and hierarchical significance onto the parts of the somatic body. Polynesians were famous for using the body as a medium of artistic expression. Their purpose was to mark a person's position in the social group in formal or public situations rather than personal embellishment. Therefore the notion of judging the body as a reflection of the individual, rather than a sign of one's rank, social status, and origins, is not the Tongan way. The somatic body mirrors ideals of Tongan society, which are reflected by the elite class and in the performance of the most elite dance (the *Tau'olunga*) and these ideals are ranked, just as is the society.

Throughout Polynesia the head is considered the most *tapu* (taboo) part of the body (along with the genitals and upper thighs). The head is the seat of thought and rationality, and the top of the head is the repository of *mana* and *tapu*.[14] Because hair is on the top of the head, it too held sanctity. With the advent of Christianity, hair now means less than it once did. Tongan women still cut their hair at the death of their father as a form of respect and submission to his role as chief of the family. In public, at church, or on formal occasions, women's hair is kept neat and tidy, worn in a bun or other restricted fashion. Hair should only be worn loose while performing a ceremonial dance or in the privacy of one's home. Long loose hair has associations with a liminal state or with sexuality. Unkempt hair is associated with a death in the family, expressing a distraught feeling. Tongan hair types range from frizzy to straight, short to long, and black to brown. The international beauty pageant places a different emphasis on hair; *papālangi* judges have a stereotype of Polynesians with straight, long, silky black hair worn freely over their shoulders. Tongan hair does not always comply with this stereotype, and so some contestants have taken to using straightening agents.

According to local standards of beauty, the face should be well defined, with well-set dark eyes framed by expressive eyebrows, a full mouth, and a high forehead. Few use makeup, since it is thought that a beautiful face does not need lipstick, rouge, or eye shadow. Eyes and expressive eyebrows are of great communicative importance in Tonga. The beauty of the face is radiated by its expressiveness—a canon of the *Tau'olunga*. Large body size was also a mark of beauty and rank in Tonga. There is an expression in Tongan which literally means "to look fat is to look well." In Tonga, fattened body and light skin were signs of high social rank. The present King Taufa'ahau Tupou IV allegedly weighed close to 400 pounds in his prime.

The Tongan body was therefore subject to cultural regimens and regulations, and was judged according to indigenous standards. Fatness symbolizes community well being, and Miss Heilala should be pleasingly plump according to this canon, where the human body represents the social body. Small hands and fingers were also a sign of high status, of membership in elite classes that did no manual labor. Soft, supple hands are also an important aesthetic element in Tongan dances.

In Tongan public life, womens' genital region and thighs are never exposed. Movement of the upper legs and hips are restricted, even in dance, and it is still considered vulgar to show movement in or expose the upper legs in Tonga. A Miss Heilala chaperon told me that "Tongan women should never show their thighs or wear bathing suits, and when they finally uncover their legs in the privacy of their own home [especially on the wedding night] they should be fair, smooth, soft, and unmarked, never 'dressed' with panty hose." Women should also sit with their legs to the side.

Tongans of high rank are distinguished, especially the women, by lighter skin protected from the sun and kept smooth and soft with specially scented Tongan oils. Though the contestants come from the more common class, they too admire lighter skin and refrain from basking in the sun, keeping their skin soft with oil. Oil has a specific meaning in Tonga, where its sheen on a bride signifies virginity. When the bride shines and glistens, she is being presented for all to bear witness to her virginity. The dancer of the *Tau'olunga* must also glisten with oil, as a symbol of her alleged state of virginity. All of the contestants must be single and in Tonga great pride is expressed in a woman who remains a virgin until she is married. When a young woman reaches twenty-one years of age her parents often give her a big party to thank her for remaining a virgin.

Ethno-aesthetic values such as shininess (*ngingila*) pervade all of the traditional Tongan arts, but the only time in the Festival pageant when the contestants can draw upon these values is in the *Tau'olunga* event. The audience waits with a kind of Durkheimian "effervescence" for the entry of the contestants who appear dripping in oil that shimmers off the reflected light as it glides down their color-rich costumes and their arms. She is a majestic image of grandeur, *sino molu*, a soft, supple body.

But this aesthetic is no longer unchallenged. A local Tongan closely associated with the pageant sums up the ways local and international aesthetics collide in the pageant:

Papalangi elements have crept into the basis of judging. What is regarded in America and Europe as a fat person would be regarded here as a kind of beauty in size, we like traditional size and stature. Slimness was never a part of our principles by which we judge beauty. We admire *sino molu*... and when we judge beauty we first look at the face and rank its ability to attract people. Hair is not as important as it is to Europeans, it ranks after the face and size.

The Tongan notion of natural beauty reflects and valorizes the ideals embodied in the essence of royalty and, at the same time, these ethno-aesthetic ideals conflict with the winning values of the international scene.

The Swimwear Event: Where Local and International Perspectives Collide

When the swim wear event was made a part of the Miss Heilala Beauty Pageant, the pageant committee tried to accommodate Tonga's notion of natural beauty, modesty, and the unique social conventions by listing the event as a sub-section of the "South Pacific Evening." Contestants are given the option of wearing traditional Tongan swimwear—a wraparound skirt or a sarong—in lieu of the "official international" one piece bathing suit with a sarong. Nevertheless, the event is still perceived locally as a cultural travesty, as immoral, and as an embarrassment. No cash prize is given. As one local Tongan explained, "Local Tongan girls would not wear bathing suits, they think this is un-Tongan." As an after-thought this Tongan added, "Nice well rounded limbs and large size do not show up too elegantly when Tongans wear bathing suits."

In 1993 some California contestants unintentionally flaunted social convention by appearing in the standard swimwear "costume" of international competitions: a one-piece bathing suit, hosiery, high heels, and a sarong or jacket. This caused eyebrows to raise. They did not walk barefoot but paraded down the platform in heels, then they turned and took off their upper garment. These actions were disruptive, and they caused a number of brothers and male cousins to immediately leave the stadium following the avoidance taboo. One of the men told me that it was very embarrassing for him and that if he had stayed he would have been forced to prevent other men from looking at his cousin and this would have caused a fight. Another man also reported being upset by the expatriate parade of bathing suits. "Women should be clothed, it is offensive to Tongans to see unclothed women. A few of the contestants are my cousins. To see a 'sister' dressed in that nature is bad to witness."

Miss Tonga/San Francisco defended the actions of the California contestants by arguing that "the girls coming from overseas anticipated

Miss Heilala 1992 with Miss Tonga-New Zealand, who is representing the Tongan Tourist Association at a dinner party. They are wearing traditional *Kiekie* around their waists.

The winning float for the Miss Heilala parade, "Tonga's Culture a Royal Heritage," featuring a contestant from California.

wearing a swimsuit, not beachwear. The bathing suit section is a big part of the whole international competition and we thought it was important here." The expatriate Tongans from California did not understand the controversy they had caused. What is interesting is that the pageant committee had been unwilling to come to terms with the conflict.

Conclusion

The Miss Heilala Beauty Pageant brings together the different ways that local Tongans and expatriates perceive beauty; sometimes the systems of aesthetics collide. The ethno-aesthetic system embedded in older social, cultural, and moral values remains dominant, and the pageant system, borrowed from abroad, is used by Tongans to assert the dominance of the local over the foreign. The standards of international beauty pageants that Miss Heilala's expatriate contestants bring with them to the pageant bring out and objectify local Tongan ideas about the body, gaze, and proper behavior between siblings. When expatriate contestants arrive from their distant diasporic homes to compete, the are forced to confront the most personal, private, and powerful features of their "Tongan" identity: kinship, the family, and the body. They are forced to question the basis of their identity, and to acknowledge the superiority of the local Tongan way.

Meanwhile, blame for the changing values seen in the Miss Heilala contest is placed on its *papālangi* elements, including its "foreign" standards of beauty and the swimsuit event that are required in the international competitions. While few tourists can actually secure seats at the Miss Heilala Pageant, and those who do are put off by the noise and crowds, Tongans rationalize this foreign contest as a concession to tourists. Nevertheless, there is accommodation and change within the pageant itself that promises some long term changes in local values. These changes can take many forms, but it is apparent that the Miss Heilala pageant may always be dealing with two kinds of cultural aesthetics, which are linked with two different attitudes toward a cultural identification bifurcated by national boundaries.

What remains clear is the fact that beauty is more than skin deep, and Tongans will continue to be at odds with the standards of natural beauty set by the international pageant. Yet the pageant works because the expatriates can participate in a way approximately equal to the locals. The Tongan details allow the locals to accept the form, at the same time vesting the whole with real relevance to their culture.

Notes

I would like to express my appreciation to H.R.H. Princess Sālote Mafile'o Pilolevu Tuita for her support of this project, and to extend my gratitude to the following people who made it possible: Joyce Anna Afeaki, Sesilia Cornett, Tupou'ahome'e Faulupa, Samantha Fisk, Mele sungu Fonongaloa, Papiloa Foliaki, Joana Sālote Forbes, Futa Helu, Rosetta Johansson, Tafolosa Kaitapu, Michelle Nui, 'Ana Michelle 'Otuafi, Rosie Havea, Maopa Helmuli Pulu, Ruperta Fulivai Sikahema Rodriguez, Dorothy Salamasina, Irene Schaumkel, Sandra Schoonderwoerd, Afuha'amango Taumoepeau, Mele Hola Telefoni and Katri Vaa'ivak. To the many Tongans who have helped answer my questions, I can only express my gratitude for their generosity in allowing me to publish what they know better than I. These acknowledgments do not in any way bind the persons mentioned to my interpretation, for it is only that—an interpretation. And finally, this essay could not have been written without patience and help of all the editors: Colleen Ballerino Cohen, Richard Wilk, and Beverly Stoeltje.

1. The initial Heilala Festivals were informal, so much so that my daughter was allowed to participate as a flower girl in 1988. In 1993 I judged the Tui Kahoa Kakala and Tui Sisi Kakala contest (traditional garlands worn around the neck or waist on ceremonial and festive occasions), and I was also given permission by H.R.H. Princess Salote Mafile'o Pilolevu Tuita to videotape aspects of the pageant. During this period I lived in the room next to the Tongan-New Zealand contestant and her chaperones, whom I accompanied everywhere they went. In 1994 I was one of the judges for the evening gown competition at the Miss Tonga/San Francisco pageant. Everyone involved knew that I was studying the pageant, and all gave me permission to use their names. I have chosen, however, to give them anonymity.

2. Tongan principles of social status and societal rank are based on primogeniture, genealogy, purity of descent line, and complex marital exchanges. Commoners (tu'a), though emancipated from forced labor in 1862, are still socially differentiated from the chiefly and/or noble ranks ('eiki). This is a stratified society where all ranks and groups are differentiated from each other by systems of exchange (Kaeppler 1971; Rogers 1977; Biersack 1982; Teilhet-Fisk 1991; Campell 1992).

3. Tongan emigration has increased dramatically since 1975. As Campbell (1992, 223) points out, "Some impression of the impact of emigration can be seen in the fact that the 1986 census gave the population of Tonga as 94, 535, only 4.6 percent higher than the 1976 census estimate. The crude rate of natural increase without emigration would have been perhaps five times that figure."

4. Tongans in general classify the expatriates as "Tongan Nationals" regardless of their actual citizenship because of their continuing strong commitment to the ideology of the Tongan family (Cowling 1990, 192-96, 202).

5. Although billed as a tourist event, the pageant attracts more expatriates than tourists. In 1993, foreign tourists comprised only 20 percent of the visitors coming to Tonga ,whereas "Tongan Nationals" make up "at least 80 percent..." (Fonua 1993, 9). Unlike most events that attract tourists, the Heilala Festival is not "staged" for an uninformed audience of tourists. Tourists are certainly welcomed and many events are explained in English, but unless they have a patient Tongan friend or tour leader who gently leads them through the gatherings and finds them a place where they can sit and/or see, tourists do not enjoy the festival. Even fewer attempt to come to the one event designed with tourists in mind, the beauty pageant.

6. When I served as a Euro-American judge in a craft competition and a beauty pageant, the point criteria were not made clear, and in one situation the total points added up to one hundred and twenty rather than the one hundred stated. The point system im-

poses a Euro-American system of evaluation that is "un-Tongan" and is, thus, basically ignored. Tallied points do not follow the aesthetic principle of *heliaki*. *Heliaki* is "characterized by never going straight to the point but alluding to it indirectly" (Kaeppler 1993; 6). It is difficult to apply the point system to an interpretation and allusion particularly in the case of a beauty pageant that embodies so many cultural elements.

7. A Tongan with a long association with the Miss Heilala Beauty Pageant reported that there must have been chiefly women in the early stages when they were raising money for a worthy project "but it is not the kind of thing chiefly girls should take part in. There is a good reason behind this: they would be ashamed if they didn't win over a girl of lower social status. The judges would be at fault."

8. This in turn generates conflict with Christian censure of smoking and drinking.

9. Some felt that the expatriates should bring their own sponsors from abroad. Most of the American Tongans agreed that they had the better sponsors, but they were quick to point out that they paid their own way over and brought their own competitive apparel. It was suggested that the problem rested in the hands of the local sponsors who did not want to compete with rival companies based in the United States that might use the sponsorship as a way of getting into a new Tongan market.

10. She encouraged and helped sponsor a number of Tongan-Americans entered in the 1993 Miss Heilala Beauty Pageant. "In the two years I have been here, I have really learned to appreciate the difficulties the Tongan people in California are experiencing. I sympathize with them. At the same time, they have a whole generation of Tongan kids growing up here, some are even identifying with blacks rather than Polynesians. They don't know what Polynesian is, their parents don't have time to tell them what Polynesian is or what even Tongan is. They have lost their identity. Tongans here learn Tongan as a second language, they learn everything Tongan as a second culture, as a foreigner."

11. The *Tau'olunga* is considered Tongan, even though Tongans freely acknowledge its origin is Samoan. "*Tau'olunga* is an amalgam of many elements. Its music is adapted from Western music traditions. Its name and manner are borrowed from Samoa. Its movements and role are Tongan" (Kaeppler 1993, 29). Tongans have embraced the *Tau'olunga* as being a chiefly dance which pays honor to the old political order.

12. This concern for preserving "traditional" materials was expressed in the 1994 pageant when Her Royal Highness used bark cloth (real and imitation) as a medium for modern fashions. She introduced a new event, the cultural Tapa night. The idea for this event stems from the work of Finau, a contemporary fashion designer who first used tapa cloth to honor the King and Queen when they came to the Polynesian Cultural Center Celebrations (Hawaii) in 1993. In 1994 the princess invited him to display his tapa cloths at the Miss Tonga/San Francisco Pageant. Some of the people were upset, because the winning dress was made from Fijian tapa, *masi*. Finau felt that the outfits should only be made from indigenous tapa cloth (or cloth printed with Tongan tapa designs) because "it elevates the value of our culture" (personal communication).

13. Kololiana 'Otuangu's article in her new publication, *Tongan Women* (1994), addresses these broader issues and suggests that "a committee should sit down and work out new rules and…decide whether the contestants should represent only a South Pacific country or whether they should open it up for participants from migrant communities in places like Australia and the United States of America. Decisions need to be made on judging criteria. Should the pageant for example pursue a *Palangi* criteria of beauty with full make up or a traditional island kind of beauty?" ('Otuangu 1994, 20).

14. Tongans share with other Polynesians a concept of *mana* and *tapu*. Mana has been interpreted as a kind of supernatural power, divine force, authority, and generative potency (Shore 1989, 139-43). To speak of mana is always to imply tapu or taboo. "As an

active quality, tapu suggests a contained potency of something, place or person. In its passive usage, it means forbidden or dangerous for someone who is *noa*" (Shore 1989, 144). This notion of being tapu is still present in Tonga today. The heads of the royal family should always sit higher than commoners. Therefore the head of the contestant must be held high and with dignity if she is to embody the essence of Tonga.

12

The Politics of Beauty in Thailand

Penny Van Esterik

Introduction

The work of beauty is seldom calculated in the assessment of gender subordination in Thailand. But one of the means that has been used to keep Thai women—both rural and urban— in their place is beauty. The attributes of gentleness, silence, and virtue are intertwined with the attributes of grace, composure, and beauty to produce a model of Thai femininity that crosses regions and classes. The Thai state is very much involved in the construction of this model and has been making use of it as part of its nation building strategies since the 1930s. It is this construction of beauty that strengthens the hold of cultural models of the feminine on Thai women. Beauty contests are one means used to encourage women to conform to a passive, morally upright, dutiful stereotype, while men continue to enjoy a double standard—expecting sexual purity of their mothers, wives, and sisters, but condoning and practising sexually exploitative behaviour with prostitutes, subordinates, and minor wives.

Beauty contests in Thailand flourish in their local, national, and international forms. Elsewhere I have explored their relation to politics and military power (Van Esterik 1993), and their connections to gender and development in Thailand (Van Esterik 1994). They are sites of complex gender negotiation, and I am currently trying to place them in their broadest context within Thai gender ideology (Van Esterik nd). But their meanings are difficult to tie down, as they influence and are influenced by global processes such as tourism, nationalism, and mass media. This paper provides an ethnographic study of international beauty contests as they intersect with local practices in Thailand, places these practices in historical perspective, and speculates on their place in Thailand's international "presentation of self."

Discussions among Thai feminists about beauty contests began long before Miss Thailand won the Miss Universe contest for the second time in 1988. In 1985 *Friends of Women Magazine* published an editorial and article opposing the idea of holding the Miss Universe pageant in Thailand. They objected to women being assessed on the basis of their appearance and treated as objects to benefit others. They contradicted the argument that the pageant would encourage tourism and foreign investment, pointing out that the pageant would encourage sexist tourists who already view Thailand as "the biggest brothel in the world." Moreover, foreign investments, they argued, are linked to factors like profit margins, market demand, and political stability, not beauty pageants. They continued their campaign against beauty contests through the 1992 Miss Universe Contest held in Bangkok, producing a comic strip insert in their newsletter. The comic shows a rural woman bantering with her male companion who urges her to enter a beauty contest. She counters his argument, saying that the contests are a waste of time, dishonest, exploitative, and turn women into traveling ads, into dolls. Other women's groups pointed out that women contribute directly to the Thai economy not through their beauty, but through their abilities and skills. They argued that beauty contests do not help women improve society and only encourage values that are detrimental to women,

Thai women's groups also objected to beauty contests because they created a situation where a North American criterion of beauty—straight nose, large eyes—is encouraged, leading to a greater homogenization of standards for evaluating women's physical appearance. Writing of the success of Vanessa Williams, the first black American Miss America, Gerald Early describes her victory as a "tribute to the ethnocentric universality of the white beauty standards of the contest; in short, her looks allow her to "pass" aesthetically (1984, 295).

But these assorted arguments fell on deaf ears, as Bangkok continues its love affair with beauty contests. For now, Thai women's groups say they are tired, that they cannot keep fighting against beauty contests, and that other issues are more important for Thai women.

In North America, demonstrations against the Miss America contest in 1968 publicized the same feminist discourse against beauty competitions, stressing how they commoditize women and exploit them for capitalist expansion through commercial endorsements and publicity appearances. They protested on the grounds that the contest promoted an impossible image of ideal womanhood, and was complicit in the idea that all women—not only participants in beauty contests—are reducible to a set of bodily attributes (Kuhn 1985:3). But beauty contests are not seriously addressed in Western feminist writings. When they are mentioned, it is mostly in response to and in protest over a particular contest. In some ways, this is not surprising because beauty contests do not dominate the thoughts of many women in North America. My interest in beauty contests was dismissed as trivial in both Thai and Canadian academe. Protests against the contests are read, particularly by men, as jealous responses of less than beautiful women. There is not a well developed feminist critique of the process of ranking women on the basis of their appearance, nor an adequate analysis of all the varied experiences of beauty contests in communities, nation states, and internationally. This book aims to fill in some of these obvious gaps in the literature.

Very little feminist analysis on beauty was done until the publication of Wolf's *The Beauty Myth* (1991). In this book, Naomi Wolf argues that images of female beauty are used as political weapons against women's advancement. The "beauty myth" carries on the work of social control of women, prescribing behavior and not just appearance (Wolf 1991,14). Thus, she argues that beauty is most directly about men's institutional power in the workplace, and elsewhere. Wolf links the perversions of the beauty myth to religion, sex, violence, and anorexia, and concludes that only by getting beyond the beauty myth can women enjoy a noncompetitive beauty that cannot be used against them. She provides a good beginning for an analysis of beauty in North America, but few insights that carry over into cross-cultural work because beauty is culturally constructed. Without an examination of how beauty is embedded in gender ideology and notions of the body in specific cultural settings, beauty is easily glossed in Euro-American terms.

Beauty Displays in Southeast Asia

Southeast Asia has a long tradition of displaying and evaluating beauty of form, for both males and females. There are sets of indigenous concepts concerning beauty that provide cultural space for several of the practices underlying beauty contests in Southeast Asia. These include body decoration and sumptuary laws regulating jewelry and dress. Further, these practices are not divorced from power. Possession of radiant beauty is evidence of legitimate power—both beauty of self and of mate. This idea, of great antiquity in Southeast Asia, has salience in recent Thai history and even in contemporary Thai politics where politicians are admired for their beauty rather than their judgment.

The appreciation of grace and elegance, and the evaluation of beauty is very deeply entrenched in Thai culture. "Thais appreciate grace and elegance; things should be beautiful to be in order, yet this order also requires hard work and dependability. Which is why it is women who are at the heart of Thai life" (Mulder 1992, 77). This may help to explain why it is feminine beauty that is extolled in court literature and poetry. Standards of feminine beauty are defined, and these include beauty of manner and behavior as well as form. Voice is also mentioned as a key attribute of women's beauty.

Transvestite beauty contests are very popular and acceptable in Thailand and the Philippines. Video documentaries such as "Lady Boys" exploits this phenomenon without exploring the challenge such contests present to the definition of gender categories in Thailand. Johnson (this volume) explores the compatibility of transvestite contests with performative traditions in the Philippines and elsewhere in Southeast Asia. Even the socialist states of Vietnam and Laos have recently begun to participate in regional beauty contests.

Beauty contests in Southeast Asia are more than examples of the exploitation and commodification of women; they epitomize a set of performative practices such as gestures, body movement, facial expressions, clothing, and make-up, which exist in popular culture and everyday practice and are exaggerated, inscribed, and more completely embodied during beauty contests. Beauty contests are sites where "bodily gestures, movements and styles of various kinds constitute the illusion of an abiding gendered self" (Butler 1990, 140). By reproducing particular kinds of gendered selves, they oppress women while naturalizing physical beauty. Hence their fascination for Thai women. I will describe these beauty practices as they were observed during a number of international, national, and local contests in Thailand in 1992, and offer suggestions of how these practices might relate to other gendered processes in the country. I will then place the current scene in historical perspective, arguing that representations of Thai cultural identity—both internally and externally—focus attention on the appearance of Thai women. Far from being invisible, they are the public embodiment of Thai culture. I begin with the international contests, specifically, the Miss Universe contest of 1992.

International Beauty Contests

The Miss Universe contest held in May, 1992, was held in the Queen Sirikit Convention Center, Bangkok, built for the World Bank meetings in 1991. Following the World Bank meetings, the Center had a new opportunity to raise money, estimated at U.S. $600,000 in tourist revenue. The pro-democracy demonstrations held that same week (see Van Esterik 1994) may have cut into that estimated profit.

The week before the contest, Thai and foreign Bangkok newspapers kept the public informed about the activities leading up to the Miss Universe Contest. For several weeks before the big event, the contest was promoted every night at 10 p.m. on television. Most articles in English newspapers downplayed the display of the women themselves, and emphasized the hard work of the contestants (rehearsals ten hours a day, their careful chaperoning to keep contestants from alcohol, cigarettes, and men) and the importance of personality as revealed by the extra interview added to the judging three years ago (to appease the feminists) (*Bangkok Post*, 21 April 1992; *Nation*, 29 April 1992).

Beauty pageants are lucrative industries, linked to the entertainment, advertising, and tourism industries at various levels. Miss Universe, Miss USA, and Miss Teen USA, are all produced by Madison Square Garden Event Productions, a Paramount Communication Company. Since 1960, the Procter & Gamble company has been the principal sponsor of the pageant, and CBS the network that has broadcast the pageants live worldwide since 1972. The press kit distributed before the event in Bangkok contained information on television ratings for the broadcast, estimating a worldwide viewing audience of 600 million in sixty countries, making the Miss Universe telecast one of the most watched programming events in the world. This is prime time politics, and it is about much more than beauty. The audience composition surveys show that most viewers were young women.

When Thailand accepted the contract to host the 1992 Miss Universe pageant, Thai Sky Television of the Siam Broadcasting and Communication Company paid one million dollars copyright fees to Miss Universe Inc. to host the event, and began the task of assembling local sponsors. These included the Bangkok Bank, Kodak, Nestle, Covermark, Nissan, Coca Cola, and the Dusit Thani hotels. Sponsors pay between U.S. $80,000 and $200,000 cash in addition to the costs of providing their products as prizes. Most sponsors said that they did it for good will and to promote a positive image of the country, although they expected to lose money.

The Miss Universe contest held in Bangkok was clearly about using women to promote Thai products and places. A three minute travelogue produced by the Tourist Association of Thailand (TAT) showed the reigning Miss Universe as she moved through the Thai tourist landscape, stopping long enough to be photographed in all the distinctive places—the beach resorts, northern Thai hill tribe villages, the ruins of Sukhothai, Ayutthaya, and Pimai, the Grand Palace in Bangkok, local temples, the floating market, Thai boxing matches, Bangkok "night life," classical dance performances, and of course shopping malls. The final television broadcast shows Miss Universe contestants riding elephants in the Queen Sirikit Convention Centre, and posing on the beaches of Pattaya and Cha'am. As the Miss Universe contestants avoided the steaming piles of elephant dung in the Rose Garden, a park just outside Bangkok, eight middle-aged women dressed in traditional costume rowed decoratively around the pond, work they were ordered to begin an hour before the arrival of the contestants to the popular tourist site. Here we have both contrived settings for displaying contrived Thai culture and people performing contrived tasks.

In the final television broadcast, eighty-five girls ages four to seven were selected to accompany the contestants. The Little Sisters of the Miss Universe Pageant exemplify the growing popularity of children's beauty contests in Thailand. Children are trained and selected for contests based on their appearance, singing ability, and dancing skills. They become "good will ambassadors" for companies that sponsor them such as Coca Cola, and are walking advertisements as they travel to different countries as part of their duties. Children's rights advocates in Thailand criticized the children's involvement in beauty contests, arguing that children should not be used to sell goods, should not be made up like little adults for other's amusement, should not be encouraged to show off, and should not be exposed to contests of questionable morality. Children, they argued, should be protected, not exploited. Mothers of the Little Sisters did not share this concern. One mother explained that her five-year-old daughter wanted to be a beauty queen when she grew up. The Little Sisters were dressed in a variety of outfits, from western dresses with elaborate lace and chiffon flounces to traditional Thai silk costumes, most with lovely jewelery. Each had a sash with the name of her "big sister's" country on it.

The children played under the watchful eyes of chaperons and trainers from "The Mall" shopping centre, a new shopping complex in Bangkok. Outside the glass walls of the rehearsal hall, anxious parents, relatives, and well-wishers "oohed" and "ahhed" over the children. "Narak" (cute) was the most common word overheard as the children gradually assembled alphabetically by country, held hands in a long chain, and walked upstairs to meet the contestants—their "big sisters"—and the press. When all was ready, the children filed in singing, to stand in front of their big sisters. They first raised their hands respectfully in a graceful "wai" salutation, but within minutes the contestants were on the floor hugging the children, kissing and cuddling them, and carrying them about, posing for the ever-present cameras. Parents strained to see their daughters finally meet the contestants, and commented favourably on their poise and grace, in great contrast to the contestants who "waied" with great awkwardness, demonstrating inappropriate respect to their little sisters. (Adults are not expected to "wai" children). Eventually, the cameras had all the "cuteness" they could absorb, and the performers moved out of the public view to a luncheon.

For all the rhetoric about the "balance between inner and outer beauty" (*Nation*, 29 April 1992) and the facade of the contests serving a higher purpose such as the provision of scholarships, attention is clearly meant to be focused on women's bodies and body parts, as women are dismembered by the press into parts perfected for advertising: "...there are pointed noses, small noses, full lips...perfect figures held up high on long legs, high hips and full bosoms and buttocks...and those tiny waists" (*Bangkok Post*, 29 April 1992). The press can hardly be blamed for focusing on body parts when they were provided with rating sheets to compare their scoring with that of the judges in the Miss Thailand World contest. Scores were assigned as follows: face (30%), figure (20%), legs (10%), walking (10%), wit (10%), personality (10%), and character (10%).

A pageant press release says that although contestants are "encouraged not to alter their own natural beauty, no restrictions are placed on cosmetic surgery." The average size of Miss Universe has decreased over time, in spite of the fact that women are getting larger. Catalina swimsuits, worn by Miss Universe for the past 29 years, are now provided in one size smaller, with "fullness at the bust needed by Asian women" (*Bangkok Post*, 29 April 1992). Asian women are now permitted the use of bra padding to provide the necessary bust fullness, and to avoid permanent cosmetic surgery "which would provoke bad press" (*Bangkok Post*, 21 April 1992). No mention, of course, of the dangers to the women's bodies of such unnecessary intrusive surgery. Wolf discusses this current practice and tells us that an American clinic advertises itself in a brochure to the effect that it can offer:

> "a Western appearance to the eyes" to "the Oriental Eyelid," which "lacks a well-defined supratarsal fold." It admires "the Caucasian or 'Western' nose," ridicules "Asian Noses," "Afro-Caribbean Noses ('a fat and rounded tip which needs correction')," and "Oriental Noses ('the tip...too close to the face')." And "the Western nose that requires alternation invariably exhibits some of the characteristics of (nonwhite) noses...although the improvement needed is more subtle." (1991, 264)

At the climax of the broadcast, a six-foot white masseuse and model representing a predominantly black country, Namibia, was chosen as Miss Universe. The contest confirmed the use of western (white) criteria defining beauty—tall, slim, curvaceous—and the advantage to English speakers. The lone ironic moment came when the only woman of colour to reach the semi-finals lost the crown by lapsing into a moment of honesty. Miss India said that her mind went blank when asked what she would do for children as leader of her country. She answered that she would build sports stadiums for children. For a moment, her mind reflected not her condition as an object of beauty for display, but her professional identity as athlete and fitness instructor. As a woman of action, she might indeed build sports stadiums. The other two candidates provided vague sentimental rhetoric about children and peace, neither having anything to do with action—with practice—so totally committed were they to their display professions, and so well coached.

The headlines on the day after the contest asked, "Are the eyes of the beholder truly colour-blind?" (*Nation*, 10 May 1992). The fact that only Miss India was dark complexioned among the ten semifinalists was overshadowed by the election of blonde Miss Namibia as the new Miss Universe. "There are white girls too," she said in answer to hostile questioning by reporters (*Nation*, 10 May 1992). According to one reporter, only the bags of the black delegates were inspected at the airport as the contestants returned home the day following the contest. Thus ended the "clean peep show that was dedicated to making money, endorsing white supremacy, and denigrating women all in one fell cultural swoop" (Early 1984, 296).

The Miss World contest began in the early fifties in England, and prides itself on being more than a beauty contest. The 1992 Miss World contest took place in Sun City, Southern Africa, at the newly opened Lost City, "an awe inspiring sort of African Disney World but with a creative cultural background" (according to the organizers, Erik and Julia Morley). "Beauty with a purpose," the contest slogan, suggests that contestants should be beautiful but should also help society in some way. There is little evidence of this intention in the Thai contest, except that the profits from the dinner and entertainment (which includes the judging of the Miss Thailand World final) are donated to the Narcotics Control Foundation. The political connections between these contests and the military are discussed elsewhere (Van Esterik 1994).

The 1992 Miss Thailand contest brought the question of representativeness and authenticity to the fore once again. As a Japanese judge struggled to question the finalists in Thai, it was revealed that three of the five Miss Thailand contestants could not understand or speak the language. The three from the United States were the runners-up to the Miss Thailand contest. Two of the three were born to Thai fathers and American mothers. They all felt they were Thai because "they were raised in a Thai atmosphere, in a house with Thai furniture," says Gina, "and we eat Thai food." Gina won the beauty contest run by Thammasat University alumni in Los Angeles. The American Thais were the obvious favorites for the Miss Thailand crown. Press reports complained that they were deprived of the crown because of their mixed looks and their failure to express themselves in Thai. Yet these "mixed looks" and facility in English are precisely the characteristics that are sought out for success in the international level contests. Their advice for the next lot of Thai-American candidates? "Take Thai speech classes and study about Thai history and culture" (*Nation Junior*, 19 April 1992).

Critics of the judges referred to the choice of Miss Ornanong Panyawong, a Thai classical dancer from Chiang Mai and the newly crowned Miss Thailand, as a "national disgrace...an insult," and objected to the crown going to a "local born, dark horse contestant...because she looked more Thai" (*Bangkok Post*, 31 March 1992). Miss Ornanong not only exemplified the classical Thai accomplished woman, she also supported her family financially as a "dutiful daughter" should. One suspects that this conflict not only reveals contradictions concerning national identity but also concerning class and region.

Fashioning Nationalism

Let me place these observations about the international beauty contests in a broader historical context. The Thai state has supported practices that use female bodies in a variety of ways not explored here—child prostitution, sex tourism, exploitative labour conditions. But the state's involvement in beauty contests adds a different dimension to the discussion. These are subtle forms of social control—but subtle forms are often the most effective. The communicative properties of bodies are intimately connected to deeply entrenched aesthetic standards for women. The properties of the good woman are extolled in Buddhist and court texts. There was "cultural space" for the elaboration of sites where women were ranked according to their appearance.

National beauty contests have been an important part of Thailand's nation building strategy since the 1930s. State involvement in national beauty contests was for the purpose of celebrating democracy and the constitution. The first government sponsored contest to choose Miss Siam was held in 1934, two years after the 1932 coup that ended the absolute monarchy in Thailand. (The winner has been named Miss Thailand since 1939.) The contest's purpose was political, and it was held as part of the Constitution Day celebrations. A public announcement directed to Thai women read:

> You have shown the country how much you respect the constitution of the Kingdom of Thailand. Therefore you sacrifice your personal happiness to come on stage for public viewing, bringing delight to the atmosphere of the Constitution Celebration. (*Bangkok Post*, 2 March 1990)

The objective of the contest was to support the new concept of democracy, to build the nation, and to increase the status of women. How the contest would accomplish the latter was never made clear. At the same time the contest would provide entertainment at the fair. It seems that democracy and the constitution needed a woman's radiant beauty to increase the power and legitimacy of democracy. Seven hundred years of Thai myth and history support this link between legitimate political power and women's radiant beauty.

The contest was held at the Rajadamnern Fair in two parks close to the Grand Palace in Bangkok, and was expected to bring a joyful atmosphere to the occasion. The contestants were chosen for their "natural" beauty, and stress was placed on their fresh, unaffected, everyday appearance. Judges would dip cotton in water to rub off any powder to make sure they had good skin. In addition, the contest would provide a setting to display the new western fashions that Thai women were supposed to adopt, such as hats, high heels, and tailored dresses. The prizes were insignificant compared with those offered in later contests—a crown trimmed with black velvet, a silver bowl, a locket—the honor was enough. The winners came primarily from the families of government officials, and tended to marry government officers.

During the years when Phibul Songkhram was Prime Minister for the first time (1938-1944), the contest served to further his nation-building and political strategy. Contest photographs showed women in military uniforms and western style hats, a fashion accessory that Phibul was promoting. The 1939 winner received a kimono from the Japanese Embassy in Bangkok, a premonition of Thailand's relation with Japan during the Second World War. But in spite of the rhetoric about uplifting the status of Thai women, the government-sponsored beauty contest displayed women in shorts at least by 1940. No contest was held during the war years, the years of Japanese occupation, and the immediate post-war years (1941-1947).

When Phibul became Prime Minister for the second time in 1948, the contest for Miss Thailand resumed with larger prizes and shorter clothing. The commercial opportunities provided by the contest were beginning to be appreciated, as the 1948 winner received a sewing machine, and the 1950 winner was photographed with her radio, which, in addition to $600 in prize money and two tickets around the world, made this a prize worth posing for. As the prizes became more substantial, the genteel image of the contest faded and by the 1950s, many contestants became mistresses of important, powerful men. Prime Minister Sarit was a particular connoisseur of beauty contest winners and used to take his mistresses (numbering over fifty), (Wyatt 1982, 285) to his "pink heaven," his bedroom.

Women were a key part of the modernizing strategy of Thailand in the early decades of this century. Concern with the correct image for Thailand is reflected in how women were represented, in an effort to assert Thai independence in the face of British and French colonial threats. King Rama VI (1910-1925) viewed the status of women as a symbol of the degree of civilization of the country (Vella 1978, 152). But his concern, like Phibul's, was for appearances: "Please understand that others are taking our measure" (Vella 1978, 153). And when appearances are manipulated, attention soon turns to women.

King Rama VI identified three major restrictions on Thai women: their limited freedom to socialize with men on equal terms, their limited access to education, and the practice of polygamy. Other problems concerned their appearance and included women's black teeth from betel chewing, short "brush cut" hair styles, and wearing the comfortable draped pants worn by both men and women. He was particularly concerned because westerners did not view these as differences in fashions, but as deliberate strategies to keep women unattractive, and thus in bondage (Vella 1978, 154). Foreign comments about the appearance of Thai women reveal misunderstandings of Thai aesthetic standards. Further, they suggest the possibility that westerners may have been confused by the lack of gender differentiation in dress. He encouraged his women friends and relatives to wear their hair long and wear more stylish wrap-around skirts rather than draped pants. Even hats were encouraged, and the new fashions were widely imitated.

Prime Minister Phibul's efforts at nation-building in the 30s also concentrated on "upgrading" Thai women in appearance as well as in substance. Like King Rama VI, he wanted them to dress and wear their hair and make-up in a manner that would appear modern and western. Particularly during the Second World War women were encouraged to dress in European style to remind the Japanese that Thai were like westerners, not like Japanese. Women were required to wear hats ("Wear a hat for your country"), stockings, and tube-like skirts rather than the draped pants worn by both men and women in rural communities and in the court. So much for the promotion of Thai dress! Beauty contests served to introduce these western dress styles and to promote them as an integral part of Thai women's appeal.

Phibul's policies were meant to "upgrade" Thai women to the status of women in western countries (Nanthira 1987). This could be accomplished by promoting women's education, guaranteeing her rights, and setting up women's groups to oversee welfare and charity events. In this way, elite women could improve common women. Much of this work was accomplished by Lady Laiat, wife of Phibun, who chaired the Women's Bureau of the Office of Cultural Affairs under the National Culture Council. The Women's Cultural Club set up bazaars, fashion shows and fairs for fundraising, as the elite women's groups still do today in Bangkok. Projects such as beauty contests attempted to encourage mass rather than elite nationalism, and always modified the image not the substance of Thai identity. On November 3, 1939, Phibul issued a law requiring people to eat Thai food, wear Thai clothes, purchase Thai products and support public activities to build Thai national identity. Thai beauty contests were developed as part of this nation building strategy as they combined efforts to promote Thai identity (including the beauty of Thai women) with efforts to appear civilized and western (having those women wear western hats and shoes).

Getting Down to Business

Beauty contestants in the 1950s began to take on contest agents, and undergo expensive beauty treatments. By coincidence, the winner of the 1953 contest used Chantana beauty shop, where the woman who was to become Thailand's most famous beauty contest agent worked as a hair dresser. Amara Asavanand, runner-up of the 1953 Miss Thailand contest, entered the Miss Universe contest on her own without national or international sponsorship, beginning the linkage to the international contests.

Just because the national Miss Thailand contest was not held between 1954 and 1964 did not mean that there were no beauty contests held in Thailand during this period, only that none were sponsored by the national government. Many Bangkok communities held local beauty contests around New Year's celebrations. These urban contests may also have inspired subtle changes in village beauty contests associated with merit-making rituals following Buddhist lent and at Songkran (New Year's). New Year's beauty contests continued to be held in cities, towns, and villages during this period; however, they had no political purpose and thus no state sponsorship.

The objectives of the Miss Thailand contest newly reestablished in 1964 were frankly commercial with some additional public relations intentions to make Thailand better known abroad. Supatra argues that the contests held during Sarit's (1959-1963) and Thanom's (1963-1973) terms as Prime Ministers served to entertain the people and close their eyes to dictatorship. Fashion shows were also staged to accomplish the same purpose (Supatra 1987, 135-36). Thailand's close military and commercial relations with the United States required investment and capitalist expansion. And even beauty queens could do their part.

The alumni association of a well-known elite school regularly sponsored a Miss Wachirawut contest as part of their fundraising strategy, but did not send the winner abroad to compete in international contests. In 1964, they decided to sponsor a Miss Thailand contest for the purpose of entering the winner as the national candidate for the Miss Universe contest. Encouraged no doubt by Miss Universe Inc. and Thai TV channel 7, the association sent Miss Thailand, Apasara Hongsakul, to the Miss Universe contest, where she won the crown and became a public celebrity. Winning the Miss Universe contest raised the status of the Miss Thailand contest. It certainly raised the stakes.

With the stakes raised, contestants were prepared to pay the beauty industry for programs that would increase their chances of winning—programs of massage, sauna, exercise, diet, dress design, and special cosmetics to make them (and no doubt any paying customer) beautiful. But these training programs were expensive. "Beauty is hard work, few women are born with it, and it is not free" (Wolf 1991, 151). Enter the professional beauty agent, who would search out suitable candidates, train them in how to walk, talk, sit, and smile to international standards, and split their prize money with them, sometimes 50-50, other times 70-30 in favour of the agent. The contestant kept gifts such as cars and trips.

By 1964, the Miss Universe standard of beauty for face, figure, and posture was adopted in Thailand. Miss Thailand, like Miss Universe should have shoulders broader than hips, a long neck, straight rounded arms, legs in proportion to hips, straight feet, hair suited to face, long fingers, clean nails, straight back, and breasts "not too large or too small." The ideal beauty should be twenty years old, at least 160 centimetres tall, and near the golden proportions 33-22-35 inches (Supatra 1987, 186).

The revolutionary ideals of the student uprising of 1973 which overthrew a corrupt regime, and the growing women's movement in Thailand discouraged the national beauty contests, which were not held from 1974 until 1984. Thai feminists were successful in arguing that the contests overstressed the appearance of women and lowered their status. During this time period, many progressive reforms were initiated, and the national climate was not conducive to the sponsorship of national beauty contests. The brutal suppression of students and progressives after the massacre at Thammasat University in October, 1976 ushered in a series of military governments with little interest in or opportunity for national spectacles. But the growth of Thai tourism in the '80s encouraged the reestablishment of the national contests in 1984. Beauty contests were used to promote everything Thai, from bananas to gemstones. In times of increasing poverty, rural women saw beauty contests as a route to economic prosperity; an advertising or entertainment executive might see them and sign them up, or provide product endorsements for them. More often, however, beauty contests were occasions for recruiting high class escorts and call girls.

Beauty contests of the '30s and '40s stressed the natural beauty of Thai women. The '80s saw opportunities and motivation for changing hair and skin colour, altering eye shape, shaving eye brows, and augmenting breast size to meet international beauty standards. In the past, youth alone was sufficient; the young were assumed to need no artificial enhancement of their maidenly beauty (Mills 1993, 152). The efforts of beauty contestants to perfect their appearance simultaneously supported the growing beauty industry including beauty shops, cosmetic companies, and fashion designers. Nose jobs and eye lifts became equally popular among urban Thai women who had the money to work on their appearance (Supatra 1987, 244).

Commercial production of beauty fit nicely with the production of representations of Thai women as part of the natural resources of Thailand.

Conclusions

What has changed in Thailand since the '30s is not the importance of beauty as an attribute of women, but individual and social attitudes towards beauty. Beauty has become effectively detached from its moral base. Thus, beauty is seen less as a natural attribute existing within the body and radiating outward, and more as something that can be purchased, placed on the surface, and enhanced. It becomes the responsibility of women to develop their own beauty potential rather than assume responsibility for meritorious acts that will result in inner beauty. When not being beautiful is a moral failure, the disjunction between indigenous meanings of beauty and that imposed by international contests is inevitable. Into this disjunction slips the knowledge and practices necessary to make oneself appear beautiful, and the industries that thrive on selling them. This reinforces the idea that beauty is a function of wealth, a belief that resonates well with Buddhist notions of karma.

In the last few decades, national beauty contests have had no overtly political purposes, at least none as explicit as those of the '30s and '40s. Yet, it is important to continue to examine the use to which Thai women's beauty has been put. These purposes include representing and essentializing Thailand in public culture primarily for purposes of international tourism, and deflecting feminist critiques of male behavior. Beauty contests set the tone for the way Thai women are evaluated and thought about and how they evaluate and think about themselves. As everyone says, "Thai women love beauty contests." Beauty contests probably have a greater influence on young Thai women than feminist writings. What is needed—and what I have only begun here—is a systematic examination of the relation between beauty, gender relations, sexuality, and power. Beauty contests are important sites for such a study.

13

Connections and Contradictions
From the Crooked Tree Cashew Queen to Miss World Belize

Richard Wilk

Introduction

There is always something strongly subjective and debatable about aesthetic judgment. In their book *Face Value* (1984), Lakoff and Scherr argue that this indefinable and unmeasurable subjectivity is not an obstacle to defining beauty, but is in fact the very core of the matter. If beauty could be judged objectively, they say, it would not be so mysterious or powerful. Because beauty can never be defined precisely, discussing or debating beauty always draws us into a conversation about basic, important matters, of values and essences. We can never agree completely on what beauty is, but it nevertheless draws us into an engagement based in common understandings of the terms of debate. Therefore, judging beauty is an exercise that simultaneously divides people and brings them together. While they will never agree completely in their judgments, they can often agree on the terms of disagreement.

Beauty contests engage diverse cultures and communities in exactly this kind of shared discourse and contention. In the foreground it is easy to see the disagreements and differences, the ways that different interests make judgments according to their personal, political and cultural agendas. At another level, however, subtle and basic forms of common agreement are being forged and established. By engaging in public judgment and debate, beauty pageants and contests can help form connections that I have called *structures of common difference* (Wilk 1995).

Imagine a world of many cultures each with their own unique definitions of gender, sexuality, and beauty. Boone's *Radiance From the Waters* (1986), on the aesthetics of feminine beauty among the Mende of Sierra Leone is an excellent model of this kind of encapsulated and culturally specific system (see also Johnson and Teilhet-Fiske in this volume). To understand Mende aesthetics you must understand Mende society, language and culture. In a world of such cultures, there are no common bridging

concepts of gender or beauty, and true translation is the task of a professional interpreter. The Mende meaning of the words we translate as
"beauty" is simply incommensurate with our own definition.

Pageants forge connections between these culturally bound and local
systems of aesthetics. While they do not resolve or eliminate differences,
they build equivalence between those diverse dialogues of gender and
beauty, so that gender and beauty emerge as if they were indeed universal
categories. Pageants engage local definitions with each other in a way that
creates common categories, though the content of the categories may be
in dispute. A debate about "what is feminine" first requires a universalized
category of "femininity." The pageants assert that beauty is one of the descriptive dimensions of that category, thereby arguing that beauty is also
natural, essential, and universal to all humanity. Engaging with the task of
aesthetic judgment in the pageant, the audience is welcome to argue about
the meaning of beauty and the importance of beauty, but not the *existence*
of beauty or its linkage to femininity.

This paper traces some of the ways that pageants build these inter-
community and cross-cultural connections within Belize, and between
Belizeans and a growing transnational and cosmopolitan media-based
consumer culture centered in the United States and Europe. I will maintain a focus on the contradictions, conflicts, and diversity that keeps bub-
bling up within this common institutional framework. By doing this I
want to suggest that just as the power of beauty is its indefinable, evanes-
cent, and subjective nature, so it is with pageantry, where the attraction for
participants and audiences is the drama of contradiction and paradox, of
the connection of opposites and the breaking of boundaries. In saying this
I do not mean to assert that Belizean beauty contests challenge or subvert
the status quo, liberate, or challenge domination. On the contrary, when
pageants make connections they often solidify the very boundaries they
cross. Their peculiar power is to make the very things they seem to challenge quite incontestable and concrete.

In other papers I have argued that pageants help organize and structure Belizeans' notions of difference, that they naturalize and essentialize
gender, age, ethnicity, and the spatial order of the nation state. Pageants
as an institution can serve the state's goals of "domesticating difference,"
of channeling potentially dangerous social divisions into the realm of aesthetics and taste. But they can also fail in getting this message across, and
can end up emphasizing and exacerbating the very divisions they are
meant to minimize or control.

In this paper I concentrate on the other kinds of divisions and differences that are not contained or channeled or resolved by the drama of the
beauty pageant in Belize, differences that are rooted in the subordinate
political and economic position that Belize occupies in the global order.

Beauty pageants can never avoid raising this issue, for their very form is an expression of the global power of the United States, where the institution was given modern form in the nineteenth century (Riverol 1992; Banner 1983). The Miss America pageant is an archetype and model for most national competitions in the world, which are now often commercial local franchises of the Miss Universe or Miss World corporations; profit making concerns owned and operated in the United States and England.

THE SETTING

Belize is a multiethnic country on the Central American mainland that remains culturally tied to the Caribbean by virtue of its colonial history. Once a source of timber for the British Empire, Belize achieved limited self-rule in 1963 and full independence in 1981. The population of about 200,000 is divided between a single city, seven smaller towns and about two hundred villages, scattered through rainforest, savanna and offshore cayes that have become major tourist attractions. The two largest cultural groups are Afro-Caribbean "Creoles" concentrated in Belize City, and a largely rural and agricultural "Hispanic" population of old and new immigrants from neighboring countries. The rest of the mix includes three groups of Maya-speaking Amerindians, German-speaking Mennonites, Garifuna (Black Caribs), Chinese, East Indians, and British and North American expatriates.

Once a sleepy backwater dominated by a tiny and exclusive expatriate elite, the country has gone through unprecedented economic and social changes during the last twenty years (see Wilk 1993; Bolland 1986). The economy has diversified into tourism and export agriculture, and local markets are dominated by imported goods of all kinds. Many Creoles have migrated to the United States, changing the ethnic balance of the country and building a transnational network of family and financial connections. A growing population of mobile "Belizean Americans" maintain ties with both countries, and wield both cultural and political influence in Belize (see Cohen this volume; Basch et al. 1994). In one of my surveys in Belize City in 1990, forty-five percent of high school students reported having an immediate relative (parent or sibling) living abroad. At the same time, Belize is becoming an "electronic suburb" of the United States through instant phone connections and television. Nine stations broadcast a steady diet of American and Mexican satellite TV, and full-service cable systems serve every settlement larger than a thousand people (Wilk 1994; Bolland 1987; Oliveira 1986).

My initial exposure to beauty pageants in Belize was mostly accidental, since I was researching the demand for imported consumer goods. While I wanted to talk about peanut butter, beans, and rice, the people I spoke with kept bringing up pageants. These were the places, they said, where local values and imported foreign ones collided on stage. And when I began to look, I found pageants literally everywhere; they extended from the annual national pageants down to Queen competitions at rural village festivals, and in high schools. In the last few years these beauty contests and pageants have rivaled dances and sporting events in popularity as public entertainment.

Initially I was drawn to study the origin and development of pageantry through newspaper archives and interviews with some of the participants in the first events. In other papers I have traced in some detail the history of beauty pageantry in Belize (Wilk 1993, 1995). I have been particularly interested in the relationship between the growth of party politics and the pageants, and also the ways that pageants have both furthered and subverted various nationalist and nation-building programs over the last half century.

Pageantry started in Belize in 1946, in the context of growing anti-British discontent with the social and economic status quo. Some members of a small, educated, urban middle class began to forge common ground with the labor union movement, and impoverished rural people suffering through the slow collapse of the logging industry. This alliance formed the core of the first successful political party, which led strikes and labor actions and then contested the first national elections in 1954 as the Peoples United Party (Shoman 1987).

The reaction among the solid Creole middle class of colonial functionaries and the thin Anglicized upper crust was a loyalist movement that sought continuing membership in the Empire. They founded the "Loyal and Patriotic Order of the Baymen" (LPOB) as a series of lodges on the Masonic model, and organized "patriotic" displays on Empire themes at an annual September celebration. Unlike the rowdy popular Carnival festivities elsewhere in the Caribbean, this celebration was serious and very British, including marching bands and schoolchildren, patriotic floats, and hours of speeches.

A group of young women attached to one of these lodges introduced the "Queen of the Bay" contest in 1946 in order to "bring up" (make more respectable) the festivities with a connection to royalty. Their Queen was supposed to represent all the characteristics associated with the values of "respectability" as it is defined throughout the Caribbean (Wilson 1973; Austin 1983). She was supposed to come from a "good" (nuclear, religious) family, be modest, educated, respectful, and above all free of any hint of sexual experience. The organizers stressed "breeding and comportment," and the pageant itself was conducted entirely in formal wear. The contestants, each nominated by one of the neighborhood "lodges" of the LPOB, marched to patriotic music, gave a brief speech and then answered historical questions that stressed loyalty to the Empire. The British Governor was the judge. Afterward an orchestra played for ball-room dancing. As one of the founders said "We were looking for a real Queen. It was to try to enlighten them. The Queen must be digni-fied!...Not like today with *bath suit!*" A typical Queen of the Bay theme in 1970 was "Preserve and Enhance our Heritage—1798-1970." At the pageant "tall, charming, beautiful and dignified Honduran beauties slow-ly go through the rituals of courtseying (sic) and walking gracefully before the appointed judges" (*Belize Billboard*, September 23 1970).

In that same founding year of 1946, in a small town in the southern part of the colony, the Garifuna, a group of mixed African-Amerindian heritage who were discriminated against in Creole colonial society, held a pageant of their own. As part of the annual celebration of their arrival in Belize ("Settlement Day") a Garifuna committee held a coronation for the "Queen of the Settlement," which was followed, according to newspaper accounts, by "native dances." This Queen had to display a very different set of skills, demonstrating her ability to speak Garifuna, her knowledge of folk culture and her ability to perform traditional dances to drums.

At the very beginning, therefore, Belizean pageantry encompassed both the values of the colonizers as interpreted through a local lens, and those of an excluded local minority struggling for respect and self-identi-ty. From this complex start, the system of pageantry rapidly expanded into the other districts, which were soon nominating their own local Queens to attend the Queen of the Bay in Belize City. By 1950 the pageant had grown in popularity to the point where "The selection of the Queen of the Bay is the greatest event of the season in British Honduras." (*Clarion*, 28 September 1950) The emerging sense of geographic nationhood was a constant theme; the pageants were presented as regional rivalry between districts, emphasizing the centrality of Belize City, where the final event took place. Some regions named their winner after a local export product, bringing in financial sponsorships from the largest industries. Stann Creek had a "Citrus Queen" and Corozal a "Sugar Queen."

The nationalist movement quickly responded with its own pageant. Though their leadership was in prison for sedition, the Peoples United Party put on the first "Miss British Honduras" pageant in 1952. The char-acter of the pageant was quite different from the Queen of the Bay, with much more emphasis on physical beauty, and less stress on respectability, including a fashion show and entertainment by popular music. Speeches were more overtly political, and the emphasis was on local and North American arts and culture rather than British models.

The PUP and the loyalist movement kept their rival pageants sepa-rate for the next thirty years. The Queen of the Bay passed from the LPOB to the conservative National Party and later the rightist United

Democratic Party, which finally won a national election in 1984. The PUP, as the dominant political party, turned Miss British Honduras into Miss Independence in 1964 and Miss Belize in 1973 when the country changed its name. The Queen of the Bay remains a conservative and patriotic event with marching, quizzes and "high fashion" prominent themes, while Miss Belize has more popular entertainment, and more emphasis on both physical beauty and talent. Both parties made the pageants part of their national political structures; district branches of the parties were responsible for arranging local contests and soliciting contributions from local businesses. Contestants were almost always the daughters of party members.

At various times the two parties have been rivals to send their Queens to international competitions. In the 1970s the opposition UDP had the Miss Universe and Miss All Nations franchises, while the PUP government sent Miss Belize to regional Caribbean pageants and Miss World. When the UDP won the national elections in 1984 they took over Miss Belize and ran both pageants for four years as ostensibly nonpartisan and national events. The UDP Minister of Youth and Culture also sponsored an official Miss Youth pageant which attracted contestants from four other Caribbean countries. When the PUP returned to power in 1989 they took back control of Miss Belize and purged the UDP supporters from various committees, putting the pageant back into the grip of party functionaries. The chair of the organizing committee in 1989 was the wife of a PUP candidate for the national assembly.

From the beginning, then, pageantry in Belize has been part of a national political struggle, both an ideological tool for promoting particular values and a means of attracting financial support and audiences for political events. Both parties have asserted, through their pageants, that their party *is* the nation, and should represent Belize to the world. In the process, the dual and divided system has often sent exactly the opposite message; that the country is deeply divided into hostile political factions that each seek to take over the state for their own interests and exclude the other. This is in fact the general practice; when in power each party distributes patronage and offices to their own supporters, and "victimizes" members of the other party, excluding them from national life (Shoman 1987). So in the process of asserting unified claims to the nation, the pageants actually achieve the opposite by making divisions and disunity clear and obtrusive (Wilk 1993). During the 1989 pageant season these divisions emerged in audience commentaries and newspaper articles where a winning Queen of the Bay was accused of being a "secret PUP" because of her family connections, while a popular but unsuccessful contestant for Miss Belize was said to have lost because her family had voted UDP.

THE PROLIFERATION OF PAGEANTS

Once the basic format of the pageant had been imported and interpreted, various groups adapted it to different purposes, drawing upon and in turn building wider audiences. At the most local and amateur level, high schools across the country use "popularity contests" as a means of raising money for school projects and functions. Both girls and boys participate; children who have been nominated by their classes circulate among merchants and businesses in their community, asking for pledges or donations. The children who raise the most money are crowned King and Queen, and preside over a party or festival day where concessions, food sales, and games raise more money for the school. The winners of these contests are often recruited to participate in other, more formal pageants, since they are already judged to have "exposure" and experience performing in public. Many Miss Belize winners got their start this way.

Even at the level of the popularity contest, the essentially ambiguous nature of the event is clear. High school students and teachers I spoke with disagreed strongly over what is important in winning. Some said physical beauty, others a popular personality, an ability to conquer shyness or to speak well in public. But at the same time they all acknowledged that social position, connections, and wealth play a role too, pointing out that the child of a banker or politician was going to have an easy time signing up merchants. These same ingredients—social connections, personal skills and presence, and physical features—contend with each other in various combinations in every pageant from the village festival to the national finals. All the competitions provide stages where these values can combine and clash, though none can ever be more than temporarily triumphant, since all are quite legitimate.

Many village and town festivities are also graced with a Queen pageant of some sort.[1] Villages often have an annual fair or agricultural show, where they may have horse races, a cricket or soccer match, a dance, food booths, and a beauty contest. Some communities have found themes that they hope will attract tourists; for example an American ecotourism company helped the village of Crooked Tree plan and finance a "Cashew Festival" in 1993, during which the village elected a Cashew Queen. In a typical year about half the country's villages have a Queen contest, usually sponsored by the elected village council in a fairly informal atmosphere with very modest prizes.

The larger towns are all district seats, and their pageants are part of the national hierarchy of the Miss Belize and Queen of the Bay festivities, dominated by the political parties. Village Queens rarely take part in these pageants, which are dominated by townsfolk. The local branch of the political party selects a pageant organizing committee, often the wives of prominent politicians, and puts them in charge of the event. The committee must often work hard to recruit contestants, and they report a continuing problem finding qualified women who are willing to participate.

There are other kinds of non-village based festivals and events that merit the selection of a Queen. The first one of these I have been able to document was in 1954 when Miss Co-Op was chosen at the Central Consumers Coop "square dance." In some years the national agricultural show features a "Miss Agriculture," while the annual Easter cycle races from the western border to Belize City have been graced by "Miss Cycling." Commercial sponsorship is much more prominent in these events than the village festivals, and the winning Queen sometimes advertises products.

Today there are only two regular ethnic pageants, Miss Garifuna and Miss Panamericana. Both emphasize the arbitrariness of national boundaries, since they link ethnic groups across national boundaries. The Miss Garifuna pageant is often partially financed from overseas, and is always attended by Garifuna from neighboring countries as well as the largest Garifuna settlement of all—Los Angeles. The Garifuna communities in the United States select their own Queens, who attend festivities back in Belize. Miss Panamericana is elected in the Hispanic northern districts on Columbus Day, and afterward travels to a number of pageants and contests in neighboring Mexico.

The most recent proliferation of pageants have been semi-commercial events, staged by the same promoters who put on musical shows and other public entertainment.[2] Their explicit goal is to attract a crowd and make money through ticket sales and commercial sponsorship. In some towns they draw in participation and services from exercise instructors, beauty shop owners, dressmakers, and others in the growing fashion and beauty industries. Lions and Rotary clubs also cosponsor these events in exchange for a share of the profits. The promoters have built popularity by broadening the participation in contests through age segmentation. In 1989 there were commercial local and national Miss Teen and Miss Preteen competitions, as well as Ms. Elegant, Ms. Middle Age, and Ms. Maturity pageants. In 1991 there was also a "Ms. Big and Beautiful." These commercial events tend to drop most of the patriotic trappings and focus on some combination of the sexual appeal of women in swimsuits, the fashion show of the latest imported dresses, and the competitive musical or dramatic performances. Most of the audience members I spoke with mentioned some combination of these qualities as the reason they attended. The performances and staging vary widely in quality and professionalism, but as a promoter told me, the audience often enjoys jeering and criticizing the bad performances and sloppy mistakes as much as they appreciate the good ones.

CONTESTS AND CONTRADICTIONS

Making the Nation

The appeal and popularity of beauty and popularity contests is obviously quite complex. What they all have in common, however, is the way they play on contradictions and complexity, bringing issues and themes that are usually concealed or latent out into the open where they take center stage.

In the largest and most popular set of pageants, the national hierarchies of the Queen of the Bay and Miss Belize, the most obvious contradictions have to do with the credibility of the nation itself (see Cohen, Van Esterik, and Moran in this volume). Belizean national culture is a very recent construction, and it is continually subject to question by a multiethnic population enmeshed in transnational networks, in the constant shadow of their giant neighbor to the north.

The national pageants play constantly on the image of the nation, ostensibly propagating the government's official policy of building a multiethnic state where ethnic diversity is both valued and subordinated to a greater loyalty. The official theme of the 1965 Miss Belize pageant, for example, was how different immigrant groups "found the tie which binds and braces all the riches of our races in one identity....Our nation is comprised of many such small communities which we are proud to call Belizeans. They have forged their destiny with the destiny of the nation."(*Belize Times*, 27 August 1965). The 1970 pageant included an "Epic of Belize Spectacle" which "portrays with Music, Mime and the Spoken Word, the exciting story of the coming of the different ethnic groups and their fusion into a single national community."(*Belize Times*, 28 August 1970). As the 1990 Miss Teen Belmopan put it in her poem *Freedom, Love, and Peace*, "Even though we all a different race, Belize da one place."

The format of the typical contest recapitulates this theme of diversity transformed into unity. Contestants enter and are introduced wearing "ethnic" costumes, often quite fanciful (sometimes from a group other than their own). But as the pageant goes on, ethnicity disappears and nationality asserts itself. First the contestants are symbolically shorn of ethnic identity in the swimsuit competition; ethnicity is metaphorically superseded by sexuality. Next they reappear transformed, as in a rite of passage, in cosmopolitan and expensive formal wear, to perform and then to answer questions on an explicitly nationalized theme. They are asked questions like "What would you, as a Belizean, have to say about your country to the audience at Miss Universe?"

But in a number of ways, the notion of Belize as a single unified nation, on a level of equality with the other nations of the world, is continually undercut and contradicted within the pageant itself.[3] The pageants question Belizean aspirations and national rhetoric in a number of ways.

One direct contradiction is provided by the appearance of contestants whose Belizean identity is questioned. Returning Belizean-Americans have sometimes been barred from participating on the grounds of unfair advantage. A recent winner was roundly criticized in public and press because one of her parents was a naturalized white immigrant from the United States. Twice, in the last five years, scandals have broken out when contestants admitted to having United States passports (which could disqualify them from representing Belize at the Miss World contest). The serious ethnic tensions of the last decade, raised by a major influx of Hispanic refugees from warfare in Central America (Stone 1990), have emerged at times in verbal abuse of Hispanic contestants, or accusations that Hispanic Belizeans are discriminated against. Accusations of ethnic favoritism on the part of judges are common among contest audiences. Regional, family, and political divisions are also common themes of complaint among contestants, audience members and newspaper reports. In 1989 a member of a local organizing committee told me that "A girl from the west (Cayo district) has never won Miss Belize and she never will, no matter how beautiful and talented she is, as long as they hold the pageant in Belize City!"

Local and Foreign

The boundaries of the nation face outwards as well as inwards, and the legitimacy of Belize is constructed on the global stage as well as among Belizeans. Just as pageants and contests raise difficult questions about the internal composition of Belize as a nation, they also bring out difficult issues concerning the status of Belize as a nation among other nations. The national hierarchy of Belizean pageants is ostensibly intended to produce a contestant who will go onward to represent the nation at the global level. But at the same time, Belizeans know that their Queen has little or no chance of even making the semifinal round at Miss Universe or Miss World. They watch these events every year on satellite television, and they know their own pageants cannot compare, that world competition takes place at another level (the same is true of most sports).

The conflict between local and foreign becomes most obvious in the pageants when we raise the question of standards of beauty. A constant refrain among the audience, organizers, and participants is the conflict between Belizean standards of beauty, and those favored by international competitions. The organizers of the national pageants complain that the contestants who please a Belizean audience can never win at Miss World or Miss Universe.

As one organizer said, "Our problem is that the girls down here are the wrong shape. They are short, and they are small on the top and big on the bottom, in the hips and thighs, while the international pageants want tall, slim girls." Another stated "We might find a tall, thin girl here who could win Miss World, but she would never survive the local contests." In 1990 the judges tried to forge a compromise with a contestant "who has the height, and has some shape. She still had enough shape for them (the audience) to be semi-satisfied. But [another contestant] was the most popular girl here in the city. She had poor skin, but hips and bust and a big rear." My informants in the audience were much more critical of the winner, claiming she was much too thin ("switchy"); saying they preferred to see a winner "quick time with a big body."

So instead of consensus, at the center of the national pageant is the collision between local standards of beauty, deeply embedded in notions of gender and sexuality, and international standards which are those of the dominant white nations of the north. The widespread awareness of this difference, and ambivalence about which is superior, is a problem for Belizean nationhood. While Belizean pageants are intensely local, full of meaning that only Belizeans can appreciate, they are performed and observed with an intimate awareness of the global gaze. Foreigners do not even have to be present to watch the local competition (though they are often included on the panel of judges) because the global standard has become an ever-present "significant other" by which the local is defined and judged.

The pageants both raise national aspirations, and crush them under the weight of global standards. The chair of the national pageant committee in 1990 said that when people come to her office they always look for Miss Belize in the picture of the 110 contestants in the Miss Universe pageant. They are always surprised that Miss Belize looks as good as most of the other women because they expect her to "stand out and be ugly. People don't think Belizeans can hold a place in the world."

This conflict between local and international standards of beauty is not something new, a recent artifact of dominant global institutions and local resistance to them. Instead, this is a long-standing confrontation in the Caribbean. In Belize the whole conception of "local culture" has emerged, first under slavery, then in the rigid racism of British peripheral capitalism. For 350 years the people of Belize have been confronted with metropolitan standards of beauty and value, embedded in dominant religious, political, and educational institutions. These standards are pervasive and all Belizeans know them—in most families light skin and straight hair are still seen as desirable, and darker individuals are often called "black pots" and "bushy." But this dominance has never been complete; there *are* other conceptions of beauty in Belize, with very different values from the metropolitan standard. This second register is not simply a negation of the first, a simple form of resistance. The forms coexist in a kind of aesthetic diglossia. This means that every beauty contest in Belize applies at least two quite different standards of judging, and quite literally, nobody can ever really win. As the 1990 judges found, trying to forge a compromise usually means pleasing nobody.

Reputation and Respectability

There are also two quite different cultural conceptions of femininity at play in Belizean beauty contests. Wilson's (1973) famous dichotomy of "reputation" and "respectability" captures some of the dimensions of this conflict, representing two different ways that women conduct is evaluated. The interplay of reputation and respectability in beauty pageantry is especially complex and intriguing, for the pageant is one of the few public events where the two kinds of value come into direct confrontation.

The selection of Miss Crooked Tree, in a conservative rural village of about 700 people, provides a good example. The young woman they chose in 1993 is well know in the village as the best student the local school has had in years; she comes from a widely respected family of an average economic position, and is above reproach by local standards of morality. She is a regular churchgoer and has no serious boyfriends; in local parlance she "holds herself up." Most people in the community, even the other losing contestants, seemed quite happy with the choice and with her conduct at Cashew Festival. She was very much the archetype of the local queen, whom Deford (1971, 13) describes as the "nice, sweet, reasonably pretty local girl, who lives in town, whom everybody knows...."

While the values of respectability that she represents may not be shared by everyone in the village, they are known to everyone and their dominance is rarely challenged in public. As the product of consensus, she is the instrument of the hegemony of the popular, through an internal process of self-representation that has its own politics.

As Stoeltje and Bauman point out (1989), at this level the pageant can be seen as a symbolic expression of a prevailing order. This order, in Crooked Tree and many other Belizean communities, is partially about the dominance of respectability over reputation, about church, school, and home versus sexuality, drugs, alcohol, dancing in clubs, and "the street." The Queen was chosen to represent respectability, in a community where everyone knows the difference between the "church gyaal" ("study brains," "homegyaal"), and the "loose woman" ("vamp up," "engine," "fire crotch") who has children by many different men ("patchwork children").

The problem is that Miss Crooked Tree is more than a respectable "church gyaal" with a high school diploma, she is also an attractive and highly eligible young woman, an object of desire. Furthermore, in order to win the pageant she has to expose herself in public to the sexual gaze of all the men in the village. Appearing on stage in a provocative dress, Miss Crooked Tree exposed herself to a kind of scrutiny and gossip that is avoided by respectable women. While reputation and respectability are usually presented as opposites, in the person of the Queen they reach a temporary and uncomfortable accommodation (revealing at a deeper level, perhaps, that the stereotypes are actually quite dependent on each other).

The contradictions are powerful because they speak to tensions within the larger society that are inscribed and impressed upon the bodies and minds of every Belizean. Beauty is a matter of cultural politics in Belize, and the duality of beauty also reflects the profound contradictions between a woman's roles in a strongly patriarchal society. What is especially intriguing is that similar issues are raised by pageantry in the United States. Susan Dworkin, writing about Bess Myerson, says "The conflict built into the foundation of all beauty contests, between the self-esteem of the woman and her public role as a sex object...[is] hot and potentially explosive" (1987, 182).

Power and Hierarchy

When public judgments are made about a complex and contentious issue like beauty or talent, attempting to reach a consensus, the issue of power cannot be far behind. I suggest that in pageants there are always at least two discourses of power. The first is the contest between local actors, factions, and interests on the public stage at the level of the pageant itself. In a village this may mean the shopkeeper against the schools, principal, or two or more religious denominations, factions, schools, or ethnic groups. The second discourse of power is about the autonomy and authority of the local stage in relation to powers at other social and political levels and in regional, national, and international institutions.

As long as Miss Crooked Tree remains in the village and goes no further, her choice speaks to village concerns, and the consensus she represents is aimed at local differences. The universalistic assertions that lie behind her selection remain implicit, tacit, unquestioned. But Miss Crooked Tree may also be called upon to represent the community to others, and may be asked to join other competitions outside the community. At this point she becomes a crucial focus for the representation of difference, for the standards she will be judged on in the wider arena are different from those used in the community. This shift in standards marks a crucial rupture, for it is the aperture through which hierarchy is asserted.

Everyone in the village knows Miss Crooked Tree, and this personal knowledge played a crucial part in the judging. The criteria spoke directly to the political structure of the village, and the local values she represented. But if Miss Crooked Tree wants to go on to compete for Miss Belize, she will be judged on a completely different basis, for purposes framed at an entirely different level. At the next pageant, she will be the outsider, and the cultural capital that made her a winner in Crooked Tree is not nearly as valuable. This is a general characteristic of pageants in most countries. Deford found the same thing in his study of Miss Wilson in North Carolina (1971); what makes a winner at the local level is rarely important at the next stage of competition (see also Lavenda, this volume). The judges and audience at a district-level competition in Belize tend to look for a different balance of reputation and respectability, of beauty and talent. And when the district winner goes on to compete at the national level for Miss Belize, Miss World Belize, or Queen of the Bay, she will be judged by still other standards.

These contradictions emphasize hierarchy and dominance. The continuing lesson is that the local is subordinated to the national, and the national to the global. The structure of pageantry makes a place for local differences at every level, but it contains those differences, channels them and ultimately transcends them, at the next level of competition.

CONCLUSIONS: GLOBALISM AND HEGEMONY

At every level, beauty contests include a process of selection and representation, of making highly public choices that assert some kind of collective identity. As such they are always arenas for the definition of locality, for inclusion and exclusion. But when local choice is exhibited at a wider stage, as part of a hierarchical structure, the pageant becomes much more than this. It is forced into a discussion, implicit or explicit, of the hierarchical relationship between the local and the regional, the national and the international.

At the national level the same issues are raised. Pageantry in Belize could be seen a classic case of cultural imperialism; an imported institution that imposes a western form of sexual objectification. Of course we know the story is actually much more complex, that local groups and interests have adapted and used the raw material of the pageant for their own very local purposes. This is a process akin to what Certeau calls "poaching," whereby consumers rework and remake the raw material of the marketplace into something distinctly their own, thereby escaping domination (1984, xiii). In this way a foreign or global institution is taken out of its original context and made local; it is reappropriated and naturalized into a different system.

The conduct of Belizean pageants is always intensely local. Understanding and decoding the events on stage requires contextual knowledge; the crowd is engaged in heated speculation about the political backing of each contestant, their family connections and hairdressers, love lives, and backstage maneuvers. Much of the performance at the pageant is explicitly aimed at turning the pageant into a uniquely Belizean event— many costumes are explicitly local, the talent displays are often nationalist skits, ethnic dances, or dialect monologues.

But are Belizeans successful in poaching the foreign form and turning it to their own purposes? Have pageants been naturalized and Belizeanized and appropriated, another global form that has been successfully adapted, domesticated, and defanged? In some subtle ways, I think not. The global has become local, but at the same time, the local has become global.

The key point here is not that the pageants and competitions eliminate differences. They are not hegemonic tools that create homogeneity. All they do is provide a common channel and a point of focus for the debate and expression of differences. They take the full universe of possible contrasts between nations, groups, locales, factions, families, political parties, and economic classes, and they systematically narrow our gaze to *particular kinds* of difference. They organize and focus debate, and in the process of foregrounding particular kinds of difference, they submerge and obscure others by pushing them into the background. They standardize a vocabulary and provide a syntax for describing and expressing differences, producing a common frame of organized distinction. They essentialize some kinds of differences as ethnic, biological, and immutable, and portray them as measurable and scalable characteristics, washing them with the legitimacy of objectivity. They use these distinctions to draw systemic connections between disparate parts of the world.

These common frames bring previously separated groups into a new arena of competition, consisting of global structures that organize diversity and turn it into *common difference*. So the diverse characteristics of multiethnic Belizeans become comparable with each other, they are brought into contention through being made structurally equivalent. At a higher level, Belize itself can then become intelligible as one national culture among all the other unique nations that make up a global pageant.

On an even more fundamental level, pageants are a spectacle—a public performance that changes the relationship between people and culture. As an audience, the diverse experiences of Belizeans find something subtly shared, even as they disagree violently about who or what should win. When culture is objectified and performed on stage, when beauty is commodified and publicly contested, it shifts the audience away from participating in culture, and towards treating objectified culture as another con-

sumer commodity. Chatterjee argues that nationalism absorbs political
life into the state (1986); here we see an institution that absorbs culture
into the state and nation, and makes the public into consumers, observers,
spectators, and "fans." Mass-mediated culture has had this effect in many
parts of the world, splitting the public according to a capitalist division of
labor into culture-producers and culture-consumers. We are building a
global class of cultural specialists, who inhabit the mediascapes,
ethnoscapes, and ideoscapes of cosmopolitan transnational culture
(Appadurai 1990). This culture industry relegates the rest of us to the role
of cultural consumers; we have the freedom to express our differences, but
only with the codes and objects the industry provides. In a subtle way this
puts us all on common ground; like the audience at a pageant, we are all
observers, and we participate only by making choices from a predeter-
mined and bounded range of options.

Notes

An earlier version of this essay was presented at the Annual Meeting of the American
Anthropological Association in November 1993. Some short sections and quotes are
drawn from papers I have presented, including one given at the 1993 meeting of the
Association of Social Anthropologists of the Commonwealth in Oxford, now published
(1995). I want to thank Anne Pyburn, Karen Judd, Colleen Ballerino Cohen, Diane
Haylock, Dacia Crawford, and all the other people whose conversation and writing has
helped me better understand beauty pageantry and Belize. Earlier drafts of this essay have
benefited from specific comments by Janet Abu-Lughod, Joel Kahn, Jonathan Friedman,
Beverly Stoeltje, and Danny Miller. Jeanine Beeler worked with me in Crooked Tree in
1992, and her insightful comments and field notes contributed a great deal to this essay.
The fieldwork for this essay was sponsored by a Fulbright research fellowship and a grant
from the Wenner-Gren Foundation for Anthropological Research.

1. It is interesting that Kings are elected in many high school popularity contests, but
males drop out of contention at the next level of competition. There is a "Mr. Belize"
pageant in some years, but it is a small event divorced from any festival or ceremonial
context. It is put on by the small bodybuilding community, and attracts a mostly male
audience, in contrast to the female competitions, which attract a mixed audience in
which women are the clear majority.
2. Finding moneymaking events is difficult for promoters in a small country like Belize.
They don't have a big enough audience to cover the costs of bringing in big-name international acts, and the few popular local bands and performers play constantly at
local clubs, so they will not draw a large high-paying crowd. Promoters also face competition from MTV. Pageants fill a crucial gap, though in 1990 one promoter told me
the audience was starting to diminish because there were so many different contests.
3. This theme is emerging quite clearly in a good deal of literature on post-colonial nation building, where nationalist projects appear as continually incomplete and ridden
with conflict, often producing unexpected or unintended consequences (summarized
concisely by Ferguson 1994). McClintock argues effectively for the centrality of gender in all nationalist discourse (1991).

References

Abrahams, Roger D. 1983. *The Man-of-Words in the West Indies: Performance and the Emergence of Creole Culture*. Baltimore and London: The Johns Hopkins University Press.

Adams, Richard N. 1989. "The Conquest Tradition of Mesoamerica." *The Americas* 46 (2): 119-36

Adorno, Theodor W. 1973. *The Jargon of Authenticity*. Trans. K. Tarnanski and F. Will. Evanston IL: Northwestern University Press.

Aguilera Peralta, Gabriel. 1980. "Terror and Violence as Weapons of Counterinsurgency in Guatemala." *Latin American Perspectives* 7 (2-3): 91-113.

Alonso, Ana María. 1994. "The Politics of Space, Time and Substance: State Formation, Nationalism and Ethnicity." *Annual Review of Anthropology* 23: 379-405.

Amphiteatrov, S. H. 1905. *Russian Women and the Liberation Movement*. Moscow.

Anagost, Ann. 1993 (Winter). "The Nationscape: Movement in the Field of Vision." *Positions* 1 (3): 586-606.

———. 1994. "The Politicized Body." In *Body, Subject and Power in China*, ed. A. Zito and T. E. Barlow. Chicago: University of Chicago Press: 131-56.

Anderson, B. 1972. "The Idea of Power in Javanese Culture." In *Culture and Politics in Indonesia*, ed. C. Holt. Ithaca: Cornell University Press.

Anderson, Benedict. 1983 [1993]. *Imagined Communities: Reflections on the Origin and Spread of Nationalism*. London: Verso.

Anderson, Ken, and Jean-Marie Simon. 1987. "Permanent Counterinsurgency in Guatemala." *Telos* 73: 9-46.

Ang, Ien. 1985. *Watching Dallas: Soap Opera and the Melodramatic Imagination*. Trans. Della Couling. London and New York: Methuen.

Anon. 1983. "La bellez de los patios." *Diario Córdoba* 13 May: 1.

Appadurai, Arjun. 1990. "Disjuncture and Difference in the Global Cultural Economy." *Theory, Culture and Society* 7: 295-310.

———. 1993. "Patriotism and Its Futures." *Public Culture* 5 (3): 411-29.

Austin, Dianne. 1983. "Culture and Ideology in the English-Speaking Caribbean: A View from Jamaica." *American Ethnologist* 10 (2): 223-240.

Averett. S., and S. Korenman. 1994. *The Economic Reality of the "Beauty Myth."* National Bureau of Economic Research, Washington, D.C. Working Paper 4521.

Aziz, Barbara Nimri. 1987. "Moving Towards a Sociology of Tibet." In *Feminine Ground: Essays on Women and Tibet*, ed. J. Willis. Ithaca: Snow Lion Publications: 76-95.

Babcock, Barbara, ed. 1978. *The Reversible World: Symbolic Inversion in Art and Society*. Ithaca: Cornell University Press.

———. 1987. "Taking Liberties, Writing from the Margins, and Doing It with a Difference." *Journal of American Folklore* 100: 390-411.

Bakhtin, M. M. 1981. *The Dialogic Imagination: Four Essays*. Ed. M. Holquist, trans. M. Holquist and C. Emerson. University of Texas Press Slavic Services vol. 1. Austin: University of Texas Press.

Balibar, Etienne. 1990. "Paradoxes of Universality." In *Anatomy of Racism*, ed. D. T. Goldberg. Minneapolis & Oxford: University of Minnesota Press: 283-94.

Banner, Lois. 1983. *American Beauty*. Chicago: University of Chicago Press.

Barlow, Tani E. 1994. "Theorizing Woman: Funu, Guojia, Jiating (Chinese Woman, Chinese State, Chinese Family)." In *Body, Subject and Power in China*, eds. A. Zito and T. E. Barlow. Chicago: University of Chicago Press: 253-89.

Barnett, Robbie. 1993 (October 7). "Wave of Arrests in Eastern Tibet." Toronto: CanTibNet Newsletter.

Barrett, Michelle. 1980. *Women's Oppression Today*.

Basch, L., N. Schiller, and C. Blanc. 1994. *Nations Unbound*. Amsterdam: Gordon and Breach.

Baudrillard, Jean. 1983. *Simulations*. Trans. P. Foss, P. Patton, and P. Beitchman. New York: Semiotext(e).

Bauman, Richard. 1992. *Folklore, Cultural Performances, and Popular Entertainments*. New York: Oxford University Press.

Bauman, Richard and Charles Briggs. 1990. "Poetics and Performance as Critical Perspectives on Language and Social Life." *Annual Review of Anthropology* 19: 59-88.

Bennett, Oliver. 1993 (November 20). "Boycott Urged of Tibet Holiday Inn." *The Daily Telegraph*: 35.

Besson, Jean. 1993. "Reputation and Respectability Reconsidered: A New Perspective on Afro-Caribbean Peasant Women." In *Women and Change in the Caribbean*, ed. J. Momsen. Kingston: Ian Randle/Bloomington: Indiana University Press: 15-37.

Biersack, Aletta. 1982. "Tongan Exchange Structures: Beyond Descent and Alliance." *Journal of the Polynesian Society* 91:181-212.

———. 1990. "Blood and Garland: Duality in Tongan History." In *Tongan Cultural History*, eds. P. Herda et al. Canberra: The Department of Pacific and Southeast Asian History: 46-58.

Bishop, Peter. 1989. *The Myth of Shangri-La: Tibet, Travel Writing, and the Creation of a Sacred Landscape*. Berkeley: Univerity of California Press.

Bivans, Ann-Marie. 1991. *Miss America*. New York: Master Media.

Blanc-Szanton, C. 1990. "Collision of Cultures: Rhetorical Reformulations of Gender in the Lowland Visayas, Philippines." In *Power and Difference: Gender in Southeast Asia*, eds. S. Errington and J. Atkinson. Stanford: Stanford University Press, 348-83.

Bloomington Herald Times. 1994. "Beauty Queen In Shop for Repairs." November 10.

Bly, Carol. 1981. *Letters From the Country*. New York: Harper & Row.

Bolland, N. 1986. *Belize: A New Nation in Central America*. Westview Press: Boulder CO.

———. 1987. "United States Cultural Influence on Belize: Television and Education as 'Vehicles of Import.'" *Caribbean Quarterly* 33 (3 & 4): 60-74.

Boone, S. 1986. *Radiance from the Waters*. New Haven: Yale University Press.

Bordo, Susan. 1993. *Unbearable Weight: Feminism, Western Culture and the Body*. Berkeley: University of California Press.

Borland, Katherine. 1994. *Performing Identities: The Politics of Culture in a Nicaraguan Community*. Ph.D. dissertation, Indiana University, Bloomington.

Bott, Elizabeth. 1981. "Power and Rank in the Kingdom of Tonga." *Journal of the Polynesian Society* 90: 7-81.

Bourdieu, Pierre. 1977. *Outline of a Theory of Practice*. Cambridge: Cambridge University Press.

Breitborde, Lawrence. 1977. *The Social Structural Basis of Linguistic Variation in an Urban*

African Neighborhood. Ph.D. dissertation, Department of Anthropology, The University of Rochester.

"Briefing Papers for Miss Heilala Contestants." 1993.

Bruner, Edward M. 1994. "Abraham Lincoln as Authentic Representation: A Critique of Postmodernism." *American Anthropologist* 96 (2): 397-415.

Bulter, Judith. 1990. *Gender Trouble.* New York and London: Routledge.

———. 1991. "Imitation and Gender Subordination." In *Inside/Out: Lesbian Theories, Gay Theories,* ed. D. Fuss. New York and London: Routledge: 13-31.

BVI Beacon 1991 (August 29). "Bisa Smith Wins Crown at Miss Caribbean Talented Teen Pageant."

———. 1994 (June 9). *Special Anniversary Issue, 1984-1994: 10 Years of Change.*

Campbell, Ian C. 1992. *Island Kindom, Tonga Ancient and Modern.* Christchurch: Canterbury University Press.

Cannel, F. 1992. *Catholicism, Spirit Mediums and the Ideal of Beauty in a Bicolano Community, Philippines.* Ph.D. dissertation, London University.

Cannon, Terry. 1990. "Colonialism From Within." *China Now* 135: 6-9.

Casaus Arzú, Marta. 1992. *Guatemala: Linaje y racismo.* San José: FLASCO.

Cash, T. and T. Pruzinsky, eds. 1990. *Body Images: Development, Deviance, and Change.* New York: Guilford Press.

Cassidy, C. 1991. "The Thin Body: When Big Is Better." *Medical Anthropology* 13: 181-213.

Certeau, M. de. 1984. *The Practice of Everyday Life.* Berkeley: University of California Press.

Chapkis, Wendy. 1988. *Beauty Secrets.* London: Women's Press.

Chatterjee, Partha. 1986. *Nationalist Thought and the Colonial World: A Derivative Discourse.* London: Zed Books.

———. 1993. *The Nation and Its Fragments: Colonial and Postcolonial Histories.* Princeton, New Jersey: Princeton University Press.

Che Man, G. K. 1990. *Muslim Separatism: The Moros of Southern Philippines and the Malays of Southern Thailand.* Quezon City: Ateneo de Manila Press.

Chen, Xiaomei. 1992 (Summer). "Occidentalism as Counterdiscourse: 'He Shang' in Post Mao China." *Critical Inquiry* 18 (4): 686-712.

"China Admits to Policy of Promoting Chinese Migration to Tibet." *Tibetan Environment and Development News* Issue 15 (October 1994). International Campaign for Tibet: 1-2.

Chodag, Tiley. 1988. *Tibet: The Land and the People.* Beijing: New World Press.

Chow, Rey. 1991a. *Woman and Chinese Modernity: The Politics of Reading Between West and East.* Minneapolis: University of Minnesota Press.

———. 1991b. "Violence in the Other Country: China as Crisis, Spectacle, and Woman. " In *Third World Women and the Politics of Feminism,* eds. C. Mohanty, A. Russo and L. Torres. Bloomington: Indiana University Press: 81-100.

Cohen, Colleen Ballerino, and Frances E. Mascia-Lees. 1993. "The British Virgin Islands as Nation and Desti-Nation: Representing and Siting Identity in a Post-colonial Caribbean." *Social Analysis* 33 : 130-51.

Cohen, Colleen Ballerino. 1995. "Marketing Paradise, Making Nation." *Annals of Tourism Research* 22 (2): 404-21

Corrigan, Annette. 1992. "Fashion, Beauty, and Feminism." *Meanjin* 51 (1): 107-22.

Cowie, Elizabeth. 1990. "Woman as Sign." In *The Woman in Question: m/f,* eds. P. Adams and E. Cowie. Cambridge: MIT Press.

Cowling, Wendy E. 1990. "Motivations for Contemporary Tongan Migration." In *Tongan Cultural History,* eds. P. Herda et al. Canberra: The Department of Pacific and Southeast Asian History: 187-205.

Crick, Malcolm. 1989. "Representations of International Tourism in the Social Sciences: Sun, Sex, Sights, Savings, and Servility." *Annual Review of Anthropology* 18: 307-44.

Csikszentmihalyi, Mihalyi. 1981. "Some Paradoxes in the Definition of Play." In *Play as Context*, ed. A. Cheska. West Point, NY: Leisure Press: 14-25.

Curthoys, Ann. 1993. "Feminism, Citizenship, and National Identity." *Feminist Review* 44: 19-38.

Daniel, E. Valentine. *Charred Lullabies*. In press.

Davis, Kathy. 1991. "Remaking the She-Devil: A Critical Look at Feminist Approaches to Beauty." *Hypatia* 6 (2).

Davis, Shelton H. 1988. "Introduction: Sowing the Seeds of Violence." In *Harvest of Violence: The Maya Indians and the Guatemalan Crisis*, ed. R.M. Carmack. Norman & London: University of Oklahoma Press: 3-36.

d'Azevedo, Warren L. 1962. "Some Historical Problems in the Delineation of a Central West Atlantic Region." *Annals of the New York Academy of Sciences* 96: 512-38.

Deford, F. 1971. *There She Is: The Life and Times of Miss America*. New York: Viking.

De Valle, Susanna B.C. 1989. "Discourses of Ethnicity: The Faces and the Mask." In *Ethnicity and Nation-Building in the Pacific*, ed. M. C. Howard. Tokyo: The United Nations University.

Development Planning Unit. 1991. *1990 Population and Housing Census, Preliminary Count*. Road Town, Tortola: Government of the British Virgin Islands.

———. 1992. *1990-1992 Employment and Earning Statistics*. Road Town, Tortola: Government of the British Virgin Islands.

Devine, Carol. 1993. *Determination: Tibetan Women and the Struggle for an Independent Tibet*. Toronto: Vauve Press.

Diamond, Norma. 1993. "Ethnicity and the State: The Hua Miao of Southwest China." In *Ethnicity and the State*, ed. J. D. Toland. Political and Legal Anthropology Series Vol. 9. New Brunswick, N.J.: Transaction Publishers: 55-78.

———. 1988 (January). "The Miao and Poison: Interactions on China's Southwest Frontier." *Ethnology*: 1-25.

Dikotter, Frank. 1992. *The Discourse of Race in Modern China*. Palo Alto: Stanford University Press.

Dirlik, Arif. 1994. "The Postcolonial Aura: Third World Criticism in the Age of Global Capitalism." *Critical Inquiry* 20: 328-56.

Dolma, Tseten (Ch. Tsetan Zholma). 1989 (April). "From Serf to Songstress." *China Reconstructs*: 14-15.

Dominguez, Virginia. 1989. *People as Subject, People as Object: Selfhood and Peoplehood in Contemporary Israel*. Madison: University of Wisconsin Press.

Dookhan, Isaac. 1975. *A History of the British Virgin Islands, 1672-1970*. Great Britain: Caribbean Universities Press/Bowker Publishing Company.

Douglas, Susan. 1994. *Where the Girls Are*. Berkeley: University of California Press.

Drewal, Margaret Thompson. 1992. *Yoruba Ritual: Performers, Play, Agency*. Bloomington, IN: Indiana University Press.

Dreyer, June Teufel. 1976. *China's Forty Millions: Minority Nationalities and National Integration in the People's Republic of China*. Cambridge: Harvard University Press.

———. 1993. *China's Political System: Modernization and Tradition*. New York: Paragon House.

Driver, Dorothy. 1988. "'Woman' as Sign in the South African Colonial Enterprise." *Journal of Literary Studies* 4: 3-20.

Duara, Prasenjit. 1993 (Winter). "Bifurcating Linear History: Nation and Histories in China and India." *Positions* 1 (3): 779-804.

Dworkin, Susan. 1987. *Miss America, 1945: Bess Myerson's Own Story*. New York: New Market Press.

Early, Gerald. 1990. "Life with Daughters: Watching the Miss America Pageant." *The Kenyon Review* 12 (4): 132-45.

———. 1984. "Waiting for Miss America." *The Antioch Review* 42: 291-305.

Eco, Umberto. 1976. *A Theory of Semiotics*. Bloomington: Indiana Univesity Press.

Endicott, K. 1970. *An Analysis of Malay Magic.* Oxford: Clarendon Press.

Errington, S. 1989. *Meaning and Power in a Southeast Asian Realm.* Princeton: Princeton University Press.

"Exhibition of Reconstruction Achievements." 1991. Brochure from museum exhibit, Lhasa, Tibet.

Evans, Mary ed. 1982. *The Woman Question.* London: Fontana.

Faludi, Susan. 1988. "Miss Teen Covina's Revenge." *Mother Jones* 13 (3): 32.

Fardon, Richard. 1985. "Introduction: A Sense of Relevance." In *Power and Knowledge*, ed. R. Fardon. Edinburgh: Scottish Academic Press.

Fei, Xiaotong. 1979. "Modernization and National Minorities in China." Occasional Papers, Center for East Asian Studies: Montreal: McGill University.

———. 1981a. "On the Social Transformation of China's National Minorities." In *Towards a People's Anthropology.* Beijing: New World Press: 36-59.

———. 1981b. "Ethnic Identification in China." In *Towards a People's Anthropology.* Beijing: New World Press: 60-77.

Feher, Michel, ed. with Ramona Naddaff and Nadia Tazi. 1989. *Fragments for a History of the Human Body.* New York: Urzone/ZONE.

Feld, Steven. 1988. "Notes on World Beat." *Public Culture* 1 (1): 31-37.

Ferguson, J. 1994. "Power or Complexity?" *Transition* 64: 132-38.

Fernandez, James. 1986. "Convivial Attitudes: A Northern Spanish Kayak Festival in Its Historical Moment." In *Persuasions and Performances.* Bloomington: Indiana University Press.

Fernández, Manuel. 1981. "Aunque la Federación de Peñas ha sido autorizada para celebrar el concurso de belleza—El feminismo municipal dejó a los patios sin Reina." *La Vox de Córdoba* 19 May: 16.

———. 1982. "Fabi Riobío, Reina de los Patios, la belleza oficial de Córdoba - Una reina en paro." *La Vox de Córdoba* 26 May: 20.

———. 1984. "La reina de la Feria en 'anorak' y sin corona." *Diario Córdoba* 23 May: 32.

"Filmstar Publicity for Lhasa Nightclub." *TIN News Update* May 27, 1992.

Fiske, John. 1989. *Understanding Popular Culture.* London: Routledge.

Fonua, Pesi. 1993. "Tongan Waits to be Discovered by Tourist." *Matanqi Tonga*: 9.

Forbes, Ann, and Carole McGranahan. 1992. *Developing Tibet?: A Survey of International Development Projects.* Cambridge: Cultural Survival and International Campaign for Tibet.

Foster, Robert. 1991. "Making National Culture in the Global Ecumene." *Annual Review of Anthropology* 20: 235-60.

Foucault, M. 1980. *Power/Knowledge: Selected Interviews and Other Writings, 1972-1977.* Ed. C. Gordon. Brighton: Harvester Press.

———. 1986. "Disciplinary Power and Subjection." In *Power*, ed. S. Lukes. New York: New York University Press.

———. 1990 [1978]. *The History of Sexuality, Volume I: An Introduction.* Trans. Robert Hurley. New York: Vintage.

Fox, Richard G. ed. 1990. *Nationalist Ideologies and the Production of National Cultures.* American Ethnological Society Monograph Series, Number 2. Washington, D.C.: American Anthropological Association.

Freedman, Rita. 1988 [1986]. *Beauty Bound.* London: Columbus Books.

Freeman, Carla. 1993. "Designing Women: Corporate Discipline and Barbados' Off-Shore Pink-Collar Sector." *Cultural Anthropology* 8 (2): 169-86.

Friedman, J. 1990. "Being in the World: Globalization and Localization." *Theory, Culture, and Society* 7: 311-28.

Geertz, C. 1960. *The Religion of Java.* New York: Free Press.

George, T. J. S. 1980. *Revolt in Mindanao: The Rise of Islam in Philippine Politics.* Oxford: Oxford University Press.

Gilbert-Neiss, C. 1977. "Letter to the Editor." *New York Times.* 18 September XI 31: 6.

Gladney, Dru C. 1991. *Muslim Chinese: Ethnic Nationalism in the People's Republic.* Cambridge: Harvard University Press.

Goldman, Irving. 1970. *Ancient Polynesian Society.* Chicago and London: University of Chicago Press.

Goldstein, Melvyn. 1989. *A History of Modern Tibet: The Demise of the Lamaist State.* Berkeley: University of California Press.

———. 1982. "Lhasa Street Songs: Political and Social Satire in Traditional Tibet." *Tibet Journal:* 56-66.

Gorbachev, M. 1987. *Perestroika: New Thinking for Our Country and the World.* London: Collins.

Gottdiener, M. 1995. *Postmodern Semiotics.* Cambridge: Blackwell.

Gowing, P. G. 1983. *Mandate in Moroland: The American Government of Muslim Filipinos.* Quezon City: New Day.

Gutwirth, Madelyn. 1992. *The Twilight of the Goddesses: Women and Representation in the French Revolutionary Era.* New Brunswick, N.J.: Rutgers University Press.

Gyatso, Janet. 1987. "Down with the Demoness: Reflections on a Feminine Ground in Tibet." In *Feminine Ground: Essays on Women and Tibet,* ed. J. Willis. Ithaca: Snow Lion Publications: 33-51.

Hall, Catherine. 1993 (Summer). "Gender, Nationalisms and National Identities: Bellagio Symposium, July 1992." *Feminist Review* 44: 97-103.

Hall, Stuart. 1992. "Cultural Identity and Cinematic Representation." In *Ex-Isles: Essays on Caribbean Cinema,* ed. M. Cham. Trenton, New Jersey: Africa World Press: 220-36.

Halle, Fannina. 1933. *Women in Soviet Russia.* New York and London: Routledge.

Hamermesh, D., and J. Biddle. 1994. "Beauty and the Labor Market." *American Economic Review* 84 (5): 1174-95.

Handelman, Don. 1977. "Play and Ritual: Complimentary Frames of Meta-Communication." In *It's a Funny Thing, Humour,* eds. A.J. Chapman and H.C. Foot. London: Pergamon: 185-92.

———. 1990. *Models and Mirrors: Towards an Anthropology of Public Events.* Cambridge: Cambridge University Press.

———. 1992. "Passages to Play: Paradox and Process." *Play and Culture* 5 (1): 1-19.

Handler, Richard. 1988. *Nationalism and the Politics of Culture in Quebec.* Madison: University of Wisconsin Press.

Hanks, William. 1989. "Elements of Maya Style." In *Word and Image in Maya Culture: Explorations in Language, Writing, and Representation,* eds. W. Hanks and D. S. Rice. Salt Lake City: University of Utah Press: 92-111.

Hannerz, Ulf. 1987. "The World in Creolization." *Africa* 57(4): 546-59.

———. 1989. "Culture Between Center and Periphery: Toward a Macroanthropology." *Ethnos* 54 (3-4): 200-216.

Harrigan, Norwell and Pearl Varlack. 1988. *The Virgin Islands Story.* Epping, Essex, England: Caribbean Universities Press.

Hart, D.V. 1968. "Homosexuality and Transvestism in the Philippines: The Cebuan Filipino Bayot and Lakin-on." *Behavior Science Notes* 3: 211-48.

"Heilala '93." 1993. *Official Handbook.*

Hendrickson, Carol. 1991. "Images of the Indian in Guatemala: The Role of Indigenous Dress in Indian and Ladino Constructions." In *Nation-States and Indians in Latin America,* eds. G. Urban and J. Sherzer. Austin: University of Texas Press: 296-306.

Herda, Phyllis. 1987. "Gender, Rank and Power in 18th Century Tonga: The Case of Tupou Moheof." *The Journal of Pacific History* 22/4: 195-208.

Herzfeld, Michael. 1986. "Of Definitions and Boundaries: The Status of Culture in the Culture of the State." In *Discourse and the Social Life of Meaning,* eds. P.P. Chock and J.R. Wyman, Washington: Smithsonian Institution Press: 75-94.

Heyu. 1988. *Tibet: A General Survey*. Beijing: New World Press.

Hooper, J. 1986. *The Spaniards: A Portrait of the New Spain*. London: Penguin.

The Island Sun. 1991a (June 1). "Miss BVI Returns to Las Vegas."

———. 1991b (August 17). "Benji V is Calypso King."

James, Kerry. 1983. "Gender Relations in Tonga 1780 to 1984." *Journal of the Polynesian Society* 92: 223-43.

———. 1990. "Gender Relations in Tonga: A Paradigm Shift." In *Tongan Cultural History*, eds. P. Herda et. al. Canberra: The Department of Pacific and Southeast Asian History: 93-100.

Jayawardena, Kumari. 1986. *Feminism and Nationalism in the Third World*. London: Zed Books.

Jewell, K.S. 1993. *From Mammy to Miss America and Beyond*. London: Routledge.

Johnson, M. n.d. *Beauty and Power: Identity, Cultural Transformation, and Transgendering in the Southern Philippines*. Ph.D. thesis, University of London.

———. 1995. "Transgender and Homosexuality in the Southern Philippines: Ethnicity, Political Violence, and the Protocols of Engendered Sexualities Amongst the Muslim Tausug and Sama." *South East Asia Research*, 3: 46-66.

Kaeppler, Adrianne L. 1971. "Rank in Tonga." *Ethnology* 10: 174-93.

———. 1978. "Melody, Drone and Decoration: Underlying Structures and Surface Manifestations in Tongan Art and Society." In *Art in Society: Studies in Styles, Sculptures, and Aesthetics*, eds. M. Greenhalgh and V. Megaw. Melbourne: Oxford University Press: 261-74.

———. 1993. *Poetry in Motion: Studies of Tongan Dance*. Tonga: Vava'u Press.

Kandiyoti, Deniz. 1994. "Identity and its Discontents: Women and the Nation." In *Colonial Discourse and Post-Colonial Theory*, eds. P. Williams and L. Chrisman. New York: Columbia University Press: 376-91.

Kapferer, B. 1988. *Legends of People, Myths of State*. London: Smithsonian Institution Press.

Keeler, W. 1987. *Javanese Shadow Plays, Javanese Selves*. Princeton: Princeton University Press.

Keesing, R. 1984. "Rethinking Mana." *Journal of Anthropoligical Research* 40: 137-56.

Keller, Bill. 1993. "Appartheid's End Transforms Beauty Show." *New York Times*. 12 September.

Kertzer, David. 1988. *Ritual, Politics, and Power*. New Haven: Yale University Press.

Kharchev, A. G. ed. 1977. *Changing Women's Roles in Society and the Family*. Moscow.

———. 1979. *Marriage and Family in the USSR*. Moscow.

Kiefer, T. 1967. "A Note on the Cross-sex Identification Among Musicians." *Ethnomusicology* 12: 107-109.

———. 1972. *The Tausug: Violence and Law in Philippine Moslem Society*. New York: Holt, Rinehart and Winston.

———. 1988. "Parrang Sabbil: Ritual Suicide Among the Tausug of Jolo." In *Understanding Islam and Muslims in the Philippines*, ed. P. Gowing. Quezon City: New Day.

Kim, Samuel S., and Lowell Dittmer. 1993. "Whither China's Quest for National Identity?" In *China's Quest for National Identity*, eds. L. Dittmer and S. S. Kim. Ithaca: Cornell University Press: 237-90.

Kindel, Stephen. 1984. "Beauty You Can Take to the Bank." *Forbes*. June 18: 136-39.

Kirshenblatt-Gimblett, Barbara. 1991. "Objects of Ethnography." In *Exhibiting Culture: The Poetics and Politics of Museum Display*, eds. I. Karp and S. Lavine. Washington, D.C.: Smithsonian Institution Press: 387-443.

Klieger, P. Christian. 1992. *Tibetan Nationalism: The Role of Patronage in the Accomplishment of a National Identity*. Berkeley: Folklore Institute.

Kuhn, Annette. 1985. *The Power of the Image*. London: Routledge and Kegan Paul.

Lacquer, Thomas. 1990. *Making Sex: Body and Gender from the Greeks to Freud*. Cambridge: Harvard University Press.

La Fontaine, J.S. 1985. *Initiation: Ritual Drama and Secret Knowledge Across the World*. New York: Viking Penguin.

Lakoff, Robin and Raquel Scherr. 1984. *Face Value: The Politics of Beauty*. Boston: Routledge and Kegan Paul.

Lavenda Robert H., Kevin Gwost, Mark Lauer, Christopher Nelson, and JacLyn Norwood. 1984. "Festivals and the Organization of Meaning: An Introduction to Community Festivals in Minnesota." In *The Masks of Play*, eds. B. Sutton-Smith and D. Kelly-Byrne. West Point, NY: Leisure Press: 34-50.

Lavenda, Robert H. 1988. "Minnesota Queen Pageants: Play, Fun, and Dead Seriousness in a Festive Mode." *Journal of American Folklore* 101: 168-75.

———. 1991. "Community Festivals, Paradox, and the Manipulation of Uncertainty." *Play and Culture* 4 (2): 153-68.

———. 1992a. "Festivals and the Creation of Public Culture: Whose Voice(s)." In *Museums and Communities: The Politics of Public Culture*, eds. I. Karp, C. M. Kreamer, and S. D. Lavine. Washington, D.C.: Smithsonian Institution Press: 76-104.

———. 1992b. "Response to Handelman." *Play and Culture* 5 (1): 22-24.

———. 1993. "The Traces of Play." TASP Presidential Address, 1992. *The Journal of Play Theory and Research* 1 (1): iii-vii.

———. 1995. "Play." In *Encyclopedia of Cultural Anthropology*, eds. D. Levinson and M. Ember. A Henry Holt Reference Book: Lakeville, CT: American Reference Publishing Company.

Lenin, V.I. *Collected Works*, V. 39. Moscow (2nd. ed.).

Levi-Strauss, Claude. 1947. *Les Structures Elementaires de la Parente*. Paris: P.U.F.

Liu, Lydia H. 1994. "The Female Body and Nationalist Discourse: Manchuria in Xiao Hong's Field of Life and Death." In *Body, Subject, and Power in China*, eds. A. Zito and T. E. Barlow: 157-77.

Lizko, N. 1994. "Do We Need a Political Party for Women?" *Gazeta Dlya Zhenschin* 11-12.

Lofgren, O. 1989. "The Nationalization of Culture." *Ethnol. Eur.* 19 (1): 5-24.

Lombardi-Satriani, Luigi Maria. 1973. *Apropriación y destrucción de las clases subalternas*. Trans. 1978, n.t. Sacramento, MX: Editorial Neuva Imagen.

Lopez, Donald S. Jr., 1994. "New Age Orientalism: The Case of Tibet." *Tricycle* 3 (3): 36-43.

Maayang, Lazarus Dempsey. 1990. "Miss Ghana Pageants: A Perilous Venture into History." *UHURU Magazine* Vol. 2: 23-29.

Mageo, J.M. 1992. "Male Transvestism and Cultural Change in Samoa." *American Ethnologist* 19: 443-59.

Majul, C. 1973. *Muslims in the Philippines*. Quezon City: University of Manila Press.

Makley, Charlene. 1994. "Gendered Practices and the Inner Sanctum: The Reconstruction of Tibetan Sacred Space Within 'China's Tibet.'" *Tibet Journal*.

———. Unpublished manuscript. "The Meaning of Liberation: Representations of Tibetan Women."

Mankekar, Purnima. 1993. "National Texts and Gendered Lives: An Ethnography of Television Viewers in a North Indian City." *American Ethnologist* 20 (3): 543-63.

Manning, Frank E. 1977. "Cup Match and Carnival: Secular Rites of Revitalization in Decolonizing, Tourist-Oriented Societies." In *Secular Ritual*, ed. S. Moore and B. Myerhoff. Amsterdam, Assen: Van Gorcum: 265-81.

———. 1978. "Carnival in Antigua (Caribbean Sea): Indigenous Festival in a Tourist Economy." *Anthropos* 73 (1/2): 191-204.

———. 1983. *The Celebration of Society: Perspectives on Contemporary Cultural Performance*. Bowling Green, OH: Bowling Green University Popular Press.

Manz, Beatriz. 1988. *Refugees of a Hidden War: The Aftermath of Counterinsurgency in Guatemala*. Albany: SUNY Press.

Marcus, George E. 1978a. "Status Rivalry in Polynesian Steady State Society." *Ethos* 6: 242-69.

————. 1978b. "The Nobility and the Chiefly Tradition in the Modern Kingdom of Tonga." *Journal of the Polynesian Society* 87: 1-166.

Martin, Emily. 1987. *The Woman in the Body*. Boston: Beacon Press.

Martin, Jane Jackson. 1968. *The Dual Legacy: Government Authority and Mission Influence Among the Glebo of Eastern Liberia, 1834-1910*. Ph.D. dissertation, Department of History, Boston University.

Maschio, G. 1989. "A Prescription for Femininity: Male Interpretation of the Feminine Ideal at the Turn of the Century." *Women and Performance* 4: 43-49.

Mascia-Lees, Frances, and Patricia Sharpe, eds. 1992. *Tatoo, Torture, Mutilation, and Adornment: The Denaturalization of the Body in Culture and Text*. Albany: SUNY Press.

Mashika, T.A. 1989. *Women's Occupation and Maternity*. Moscow.

Maurer, William M. 1994. *Recharting the Caribbean: Land, Law and Citizenship in the British Virgin Islands*. Ph.D. dissertation, Stanford University.

McClintock, Anne. 1991. "'No Longer in a Future Heaven': Women and Nationalism in Southern Africa." *Transition* 51: 104-23.

————. 1992. "The Angel of Progress: Pitfalls of the Term 'Post Colonialism.'" *Social Text* 31-32: 84-99.

————. 1993 (Summer). "Family Feuds: Gender, Nationalism and the Family." *Feminist Review* 44: 61-80.

McEvoy, Frederick D. 1977. "Understanding Ethnic Realities Among the Grebo and Kru Peoples of West Africa." *Africa* 47: 62-79.

Menchú, Rigoberta. 1983. *I, Rigoberta Menchú: An Indian Woman in Guatemala*. Ed. E. Burgos-Debray, trans. A. Wright. London and New York: Verso.

Miller, D. 1994. "Style and Ontology." In *Consumption and Identity*, ed. J. Friedman. Harwood Academic Press: 45-70.

Miller, Daniel. 1994. *Modernity, An Ethnographic Approach: Dualism and Mass Consumption in Trinidad*. Oxford and Providence: Berg Publishers.

Millet, K. 1977. *Sexual Politics*. London: Virago.

Mills, Mary Beth. 1993. *We Are Not Like Out Mothers: Migrants, Modernity, and Identity in Northeast Thailand*. Ph.D. diss. University of California at Berkeley.

Mintz, Sidney. 1989. *Caribbean Transformations*. New York: Columbia University Press.

Mitchell, T. 1991. *Blood Sports: A Social History of Spanish Bullfighting*. Philadelphia: University of Pennsylvania Press.

Moore, Sally Falk and Barbara Myerhoff. 1977. "Introduction: Secular Ritual: Forms and Meanings." In *Secular Ritual*, eds. S. Moore and B. Myerhoff. Assen/Amsterdam: Van Gorcum.

Moran, Mary H. 1990. *Civilized Women: Gender and Prestige in Southeastern Liberia*. Ithaca: Cornell University Press.

————. 1995. "Warriors or Soldiers? Masculinity and Ritual Transvestism in the Liberian Civil War." In *Feminism, Nationalism, Militarism*, ed. C. Sutton. Arlington: American Anthropological Association.

Mueggler, Erik. 1991 (April). "Money, the Mountain, and State Power in a Naxi Village." *Modern China* 17 (2): 188-226.

Mukerji, Chandra and Michael Schudson, eds. 1991. *Rethinking Popular Culture: Contemporary Perspectives in Cultural Studies*. Berkeley: University of California Press.

Mulder, N. 1992. *Inside Southeast Asia: Thai, Japanese, and Filipino Interpretations of Everyday Life*. Bangkok: Duang Komol Books.

Murray, S. O. ed. 1992. *Oceanic Homosexualities*. London: Garland Publishing.

Nájera-Ramírez, Olga. 1989. "Social and Political Dimensions of Folklorico Dance: The Binational Dialectic of Residual and Emergent Culture." *Western Folklore* 48: 15-32.

Nanda, S.J. 1992. *Neither Man Nor Woman: The Hijras of India*. Belmont, CA: Wadsworth Publishing.

Natarajan, Nalini. 1994. "Woman, Nation, and Narration in *Midnight's Children*." In *Scattered Hegemonies: Postmodernity and Transnational Feminist Practices*, eds. I. Grewal and C. Kaplan. Minneapolis: University of Minnesota Press: 76-89.

Nelson, Diane. 1993. "Gendering the Ethnic-National Question: Rigoberta Jokes and the Out-Skirts of Fashioning Identity." Paper presented at the annual meetings of the American Anthropological Association. Washington, D.C.

"News From Tibet." 1992. Holiday Inn-Lhasa publicity leaflet.

New York Times. 1975. "Unrest Growing in El Salvador: Demonstrations Put Down After Protest of Cost of Beauty Pageant." August 10.

———. 1976. "Miss World is Crowned, Nine Quit Over Race Issue." November 20.

———. 1993. "Hey, Who Let Her Song in Here?" September 26.

Nichter, M., and M. Nichter. 1991. "Hype and Weight." *Medical Anthropology* 13: 249-84.

Nimmo, H.A. 1976. "The Relativity of Sexual Deviance: A Sulu Example." *Papers in Anthropology* 19: 91-97.

Noble, L.G. 1976. "Muslim Grievances and the Muslim Rebellion." In *Rebuilding a Nation: Philippine Challenges and American Policy*, ed. C.H. Lande. Washington, D.C.: The Washington Institute Press.

Norbu, Dawa. 1991. "China's Policy Towards its Minority Nationalities in the Nineties." *China Report* 27 (3): 219-233.

———. 1994 (May). "Motivational Crisis in Tibetan Education System: Some Personal Reflections." *Tibetan Review* 24 (5): 3-14.

Norbu, Jamyang. 1989[1986]. "On the Brink." *Illusion and Reality*. New Delhi: TYC Books: 71-77.

Norbu, Thubten Jigme, and Colin Turnbull. 1968. *Tibet*. New York: Simon and Schuster.

Nöth, Winfried. 1990. *Handbook of Semiotics*. Bloomington: Indiana University Press.

Oliveira, O. 1986. "Satellite Television and Dependency: An Empirical Approach." *Gazette* 38: 127-45.

O'Neal, Michael E. 1983. *British Virgin Islands Transformations: Anthropological Perspectives*. Ph.D. dissertation, The Union Graduate School, Cincinnati, Ohio.

Orosa, S.Y. 1923. *The Sulu Archipelago and Its People*. New York: World Book Company.

Ortner, Sherry. 1989-90 (Winter). "Gender Hegemonies." *Cultural Critique*: 35-80.

'Otuangu N., Kololiana. 1994. "Let's Talk." *Tongan Women* (1st Edition): 20.

Pandey, Gyanendra. 1990. "The Colonial Construction of 'Communalism': British Writings on Banaras in the Nineteenth Century." In *Mirrors of Violence: Communities, Riots, and Survivors in South Asia*, ed., V. Das. Delhi: Oxford University Press: 94-134.

Papanek, Hanna. 1994. "The Ideal Woman and the Ideal Society: Control and Autonomy in the Construction of Identity." In *Identity Politics and Women: Cultural Reassertions and Feminisms in International Perspective*, ed. V. Moghadam. Boulder: Westview: 42-75.

Parker, Andrew, Mary Russo, Doris Sommer, and Patricia Yaeger eds. 1992. *Nationalisms and Sexualities*. New York and London: Routledge.

———. 1992. "Introduction." In *Nationalisms and Sexualities*, eds. Parker et. al. London: Routledge: 1-18.

Pateman, Carole. 1988. *The Sexual Contract*. Cambridge: Polity.

Peacock, J. L. 1968. *Rites of Modernization: Symbolic Aspects of Indonesian Proletarian Drama*. Chicago: University of Chicago Press.

Peña Hernández, Enrique. 1968. *Folklore de Nicaragua*. Guatemala, C.A.: Talleres Piedra Santa.

Pettersen, Carmen L. 1976. *Maya of Guatemala: Life and Dress/Maya de Guatemala: Vida y Traje*. Guatemala: Museo Ixchel.

Phuntsog (Sipur), Nawang. 1994 (August). "Tibetan-centric Approach to Schooling." *Tibetan Review* 24 (8): 17-20.

Pinchback, Ivy. 1981 [1930]. *Women Workers and the Industrial Revolution 1750-1850*. London: Virago.

Pinigina, L. ed. 1994. *Between Us, Girls*.

Pitt-Rivers, J.A. 1963. *Mediterranean Countrymen: Essays in the Social Anthropology of the Mediterranean*. Westport, CT: Grrenwood Press.

Pomeroy, Sarah. 1975. *Goddesses, Whores, Wives, and Slaves: Women in Classical Antiquity*. New York: Schocken.

Popol Vuh. 1947. *Popul Vuh: las antiguas historias de Quiché*. Trans. A. Recinos. Mexico and Buenos Aires: Fondo de Cultural Económica.

Pukhova, Z. 1988 (July). (Chairman of the Committee of Soviet Women.) "Speech." *Pravda* 2.

Radakrishnan, R. 1992. "Nationalism, Gender, and the Narrative of Identity." In *Nationalisms and Sexualities*, eds. Parker et.al. London: Routledge: 77-95.

Radway, Janice. 1984. *Reading the Romance: Women, Patriarchy, and Popular Culture*. Chapel Hill: University of North Carolina Press.

Riverol, Armando R. 1992. *Live from Atlantic City: The History of the Miss America Pageant Before, After and In Spite of Television*. Bowling Green, OH: Bowling Green State University Popular Press.

Rodriguez, L. 1992. "La mujer cordobesa y las fiestas demayo." *Diario Córdoba* 17 May: 12.

Rofel, Lisa. 1993. "Where Feminism Lies: Field Encounters in China." *Frontiers* 13 (3): 33-52.

Rogers, Garth. 1977. "'The Father's Sister is Black': A Consideration of Female Rank and Power in Tonga." *Journal of the Polynesian Society* 86: 157-82.

Rosenberg, Chanie. 1989. *Women and Perestroika: Present, Past and Future for Women in Russia*. London: Bookmarks.

Rosensweig, Roy. 1983. *Eight Hours for What We Will: Workers and Leisure in an Industrial City, 1870-1920*. New York: Cambridge University Press.

Rossel, Pierre (ed.). 1988. *Tourism: Manufacturing the Exotic*. Document 61. Copenhagen: International Workgroup for Indigenous Affairs.

Royce, Anya Peterson. 1982. *Ethnic Identity: Strategies for Diversity*. Bloomington: Indiana University Press.

Samuel, Geoffrey. 1982. "Tibet as a Stateless Society and Some Islamic Parallels." *Journal of Asian Studies* 41(2): 215-29.

Santiago Vallecillo, Maria del Carmen. 1982. "Cartas al director: !!Mujeres para qué!!" *Diario Córdoba* 16 May: 4.

Schirmer, Jennifer. 1993. *Whose Rights are they Anyway? The Guatemalan Military's Looting of Human Rights Discourse*. Paper presented at the annual meetings of the American Anthropological Association in Washington, D.C.

Schivelbusch, Wolfgang. 1988. *Disenchanted Night*. Berkeley: University of California Press.

Schneider, David M. 1969. *Kinship, Nationality and Religion in American Culture: Toward a Definition of Kinship*. Paper presented at the annual meeting of the American Ethnological Society.

Schultz, Emily. 1990. *Dialogue at the Margins: Whorf, Bakhtin, and Linguistic Relativity*. Madison, WI: University of Wisconsin.

Schwartz, Ronald David. 1991a. "Travellers Under Fire: Tourists in the Tibetan Uprising." *Annals of Tourism Research* 18: 588-604.

———. 1991b. "Democracy, Tibetan Independence, and Protest Under Chinese Rule." *Tibet Journal*: 3-27.

Segal, Daniel A. 1991. "'The European': Allegories of Racial Purity." *Anthropology Today* 7 (5): 7-9.

Segalen, Martine and Josselyne Chamarat. 1983. "La Rosiere et la 'Miss': Les 'Reines' des Fetes Populaires." *Histoire* 53: 44-55.

Shakabpa, Tsepon W.D. 1967. *Tibet: A Political History*. New York: Potala Publications.

Shakya, Tsering. 1993. "Whither the Tsampa Eaters?" *Himel* 6 (5): 8-11.

Shastri, Pema Tsewang. 1994 (July). "Letter: The Seeds of Future Tibet." *Tibetan Review* 24 (7): 21.

Sheldon, W, E. Hartl, and E. McDermott. 1949. *Varieties of Delinquent Youth: An Introduction to Constitutional Psychiatry*. New York: Harper & Bros.

Shohat, Ella. 1992. "Notes on the 'Post-Colonial.'" *Social Text* 31-32: 99-113.

Shoman, A. 1987. *Party Politics in Belize, 1950-1986*. Benque Viejo, Belize: Cubola Press.

Shore, Bradd. 1989. "Manu and Tapu." In *Developments in Polynesian Ethnology*. Honolulu: University of Hawaii Press: 137-73.

Silverstein, B. L. Perdue, and B. Peterson. 1986. "The Role of the Mass Media in Promoting a Thin Standard of Body Attractiveness for Women. *Sex Roles* 14: 519-32.

Simons, Anna. 1994. "Somalia and the Dissolution of the Nation-State." *American Anthropologist* 96: 818-24.

Skurski, Julie. 1994. "The Ambiguities of Authenticity in Latin America: *Doña Barbara* and the Construction of a National Identity." *Poetics Today* 15.

Smith, Carol A. 1992. "Race/Class/Gender Ideology in Guatemala: Modern and Anti-Modern Forms." Paper presented at the "Ethnicity and Power" conference.

Smith, Valene. 1978. *Hosts and Guests: The Anthropology of Tourism*. Philadelphia: University of Pennsylvania Press.

Stewart, John 1986. "Patronage and Control in the Trinidad Carnival." In *The Anthropology of Experience*, eds. V. Turner and E. Bruner. Urbana and Chicago: University of Illinois Press: 289-315.

Stoeltje, Beverly. 1983. "Festival in America." In *Handbook of American Folklore*, ed. R. Dorson. Bloomington, IN: Indiana University Press: 239-45.

——. 1987a. "Cultural Queens: Modernization and Representation." Paper presented at annual meetings of The Association for the Study of Play, Montreal.

——. 1987b. "Riding, Roping, and Reunion: Cowboy Festival. In *Time Out of Time: Essays on the Festival*, ed. A. Falassi. Albuquerque, NM: University of New Mexico Press: 138-51.

——. 1988. "Gender Representations in Performance: The Cowgirl and the Hostess." *Journal of Folklore Research* 25 (3): 219-41.

——. 1992. "Festival." In Folklore, Cultural Performances, and Popular Entertainments, ed. R. Bauman. New York: Oxford University Press: 261-71.

——. 1993. "Power and the Ritual Genres: American Rodeo." *Western Folklore* 52: 135-56.

——, and Richard Bauman. 1989. "Community Festival and the Enactment of Modernity." In *The Old Traditional Way of Life*, eds. R. Walls and G. Shoemaker. Bloomington: Trickster Press: 159-71.

Stoler, Ann. 1989a. "Rethinking Colonial Categories: European Communities and the Boundaries of Rule." *Comparative Studies in Society and History* 13 (1): 134-61.

——. 1989b. "Making Empire Respectable: The Politics of Race and Sexual Morality in 20th-Century Colonial Cultures." *American Ethnologist* 16 (4): 634-60.

——. 1991. "Carnal Knowledge and Imperial Power: Gender, Race, and Morality in Colonial Asia." In *Gender at the Crossroads of Knowledge: Feminist Anthropology in the Postmodern Era*, ed. M. di Leonardo. Berkeley: University of California Press: 51-101.

Stone, M. 1990. "Backabush: Settlement on the Belmopan Periphery and the Challenge of Rural Development." *Third Annual Studies on Belize Conference*, SPEAReport 6. Belize City: SPEAR: 82-134.

Sun, Lena. 1994 "Ethnic Animosities Reborn as Chinese Traders Flood Tibet." *Washington Post* 15 September: A27.

Supatra Kobkidsuksakul. 1988. *Miss Thailand, 1934-1987*. MA thesis. History Department. Thammasat University, Bangkok, Thailand.

Swain, Margaret Byrne. 1990. "Commoditizing Ethnicity in Southwest China." *Cultural Survival Quarterly* 14 (1): 26-29.

Synnott, Anthony. 1989. "Truth and Goodness, Mirrors and Masks, part 1." *British Journal of Sociology* 40 (4): 607-36.

Tan, S. 1977. *The Filipino Muslim Armed Struggle, 1900-1972*. Manila: Filipinas Foundation.

Tefft, Sheila. August 12, 1993. "Goodby Mao Cap, Hello Tiara: Beauty Pageantry Sweeps China." *Christian Science Monitor*.

Teilhet-Fisk, Jehanne. "To Beat Or Not to Beat, That is the Question: A Study on Acculturation and Change in an Art-Making Process and Its Relation to Gender Structures." *Pacific Studies* 14: 41-68.

Thomis, Malcolm. 1982. *Women in Protest, 1800-1850*. London: Croom Helm.

Thompson, Michael. 1979. *Rubbish Theory: The Creation and Destruction of Value*. Oxford: Oxford University Press.

Thurston, David. 1992. "Hell and High Water." *M Magazine*. Hong Kong: South China Morning Post.

"Tibet Government Bans BBC, Star TV." *Canada TibNet* reprint of Tibet TV broadcast March 9, 1994.

Tierney, Ben. 1991. "Letter From Tibet: First Miss Fashion Parade Evaluation Dons Fur Mantle." *Vancouver Sun*: 12 December: A3.

Turner, Terrence. 1977. "Transformation, Hierarchy and Transcendence: A Reformulation of Ven Gennep's Model of the Structure of Rites de Passage." In *Secular Ritual*, ed. S. Moore and B. Myerhoff. Assen/Amsterdam: Van Gorcum.

Turner, Victor. 1967. *The Forest of Symbols*. Ithaca: Cornell University Press.

———. 1986. *The Ritual Process: Structure and Anti-Structure*. Ithaca: Cornell University Press.

———. 1974. "Liminala to Liminoid in Play, Flow, and Ritual: An Essay in Comparative Symbology." *Rice University Studies* vol. 60. Houston, TX: Rice University: 53-92.

———. 1986. "Carnival in Rio: Dionysian Drama in an Industrializing Society." *The Anthropology of Performance*. New York: PAJ Publications: 123-138.

Van Esterik, Penny. 1993. "Beauty and the Beast: The Cultual Context of the May Massacre, May 1992. "Thai Studies Project working paper No. 10. York University.

———. 1994. "Gender and Development in Thailand: Deconstructing Display." In *Women, Feminism, and Development*, eds. H. Dagenais and D. Piche. Montreal: McGill-Queens University Press.

———. n.d. *Gendered Surfaces*. ms. York University.

Van der Kroef, J. M. 1954. "Transvestism and the Religious Hermaphrodite in Indonesia." *University of Manila Journal of East Asiatic Studies* 3: 257-65.

Van Walt, Michael. 1987. *The Status of Tibet*. London: Wisdom Publications.

Verdery, Katherine. 1990. "The Production and Defense of 'the Romanian Nation,' 1900 to World War II." In *Nationalist Ideologies and the Production of National Cultures*, ed. R.G. Fox. Washington, D.C.: American Anthropological Association: 81-111.

Vogt, Evon. 1955. "A Study of the Southwestern Fiesta System as Exemplified by the Laguna Fiesta." *American Anthropologist* 57: 820-39.

Wang, Furen, and Suo Wenqing. 1984. *Highlights of Tibetan History*. Beijing: New World Press.

Warner, Marina. 1985. *Monuments and Maidens: The Allegory of the Female Form*. New York: Antheneum.

Whitham, F. L. 1992. "Bayout and Callboy: Homosexual-heterosexual Relations in the Philippines." In *Oceanic Homosexualities*, ed. S. Murray. London: Garland Publishing.

Wilk, Richard. 1993. "Beauty and the Feast: Official and Visceral Nationalism in Belize." *Ethnos* 53 (3-4): 1-25.

———. 1994. "Colonial Time and TV Time." *Visual Anthropology Review* 10 (1): 94-102.

———. 1995. "Learning to be Local in Belize: Global Systems of Common Difference." In *Worlds Apart: Modernity Through the Prism of the Local*, ed. D. Miller. London: Routledge.

Williams, Brackette F. 1989. "A Class Act: Anthropology and the Race to Nation Across Ethnic Terrain." *Annual Review of Anthropology* 18: 401-44.

———. 1990. "Nationalism, Traditionalism, and the Problem of Cultural Inauthenticity." In *Nationalist Ideologies and the Production of National Cultures*, ed. R.G. Fox. Washington, D.C.: American Anthropological Association: 112-29.

———. 1991. *Stains on My Name, War in My Veins: Guyana and the Politics of Cultural Struggle*. Durham, NC: Duke University Press.

———. 1993. "The Impact of the Precepts of Nationalism on the Concept of Culture: Making Grasshoppers of Naked Apes." *Cultural Critique* (Spring): 143-91.

Williams, Raymond. 1977. *Marxism and Literature*. Oxford: Oxford University Press.

Willis, Janice D. (ed.). 1987. *Feminine Ground: Essays on Women and Tibet*. Ithaca: Snow Lion.

Wilson, Peter. 1973. *Crab Antics: The Social Anthropology of English-Speaking Negro Societies of the Caribbean*. New Haven: Yale University Press.

Wolf, Eric. 1957. "Closed Corporate Communities in Mesoamerica and Central Java." *Southwestern Journal of Anthropology* 13: 1-18.

Wolf, Naomi. 1991. *The Beauty Myth*. New York: Doubleday.

Woolrich, Peter. 1992. "I'm On the Top of the World." *You Magazine*.

Working With the Dragon: Holiday Inn and China in Tibet. December 1993. London: Tibet Support Group, U.K.

Wu, David Yen-ho. 1991. "The Construction of Chinese and Non-Chinese Identities." *Daedalus* 120 (2): 159-79.

Wyatt, David. 1984. *Thailand: A Short History*. New Haven: Yale Unviversity Press.

Yan, Min. 1984 (April 3). "On Actual Inequality Among Nationalities Left Over by History." Beijing Renmin Ribao, China—PRC National Affairs (radio broadcast).

Yuval-Davis, Nira and Floya Anthias, eds. 1989. *Woman-Nation-State*. London: MacMillan.

Zhang, Xudong. 1994. "On Some Motifs in the Chinese 'Cultural Fever' of the Late 1980s: Social Change, Ideology, and Theory." *Social Text* 39: 129-56.

Zubieta, Rafael G. 1981 (May). "Una reina de 18 años soltera y sin compromiso. 'Me parece absurdo que pretendan suprimir tradiciones como estas.'" *Diario Córdoba* 21: 14.

———. 1981 (May). "Un Ayuntamiento feminista." *Diario Córdoba* 5: 6.

Contributors

Katherine Borland received her Ph.D. in Folklore from Indiana University in 1994. Currently, she is executive director of Delaware Futures, where she works with academically promising but underachieving low income high school students.

Colleen Ballerino Cohen is Associate Professor of Anthropology and Women's Studies and Director of Women's Studies at Vassar College. Her articles appear in *Signs, Social Analysis, Journal of the History of Sexuality*, and a special Gender Issue of the *Annals of Tourism Research*, and in edited collections. Since 1989 she has conducted ethnographic research on national culture and identity in the British Virgin Islands, and is presently completing a book based on this research.

Mark Johnson is a temporary lecturer in Anthropology, University College London, and is completing his Ph.D. thesis entitled, "Beauty and Power: Identity, Cultural Transformation, and Transgendering in the Southern Philippines." He has also published a paper on this research, "Transgender and Homosexuality in the Southern Philippines: Ethnicity, Political Violence and the Protocols of Engendered Sexuality."

Robert H. Lavenda is Professor of Anthropology at St. Cloud State University, in Minnesota. He has written extensively about festivals and carnivals in Latin America and Minnesota, and is co-author of two text-books in anthropology. He is a past president of the Association for the Study of Play.

Carlota McAllister is pursuing a Ph.D. in anthropology at Johns Hopkins University. She completed her Master's in anthropology at the University of Arizona with a thesis on the Rabín Ahau. Currently, she is concerned with violence as it constitutes sociality in Guatemala.

Carole McGranahan is a graduate student in the Program in Anthropology and History at the University of Michigan. She is co-author, with Ann Forbes, of *Developing Tibet?: A Survey of International Development Projects* (1992). Currently, she is preparing for dissertation research on history and memory in eastern Tibet.

Mary H. Moran is Associate Professor of Anthropology at Colgate University. She is the author of *Civilized Women: Gender and Prestige in Southeastern Liberia* (Cornell University Press, 1990) and articles in *Feminist Studies, Canadian Journal of African Studies, Women's Studies Quarterly, Liberian Studies Journal,* and several edited volumes. Her current projects include a book-length manuscript on the articulation of local and national political discourses in Liberia and an edited volume entitled, *History, Conflict, and Identity on the Windward Coast.*

Lena Moskalenko holds a doctorate from the Moscow State University on the subject of the development of small businesses under the Law on Cooperation of 1988. Currently, she is engaged in research on individualism at the University of Middlesex in London. She also teaches sociology and politics at the University of Kent in Canterbury.

Richard Sanders and Sarah Pink are both doctoral students at the University of Kent in Canterbury, UK. In addition, Richard has been teaching sociology to architectural students at the Kent Institute of Art and Design in Canterbury, while Sarah has been organizing the Royal Anthropological Society's 1994 Film Screening at the University of Kent and teaches social anthropology and visual anthropology there.

Beverly Stoeltje teaches feminism, nationalism, and ritual genres at Indiana University, where she is Associate Professor of Folklore, and is on the faculty of the African Studies Program, Women's Studies Program and the Research Center for Linguistics and Semiotic Studies. She was a Fulbright Fellow in Ghana 1989-90. She has published on Asante Queen mothers, women in the American West, American Rodeo and Festival; she was guest editor of a special issue of the *Journal of Folklore Research,* "Feminist Revisions in Folklore Studies," and is currently editing a volume on the *Vox Populi.*

Jehanne Teilhet-Fisk, Emeritus Professor of Art History, University of California at San Diego, is a Professor of Art History at Florida State University. Her publications include, *Paradise Reviewed: An Interpretation of Gauguin's Polynesian Symbolism, Dimensions of Polynesia,* "The Equivocal Nature of a Masking Tradition in Polynesia," "The Role of Women

Artists in Polynesia and Melanesia," "Tongan Grave Art," and "To Beat or Not to Beat, That is the Question: A Study on Acculturation and Change in an Art-Making Process and its Relation to Gender Structures."

Penny Van Esterik teaches anthropology at York University in Toronto, Canada. She has a long involvement with gender and development activities in Thailand in addition to interests in breastfeeding, women's work, and food issues. Recent publications include *Beyond the Breast-bottle Controversy* (Rutgers University Press), and *Taking Refuge: Lao Buddhists in North America* (Arizona State University, Monographs in Southeast Asian Studies).

Richard Wilk is a cultural anthropologist, presently an Associate Professor at Indiana University. He has done archaeological, ethnohistoric, ecological, and applied research in Belize for more than twenty years. He has written and edited books on household organization, and is currently completing a textbook in economic anthropology.

Index